The Image of

The Image of Disability

Essays on Media Representations

Edited by JL SCHATZ *and*
AMBER E. GEORGE

McFarland & Company, Inc., Publishers
Jefferson, North Carolina

ISBN (print) 978-1-4766-6945-8
ISBN (ebook) 978-1-4766-3299-5

LIBRARY OF CONGRESS CATALOGUING DATA ARE AVAILABLE

BRITISH LIBRARY CATALOGUING DATA ARE AVAILABLE

Front cover image © 2018 alexsl/iStock

Printed in the United States of America

*McFarland & Company, Inc., Publishers
Box 611, Jefferson, North Carolina 28640
www.mcfarlandpub.com*

Table of Contents

Preface

JL SCHATZ *and* AMBER E. GEORGE

This book rose out of the work initially done at the 1st Annual Eco-Ability conference that was hosted at Binghamton University in 2013. While the conference itself focused on the connection between disability studies, environmental justice, and animal liberation, many of the participants and attendees had an interest in how both disability and animal liberation was represented in the media. Collectively, they lamented the lack of analysis and attention given to the topic. In the years that followed, we resolved to correct that imbalance given how important the media is in shaping the lives of people throughout the world. In turn, we worked with the Institute for Critical Animal Studies and the *Journal of Critical Animal Studies* in order to publish works that tied activism to media representation while finding a collection of scholars to work with more exclusively on disability studies and the media.

This book pulls together a series of scholars and activists in order to demonstrate the importance of fiction in impacting the lived reality of people with disabilities. This book explores disability from the ever-shifting and changing definitions of biological impairment, espoused by the medical model, to that of disability as a cultural phenomenon that originates from social and political factors that give rise to medicalization. Our collection disrupts and challenges predominant negative assumptions about disability from an intersectional perspective in order to engage our readership in a more thoughtful understanding of disability. We offer an in-depth analysis of the triumph-over-adversity stereotype along with many others that impede the success of disability rights activists, scholars, and those seeking independence from harmful prejudices.

Contributors explore new perspectives on disability including analyses of people with disabilities as producers, consumers, and products of media. Moreover, disability is expanded on through disability identity, culture, and

1

intersections with other disciplines such as critical race theory, gender studies, and other such viewpoints. Ultimately, our book encourages disabled scholars and allies to re-imagine and create media in a way that can disrupt the status-quo and lend itself toward a more liberatory politics.

Introduction

JL SCHATZ *and* AMBER E. GEORGE

It is only recently that disability studies has begun to gain prominence in both academia and public rights discourse. And, while there have been appeals for inclusion in regard to ramps and parking spaces for some time, larger social environments that stigmatize disability have mostly gone unquestioned. Even with the rise of disability studies, very little work has been done on the media representations that reinforce ableism, outside of the obscure article or conference presentation. This is unfortunate because "ableism dominates the thinking of our society as a whole and it clearly operates as a discourse of power and domination. Furthermore, ableism becomes most visible as a 'mental framework' transmitted through rhetorical devices including language, imagery, and systems of representation" (Cherney 2011). As such, it is crucial to explore how ableism reproduces itself through the media since it is there where the normative construction of the body and mind is reinforced within society. However, even more importantly, the media provides a space where change can occur because "where there is power, there is resistance" (Foucault 1978, 95). Since it's nearly impossible to escape the media's influence, it becomes even more important to use its power to alter the disciplining techniques that make disability demonized. Ultimately, because "culture is the realm that allows us to draw broad and pertinent connections between policy, representation, and lived experience … politics must displace disability as the anchor of physical 'truth,' developing new claims of justice and self-determination for racial, ethnic, and gender politics that do not rely on a methodological or symbolic distancing from disability" (Samuels 2014, 213–214). Our book does precisely that through a critical reading of disability in the media.

Representations of disability within academic approaches tend to get tangled in debates between social and medical models of disability. We believe many of these authors tend to forget that the bodies behind the media representations

3

are real and simultaneously linked to representations on the screen. No one denies that physical and mental impairments are real, however, how individuals understand these impairments is what makes them disabling in society while also impacting the social and medical treatment of people with disabilities. As poet and disability activist Eli Clare (2001) writes, "Words shaped by how my body—and I certainly mean to include the mind as part of the body—moves through the world. Sometimes we who are activists and thinkers forget about our bodies, ignore our bodies, or reframe our bodies to fit our theories and political strategies.... But in defining the external, collective, material nature of social injustice as separate from the body, we have sometimes ended up sidelining the profound relationships that connect our bodies with who we are and how we experience oppression."

In other words, the more that media sources expect people with disabilities to perform their disability in pre-scripted, ableist ways, the more the media will recreate these representations in reality to create a self-fulfilling prophecy that reconstitutes ableism repeatedly. Fortunately, "ableist culture sustains and perpetuates itself via rhetoric; the ways of interpreting disability and assumptions about bodies that produce ableism are learned," which means they can be unlearned (Cherney 2011).

While disability studies have glossed over media studies, cultural studies departments have likewise largely left disability absent from their research analyses and course offerings. This is troubling given all the attention that is given to other social identities such as gender, race, sexuality, and even species-based representations in advertising and film. This is not to say such attention is undeserved. However, it is to say that when disability is left unattended, cultural studies forfeits a crucial opportunity to deconstruct how hegemonic understandings of the world are forged via disability. So long as this is the case,

> what abilities one favours and what ableisms one exhibits is a dynamic that also defines human-nature relationship ... which in turn has an impact on which strategies and priorities are envisioned and employed for gaining water, energy climate and disaster security and avoiding insecurity.... Ableisms historically have been used and still are used by various social groups to justify their elevated level of rights and status in relation to other social groups, other species and the environment.... An ability lens is essential for examining equity and equality discourses [Wolbring 2012].

In doing so, it becomes paramount to counter ableist representations and foster new realities by rereading dominant discourses. As such, this book fosters "a strategy of crafting new words ... [to] challenge ableism, and consider [its] implications ... in the context of disability rights and activist politics working to secure them" (Cherney 2011).

The essays of this book are diverse and span the intersections between the media, disability, gender, sexuality, and so on. Our aim in producing such a rich sense of intersectional analysis on disability within the media is to create a source for both critique and praxis. For this to be possible, it is important to understand how "one of the ways oppression is uniquely addressed is through discussing personal experiences about one's relationship between disability, animals, and nature. It is through reflection on personal experiences that theory and movements are founded, not purely through supposed value-neutrality and objectivity" (Nocella II, George, and Schatz 2017, xxi). These personal experiences include social environments fostered by the media landscapes in which people live. The feelings we have toward the media and each other are undoubtedly subjective because one can never predict how representations may impact any given person. Nevertheless, the subjective experiences of ableism and the hegemonic norms they reinforce are just as important in addressing disability as the medical and structural advances that address issues of impairment. So much of current medical models focus on the compulsory desire to cure disability "predicated on the idea that all persons, when possible, must be made 'normal,' must be 'fixed,' through a process of medical intervention" (Flynn 2017). This compulsion to cure "co-opts discourses of empowerment (for instance, discourses of survivorship or recovery) ... for financial and/or political ends" (DeVolder 2013). Fortunately, "since the norm is always in danger of being disrupted, it has to be continually established, performed and reinforced (Butler 1993; Mcruer 2006).... Our challenge is to interrupt its iteration (Gilmore 2010), to work the weakness of the norm (Butler 1993) and to open up space for an influx of stories, knowledge and perspectives that we cannot even begin to imagine" (DeVolder 2013). A multidimensional collection, such as this, of the very examples that circulate throughout popular culture is perfectly situated to perform such an interruption given that the very terrain such analysis is founded upon informs the reality that it is representing.

To do this, we have divided the book into three parts, the first of which focuses on the fictional representations of disability in movies and television. The authors in this part investigate how fiction informs contemporary understandings of disability and how it serves to either reproduce or deconstruct ableist norms. Fiona Whittington-Walsh explores these representations in connection with the fourth season of *American Horror Story*, titled *Freak Show*. She demonstrates how *American Horror Story* uses the same tropes from historical freak show circus performances to demonize those who are "freaks." Despite ardent legal regulation and ostracizing from able-bodied/minded norms, Whittington-Walsh argues people in freak show communities created a sense of self-value outside the boundaries of society.

Mia Harrison examines how power and punishment operate within the popular HBO television series *Game of Thrones*. She contends that the representation of disability goes beyond Peter Dinklage's performance of Tyrion Lannister, commonly referred to as the dwarf. In doing so, Harrison exposes how disability permeates the show while demonstrating the importance of broadening media analysis beyond the obvious examples when advancing disability studies.

Bill Beechler, Jr., explores Marvel's portrayal of Hawkeye as a character who is deaf and has been represented differently over the history of his comic and film career. He notes that in many depictions, Hawkeye's deafness is erased or simply cured by a hearing aid implant, thereby downplaying Hawkeye's disability as part of his identity. However, when storybook creators paid attention to Hawkeye's deafness, they did so in ways that inspired children not to feel subhuman if they couldn't hear. In the end, Beechler covers how disability can be represented positively within the media when given proper attention.

Sara Beth Brooks and Tyler Snelling investigate how the notion of killjoy operates within the television show *South Park* regarding Jimmy's disability and PC culture. They contend that the promise of disability inclusion, and PC policing, is used to form a cruel optimism for people with disabilities. Since Jimmy and other people with disabilities on the show fail to conform to what a typical disability rights advocate should look like, they are constructed as agents of their own oppression. Ultimately, this analysis deconstructs the effects of internalized ableism due to such practices.

In the second part of the book, the authors investigate how notions of disability are tied up within representations of gender. The authors once again use film and television for their analysis to explore the intersection while acknowledging the difficulty of theorizing disability as a standalone concept. JL Schatz explores the connection between masculinity and able-bodiedness in the television show *Breaking Bad*. He argues that "being a real man" means negating disability identity because of ableist notions of dependency and the force of hegemonic masculinity. To counter this effect, Schatz argues that people should embrace a relational autonomy that doesn't privilege the ableist norms of hegemonic masculinity.

Hailee M. Yoshizaki-Gibbons and Meghann E. O'Leary explore the hypersexualization of bipolar women in both film and television. They argue that representations of bipolar disorder render women sexually available, yet also incapable of freely giving or withdrawing consent. These portrayals are examples of the pervasive way people with disabilities experience sexual repression by able-bodied white men. Yoshizaki-Gibbons and O'Leary caution us to consider how this hypersexualization impacts individuals and society in violent ways.

Sonya Freeman Loftis looks at how autism relates to asexuality in ableist ways within the television show *The Big Bang Theory*. She contends that the way the main character is represented as being autistic without ever labeling it as autism within the show is a form of ableism, which causes characters with a disability to be the punchline in the comedy. Further, the comedic tropes within the show deliberately play up the stereotypical representation of people with autism as being asexual and robot-like through a negative portrayal, which adversely impacts the reality of people with autism.

In the third part of the book, the authors explore how the representation of disability impacts people beyond the screen. In doing so, they demonstrate how media representations are anything but neutral because they have a direct consequence for people with disabilities in the real world. Susan G. Cumings looks at how invisible disabilities can be made visible in social media campaigns when led directly by people with disabilities themselves. In these campaigns, which identify disabilities that are often ignored by society, disabled activists can positively portray themselves beyond the stereotypical representations that so often permeate the media. In exploring these campaigns, Cumings also delves into the difficulty activists have confronted and the many stereotypes unique to people living lives with invisible disabilities.

Jason Ho Ka Hang examines how disability representations in film translate into reality within East Asia. In doing so, he argues that these films serve not only as representations but also inform how governments and individuals treat people with disabilities. As such, he argues that it is imperative that these representations not reproduce ableist stereotypes because, when they do, it directly impacts those who are being represented. While the analysis in this essay is unique to the East Asian experience, Ka Hang recommends paying attention to the nuances of how disability operates differently in a global context.

Clare Harvey looks at how Oscar Pistorius was represented before, during, and after his murder trial. In turn, she argues that Pistorius' disability was used to paradoxically both champion him as a supercrip as well as render him vulnerable and weak. As such, during the trial, disability was used to inform the way jurors approached deliberation because it was built upon their preconceived conceptions of disability. Ultimately, Harvey argues that the media representations helped to solidify stereotypes that demonize people with disabilities either as villains or needing help.

Zhraa A. Alhaboby, Hala Evans, James Barnes and Emma Short analyze cyber victimization specifically within the context of disability. Unlike other forms of bullying, the cyber victimization of people with disabilities is often even more insidious because it plays upon hegemonic tropes that a life with a disability is a life not worth living. In the end, Alhaboby, Evans, Barnes and Short provide ways to counter the current cyber environment where such victimization occurs while at the same time interrogate how current harassment and representation online reinforces a destructive form of ableism.

Ultimately, by examining disability representations as they intersect with the media and other identity categories, this book in its entirety is meant as an interruption to challenge the ableist norms that structure society. "Much can be gained by viewing disability as always already a form of rhetorical action.... Such a conception allows us to understand not just that disability is a socio-discursive construct but also, then, how and to what end that construct is routinely and strategically deployed" (Carpenter 2011). Again, this is not meant to downplay the importance of medical approaches to understanding disability or to ignore the reality of impairment. "Social representations obviously affect the experience of the body ... but the body possesses the ability to determine its social representation as well, and some situations exist where representation exerts no control over the life of the body" (Siebers 2013, 190–191). Thus, our aim is not to overstate the power of discourse. "Rather, embodiment seen complexly understands disability as an epistemology that rejects the temptation to value the body as anything other than what it was and that embraces what the body has become and will become relative to the demands on it, whether environmental, representational, or corporeal" (Siebers 2013, 190–191). In other words, we aim to counter the silence that media representations often generate about the corporeal reality of disability and its response to individual impairments. To this end, so long as media representations are unobserved, any medical or structural advancements will only be co-opted into the same compulsory desire to produce normalcy by reproducing the ableist assumptions for such advancements initially. Correcting this imbalance in analysis can help to understand disability better and produce new realities where such advancements are about more than just eliminating or assimilating those who are perceived as undesirable within society.

REFERENCES

Carpenter, Rick. 2011. "Disability as Socio-Rhetorical Action: Towards a Genre-Based Approach." *Disabilities Studies Quarterly*. http://dsq-sds.org/article/view/1666/1605.

Cherney, James. 2011. "The Rhetoric of Ableism." *Disability Studies Quarterly*. http://dsq-sds.org/article/view/1665/1606.

Clare, Eli. 2001. "Stolen Bodies, Reclaimed Bodies: Disability and Queerness." *Public Culture* 13(3): 359–365.

DeVolder, Beth. 2013. "Overcoming the Overcoming Story: A Case of 'Compulsory Heroism.'" *Feminist Media Studies* 13(4): 746–754.

Flynn, Susan. 2017. "Ex Machina: Possessing and Repossessing the Body." *Ethos: A Digital Review of Arts, Humanities, and Public Ethics* 3(1): 32–45.

Foucault, Michel. 1978. *The History of Sexuality, Vol. I: An Introduction*. New York: Vintage.

Nocella, Anthony, II, Amber E. George, and JL Schatz. *The Intersectionality of Critical Animal, Disability, and Environmental Studies: Toward Eco-ability, Justice, and Liberation*. Lanham, MD: Lexington Books.

Samuels, Ellen. 2014. *Fantasies of Identification: Disability, Gender, Race.* New York: New York University Press.

Siebers, Tobin. 2013. "Disability and the Theory of Complex Embodiment—For Identity Politics in a New Register." In *Disability Studies Reader*, edited by Lennard Davis, 272–291. Abingdon: Routledge.

Wolbring, Gregor. 2012. "Ableism, Disability, and the Academy." http://fedcan.ca/fr/blog/ableism-disability-studies-and-academy.

"One of Us" or Two?

Conjoined Twins and the Paradoxical Relationships of Identity in American Horror Story: Freak Show

FIONA WHITTINGTON-WALSH

Dear Diary,
   It was the 3rd of September that the world as I had known was forever doomed. The shadows that had sheltered me were blinded by the light of scrutiny. I knew I was about to enter the gates of hell. But like the inescapable pull of gravity there was nothing I could do about it.

[Dot]

Nineteen fifty-two, Jupiter, Florida, sets the stage for the unfolding terror of the fourth season (2014–2015) of F/X's hit anthology TV show *American Horror Story* (*AHS*), titled *Freak Show*. The first episode of *AHS: Freak Show* begins with the voice of Dot (Sarah Poulson) reading her diary entry for the 3rd of September. At first, the audience is denied seeing her; a black curtain has cloaked the world in darkness mirroring her mood. The only accompaniment to her voice is the dream-like soft ringing of xylophone keys. As she continues to read the entry, she appears—alone; filling the right side of the screen. Because the audience is privy to her innermost thoughts, her voice reading a diary entry, they are positioned as being intricately connected to her and whatever journey she is about to experience. She is moving, with her audience in tow, toward the carnival world of freak shows and despite the tinkling music, they understand that they are most certainly entering a nightmare.

AHS: Freak Show creators Ryan Murphy and Brad Falchuk have long had a fascination with disability. Characters and actors with disabilities have appeared on all seasons of *AHS* as well as their other collaborations including

11

Glee and *Nip Tuck*. *Freak Show* is, however, the first time that disability has been the central theme. *Freak Show* stars some of the anthologies regulars such as Jessica Lang (Fräulein Elsa Mars) and Evan Peters (Jimmy, the Lobster Boy). The season also introduces new actors including some with disabilities and/or differences.

AHS: Freak Show tells the story of a tiered band of circus sideshow performers who have been collected by Fräulein Elsa (a German dominatrix/entertainer) as they set up camp on the outskirts of the town Jupiter, Florida. They are hopeful for a long, successful stay. Their stay, however, is ruined by a series of murders committed at first by a deeply disturbed clown, Twisty, who is not part of the side show. Twisty starts the carnage off by brutally attacking two lovers having an idyllic picnic, murdering the young man and kidnapping the woman. The first episode, "Monsters Among Us," ends with Elsa's performers murdering a local detective and cutting up his remains to hide the crime. Twisty, hiding in the shadows and behind a mask, watches as does the audience.

In the opening scene described at the beginning of this essay, Dot is the only character the audience meets even though she is conjoined with her twin sister, Bette (Sarah Poulson). *AHS: Freak Show* utilizes several modes of representation found in actual freak shows while building a paradoxical experience for the audience. In their separate, individuated state, such as when we hear only their individual diary entries, the sisters are very much human, just like "us," yet in their full embodied state they are monstrous because they are two.

Conjoined twins challenge our notion of the individual and that of identity while blurring the boundaries of "self" (Fiedler 1978; Thomson 1996). In Western, patriarchal capitalist society, identity is not conceptualized beyond an individuated state. In her seminal work *A Cyborg Manifesto*, Donna Haraway (1991) maintains that our identity is tangled in a "maze of dualisms in which we have [had to] explained our bodies" (181). Our identity is created for us out of these dualisms. A fundamental part of this is to negate the "original unity" our connection to mother and to nature and to each other. Rather than recognizing this, these dualisms create a paradox in our identity. They contradict our actual social experiences. These dualisms are abstract concepts and are support by an ideological system that, as Karl Marx (1988) contends, gives "them" subjectivity and causal powers, while we are relegated as objects. The production of ideology flips reality on its head: what is real, us, appears unreal, and we construct our identity out of the abstract. The system of ideological production benefits the capitalist elite, the bourgeoisie, who, as Dorothy E. Smith (1987) furthers, are predominantly male.

In contrast, people with disabilities have historically been represented not in an individuated state but as a paradoxical mixture of human and monster. All other dualisms disappear behind the monster façade. People with disabilities are not seen as male or female, sexual or desirable. They are represented as less than human, not worthy of life. This essay examines these paradoxes to identity as displayed in *AHS: Freak Show.* The paradoxical relationship of identity that is showcased presents characters that are hybrids of both human and monster as well as embodying myth and history. Real events and people from 1952 form the foundation of the tale of monsters that further blurs the boundaries of the self. These events make their way into the characters on *AHS: Freak Show* and help substantiate the fact that the American dream is only myth that uses disability as a metaphor for nightmare.

The Spectacle of Disability

Central to the cultural construction of disability in television and film is that "impairment" is seen through "the lens of spectacle" (Chivers and Marcotić 2010, 9) whereby the disabled characters become objectified and seen as less than human. The foundation to this spectacle is the medical model of disability complete with its medical gaze, which positions people with disabilities as both objects of scientific medical inquiry *and* societal pity (Longmore 2001; Darke 2010).

Within film studies the omnipotent gaze is also deeply connected to the power knowledge system and, as feminist scholars of film theory maintain, involves active participation by the spectator (Mulvey 1975). The power imbalance is created when the object of the scopophilic ("pleasure from looking") gaze is fetishized and as anti-racist/colonial theorists add, involves the process of mimetic representation which solidifies complete domination and control over the "other" (Hall 1997). Scholars examining disability in film and television maintain that this masculinized, colonial gaze is also an "ablest" gaze whereby the objects under surveillance are further devalued as monstrous and not worth living (Whittington-Walsh 2002; Smith 2011).

AHS is a horror television series. Horror is a genre where evil, that which signifies the deformity of the soul, is almost always associated with physical and/or cognitive aberrations (Longmore 1985; Carroll 1990; Smith 2011). Nicole Markotić (2001) explains that the message is simple in that "people who look different are different, and that is why we the viewing audience are and should be afraid of them" (67). Noel Carroll (1990) posits that one of the core principles behind the "philosophy of horror" is the presence of monstrosity. Horror films utilize key paradoxes most notably the fact that audiences are frightened by something they rationally understand does not exist, while at the same time the very thing that repels also attracts (Carroll 1990). Angela M. Smith (2011) furthers that key to the implementation of the horror is "notably monstrous bodies, acts of violence, and the jeopardizing of the female body" (87). The classic film horror monster is almost always male and poses a "temporary sexual threat to female bodies" (Smith 2011, 24) and therefore the progeny of the nation.

Within Western cultural representations, people with disabilities and differences were not always represented as monsters. Mikhail Bakhtin (1984) writes about the collective body of the "grotesque" which was celebrated during medieval carnival festivals and written about in the novels of François Rabelais. The grotesque celebrated all that was found within the body and its connection to the collective and the natural world. The life cycle of the body, from birth to death, was celebrated in connection with the earth and harvest. The body of the grotesque was *un*finished and intrinsically female because it was always in a state of becoming another body. It is a hybrid of at least two bodies. This collective body of the people challenged the aesthetics of modern beauty and embodiment.

The grotesque was based on images created by the people for the people and is both flesh and text and more human than the ideal, normal body that was represented in the bourgeois body. The bourgeois body is a body that denies its "original unity," its connection to both the female body and nature. The bourgeois body, therefore, is predominantly male and, as Haraway (1991) argues, a product of science and technology, not of history or social relations. Under Western patriarchal capitalism, manhood requires a distancing from dependence on all that was the grotesque body in order to engage in the capitalist pursuit of individual happiness. The bourgeois body is strictly an individual body, cut off from the "ancestral body of the people" (Bakhtin 1988, 29).

With the rise of capitalism, the carnival celebrations eventually were replaced with state sanctioned festivals and the bourgeois body, complete with its individuated state of being, became subject, while all other bodies relegated as objects. This author maintains that bodies of difference, those denied subjectivity, found their way onto the margins of the circus. Capital takes over from the collective celebrations. The grotesque that was cosmic and natural, both flesh and illusory, became bodies constructed as freaks. Existing for hundreds of years, freak shows were one of the first forms of disability spectacle where bodies seen as different were subjected to the gaze of awe, wonder, and disgust.

Leslie Fiedler (1978) explores how audiences experience bodies that deviate from what is considered "normal" in both sideshow performances and film narratives. Those who are called "freaks" are hybrids of both monster and human, a combination of both flesh and myth: "The true Freak ... stirs both supernatural terror and natural sympathy, since, unlike the fabulous monsters, he is one of us, the human child of human parents, however altered by forces we do not quite understand into something mythic and mysterious" (Fiedler 1978, 24).

But of course, no one is born a freak. Freak is a performance. Robert Bogdan (1988) argued that there were two distinct ways that "human abnormalities" were exhibited in freak shows: the exotic and aggrandized modes of representation. In the *exotic mode of representation*, the performer was positioned in a way that would appeal to the audience's interest in newly "discovered" cultures and the people who inhabit those cultures. They were both exotic and primitive becoming physical examples of social Darwinist theories. The *aggrandized mode of presentation* represented the performer as high status, appearing to be "just like us" while possessing remarkable talents despite a physical or intellectual difference.

Chang and Eng Bunker are the most famous freak performers who today are still billed as the "original Siamese twins." It is their modes of performance that continue to shape our understanding of conjoined twins, informing everything from media accounts and doctor testimonials (Whittington-Walsh 2007). Born in 1811 in Siam, the brothers were exhibited throughout their lives eventually successfully managing themselves, marrying two sisters, and retiring onto a plantation complete with slaves in North Carolina. During the American Civil War, they came out of retirement and went back on the road for one last exhibition tour and capitalized on the national fear surrounding the "enemy within." Dropping the "*and*" and representing themselves as "one," the brothers used the stage name "Chang/Eng" and subsequently became a symbol for the struggle for national unity (Whittington-Walsh 2007). Eng was the embodiment of the Union side, Chang the Confederate. Eng was a prohibitionist, Chang a drunk. Eng assimilated to the bourgeois morality concerning sexual restraint, while his brother apparently "loved the ladies" (Fiedler 1978, 204).

It is very difficult to determine what is performance and what is historical fact. Most of what is written about Chang and Eng utilizes the modes of representation that make the foundation of the freak performance. For example, even though both Chang and Eng had their own separate homes and families (taking turns living under each other's roofs), all written "accounts" credit the brothers as fathering 21 children as a unit. It is, however, the brothers' enemy within narrative that is continuously showcased in cultural representations and news stories about conjoined twins where one sibling is characterized as a parasite. For example, the 1951 film *Chained for Life*, starring conjoined sisters Daisy and Violet Hilton, focused on the perplexing ethical dilemma of one twin being accused of murder and therefore potentially condemning her innocent sibling to death. In news stories one twin is generally represented as sucking the life of the other, therefore becoming an enemy within to the stronger sibling who is understood to be the legitimate occupier of the body. While separation was understood as a threat and interpreted as a horrible course of events for the nation, the possibility of separation for Chang and Eng and all conjoined twins is the only way of achieving "freedom, fraternity, and equality."

Freak shows lost significance as a form of entertainment spectacle in the early 20th century largely because the medical model started pathologizing disability. This caused the gazing crowds to no longer be looking at a *freak* but were now gazing upon someone needing to be cured (Bogdan 1988). Subsequently, film replaced the live exhibition by showcasing disability, "flesh becoming shadow" (Fiedler 1978, 16). Film and television continue the disability spectacle by inundating audiences with disability themes, especially within the horror genre (Fiedler 1978; Whittington-Walsh 2002).

"Monsters Among Us"

Tod Browning's 1932 film *Freaks* is one of the most infamous examples of disability representation in film and as this author contends is the inspiration for *AHS: Freak Show*. The film stars actual sideshow performers including Daisy and Violet Hilton. The setting is the pastoral French countryside at the height of the Great Depression and on the cusp of the wave of fascist terror. Nineteen thirty-two saw the birth of Heinrich Himmler's wedding laws which were designed to increase racial purity using the principles of eugenics (Whittington-Walsh 2002). Between 1939 and 1945, hundreds of thousands of children and adults with disabilities were murdered in Germany in its quest to eliminate all threats to German progeny (Evans 2004).

However, Germany wasn't alone in its desire to improve the health and purity of its nation. Many western countries had active eugenics policies where compulsory sterilization and mass institutionalization were routinely practiced. From 1896 to the 1970s, the United States utilized eugenics to not only control progeny but also to create a new class consisting of anyone who was deemed "different" and therefore undesirable (Smith 2011, 16). Victims were selected and deemed deficient based on disability, race, sex, ethnicity, and social class. Disability within film media still plays upon these tropes since they are from an *ableist* perspective, whereby "impairment" is understood to be "naturally horrific and undesirable" (Smith 2011, 31).

Freaks is a spin on the classic love story and horror genre. It tells the story of a small statured performer, Hans (Harry Eales), who falls in love with an averaged sized trapeze artist, The Peacock of the Sky, Cleopatra (Olga Baclanova). Cleopatra discovers Hans has inherited millions and with the aid of the strong man, Hercules (Henry Victor), agrees to marry Hans and plans to poison him to get all his money. Despite her beauty, Cleopatra is the embodiment of evil. *She* is the monster. Browning disrupts the philosophy of horror by having non-disabled, "beautiful" bodies being the markers of evil, *not* disability. Hans becomes wise to Cleopatra's plan and shortly after their marriage, he and his fellow sideshow performers take revenge and kill Hercules and mutilate Cleopatra into a freak. The Peacock of the Sky is turned into a chicken woman, squawking in a large box for all to gaze upon.

This author's early work (Whittington-Walsh 2002) maintains that the film is rare in the history of disability representation not only in the casting of actual circus sideshow performers, but also in Browning's cinematic technique. The audience remains backstage and never watches the characters with disabilities performing but only witnesses the non-disabled characters perform. This is highly significant in positioning the audience not as usual bearers of the gaze, those that paid the entrance fee and expect a good show. They are privy to the mundane everyday world where people eat, do laundry, have babies, and court one another. Browning represents the performers as human, not freak. He allows the disabled characters to return the gaze and showcase how it is the non-disabled characters who are the monsters (Whittington-Walsh 2002).

Show Time!

Nineteen fifty-two, 30 years after Tod Browning's film, is significant for the backdrop for the horror of *AHS: Freak Show*. Nineteen fifty-two saw Christine Jorgensen become the "first" highly public recipient of trans-sexual surgery and the worst polio epidemic hit the United States. The number one film at the box office and winner of the best picture Oscar that year was Cecil B DeMille's *Greatest Show on Earth*. Actors with disabilities are not in DeMille's sanitized circus world except for a few small statured performers as clowns. The film glorifies the idea of a pastoralized, small town American life, which was in reality, just fantasy. In winning the Oscar for best picture, it "beat" Fred Zimmerman's film *High Noon*, a film that many believe uses the western drama as an allegory for the persecution and blacklisting of intellectuals and filmmakers by Senator Joseph McCarthy (Bynum 2004). Nineteen fifty-two saw the height of the witch-hunt with some Hollywood celebrities exposing colleagues as communists and therefore enemies within.

On April 22, 1952, at 9:30 a.m, five million Americans watched Los Angeles television station KTLA's live national feed of an atomic bomb test in Yucca Flats, Nevada. These tests had profound negative health consequences including topical burning of exposed skin due to "snow" fallout, and significant increases in rates of cancer and stillbirths (Johnson 1984; Miles 2013). Information regarding the radioactive exposure was suppressed by the American government through a sophisticated censorship campaign in combination with an all too trusting population (Miller 1986).

Nineteen fifty-two also saw the first "successful" separation of conjoined twins. Rodney and Roger Brodie were born in 1951 conjoined at the head but had separate brains and nervous and circulatory systems. On December 17, 1952, they were separated in a 12-hour and 40-minute surgery. During surgery, it was discovered that the boys shared the sagittal sinus, the canal that drains blood from the brain to the heart. It was determined before surgery that Rodney was given a better chance for survival so he retained the sagittal sinus. Rodney was identified as the legitimate citizen and Roger was the enemy, a parasite that needed to be sacrificed for his brother to live. Having never regained consciousness, Roger died 20 days after surgery, while Rodney, suffering from neurological damage post-surgery, died nine years after his brother in 1962.

These events are significant for *AHS: Freak Show* and demonstrate the paradoxical reality of post-war American life. While the circus in DeMille's sanitized epic received a warm, American pie welcome, Fräulein Elsa's Cabinet of Curiosities receives no such welcome. In the first episode, Elsa must renegotiate the terms of rent from the farmer who owns the field with sexual favors. It appears his wife does not appreciate having "freaks" around. Most significantly, at the end of the first episode, right before the local Detective's murder he tells the troupe: "Come tomorrow morning, my boys are going to come over here and run you out of town. There's no place in Jupiter for *Freaks.*"

While the troupe doesn't belong in Jupiter, Jupiter doesn't belong behind the stage. Outsiders arrive and attempt to mingle with the circus community only to discover they, like the audience, don't belong. One such outsider is Dandy Mott (Finn Wittrock) a wealthy young man who on opening night buys out the entire show only to sit in the audience alone with his mother (Frances Conroy) peering through opera glasses at the spectacle in front of him. Dandy dresses like a young sophomore sorority jock complete with cardigans thrown over his shoulders. He carries himself with an air of arrogance but at the same time walks slightly pigeon toed, which makes his gait somewhat childlike. Dandy becomes obsessed with Dot and Bette and fantasizes about marrying them. While Cleopatra was willing to do anything to have wealth and an opulent life in Tod Browning's *Freaks*, Dandy already has that life yet he remains bored with it. He has inherited a fortune from his father, has behavioral outbursts like a child, and his bedroom is full of giant-sized toys. The sideshow performers also give Dandy a dual identity by referring to him as the "man/child."

Good-looking, abled-bodied, white and powerful, Dandy is an example of bourgeois embodiment. He is isolated and separate from other bodies. He doesn't belong to the ancestral body of the people. But of course, the ideology of this normal embodiment is just that, ideology, not a reality. Due to generations of paternal inbreeding, Dandy is inherently evil and joins his kindred spirit Twisty in kidnappings, torture, and murder. To rationalize her son's behavior, Dandy's mother explains to him that his father's family (which due to the inbreeding must also be her own) believes in the purity of their genes and does not want to pollute it with "others." Dandy is the perfect specimen of a eugenics breeding program. He is the result of careful in-breeding which makes him a monster as per Smith's (2011) contentions. He is male, commits violent acts, and poses a threat to women. *His* genes, with generations of inbreeding, pose a threat to Dot and Bette and therefore the progeny of the nation.

This representation of the bourgeois body as monstrous and Dot and Bette as symbols for the purity of the nation ends with Dandy's character. Despite the attempt to create a bond between the disabled characters and the audience as Browning achieved, the audience of *AHS: Freak Show* is positioned as outsiders, never belonging as "one of us," and never feeling a connection to the disabled characters. The main reason for this failure is that *AHS: Freak Show* relies on many of the classic tricks utilized in the side shows and reinforces the performance modes outlined by Bogdan. While following along with the showman's rules of denying the audience what they want to see (and what they have paid to see), Murphy and Falchuk give the audience a show before they enter the bright lights of the main tent. The disabled characters are always performing, constantly drawing their performances from the rich history of freak shows as inspiration.

In episode one, after Dot's introductory statement, the audience is transferred to the outside of a rural house where the milkman is delivering a case of milk. Surprised by numerous bottles of rancid milk still sitting on the porch where they had last been delivered, he tentatively enters the house and discovers it is a house of horrors. He finds Mrs. Tattler dead, murdered in the kitchen. He proceeds to search the house and finds the real horror hiding in the upstairs closet where he hears two people whispering from behind the door. He opens it and screams in horror at what he sees. The audience, however, sees nothing.

The denial of what the audience covets continues as they are transferred onto a gurney rushing into a hospital surgery room. At this point, less than three minutes into the first episode, *AHS: Freak Show* is trying to create a connection between "us" and "them" by positioning the audience at the head of the gurney looking down two long legs and two feet. The audience's gaze is drawn to the feet; the left clean and well-manicured decorated with red nail polish while the right is the binary opposite; dirty, un-manicured, with traces of dried blood. The attempt at creating the connection, however, fails. The audience is left in the hall as the gurney rushes through the doors. The medical model is the antithesis to the spectacle of sideshows so we are not allowed to follow through the doors. They are also left in the hall to build up excitement over what they are missing out on. An orderly rushes out of the surgery room and a nurse comes out to vomit into a garbage can.

Elsa manages to sneak her way into Dot and Bette's hospital room dressed as a candy striper, pushing a cart of goodies and carrying two helium balloons. The camera is peering down on Elsa from the ceiling as if attached to one of the balloons that has escaped and floated upwards. Slowly, the camera sinks back down only to land *behind* the curtain that is surrounding the bed. There is a gap in the curtain and the audience can see Elsa tentatively approach the bed. The camera cuts back to outside of the curtain with Elsa and follows her as she makes her way closer. There are two silhouettes illuminated from behind the curtain but the position of the curtain opening, while denying the ability to see who lies behind it, appears to separate the two silhouettes. They appear as two. Elsa moves towards the left side of the bed and slowly peeks through another gap in the curtain. Finally, the audience sees what she sees, Dot sleeping. She widens the gap in the curtain to slowly reveal both Dot *and* Bette. Elsa murmurs under her breath in German. She quickly opens the rest of the curtain startling the twins awake. It is as if Elsa is bringing them to life by ripping the curtain open and announcing, "Show Time!" The monsters that lie within are finally revealed. They are both one and two.

Chang and Eng's freak mythology shapes the experiences of Dot and Bette. The sisters are the materialization of the enemy twin, which has as its foundation the paradoxical relationship between good and evil, human and monster. After Elsa wakes the twins up in the hospital room we are thrown back and forth from seeing Dot and Bette through Elsa's eyes to seeing Elsa from the sisters' two sets of eyes. Elsa quickly determines that Bette is naïve and responds favorably to idyll chit-chat and shallow compliments. Dot is the opposite and displays animosity towards the intruder. Elsa lights a cigarette and Bette takes a draw while Dot coughs as the smoke leaves her mouth. The conversation between Elsa and Bette turns to sexuality. Elsa makes a confession to the sisters: "One of your doctors shared your x-ray reports with me. It says you have two hearts but only one reproductive system [chuckles]. Complicated, no? [Pause] Has anyone tasted your cherry pie?" Dot is repulsed by the conversation and thinks that Elsa is a "psycho-pervert." The sisters have a brief conversation together in their minds where Bette responds to Dot's revulsion of Elsa by stating, "I think she is just down to earth is all," and giggles.

While they may in their individuated state appear "like us" together they possess remarkable talents such as having a conversation with each other in their minds that further distinguishes them from us. Elsa continues with her line of inquiry, "So you're virgins; sad for you. Do you at least pleasure yourselves?" Here we clearly see the freak mythology that mirrors Chang and Eng's performance. Bette responds to Elsa by saying, "She never wants to," to which Dot retorts to her sister in her mind, "I hate you." Bette, ignores her sister's statement, perhaps she has heard it many times before, and continues her conversation with Elsa: "If I do, she closes her eyes and pretends she doesn't feel anything. She told me she leaves her body [whispering with her hand covering the side of her mouth closest to Dot] I think she's lying. I think she likes it." Dot yells out loud, "Shut your disgusting mouth, you slut!"

One of the prevailing stereotypes of people with disabilities and one that is included in cultural representations is that people with disabilities are asexual, neither possessing a sexuality nor being sexually desirable. In *Freaks*, Browning allowed all the characters to possess sexual agency. Both Daisy and Violet Hilton had lovers and got married in the film, something that was denied to them in their real lives. While numerous characters on *AHS: Freak Show* are shown having sex it is always seen as an example of depravity and monstrousness. For example, the first episode has a bizarre opium-hazed orgy film that the audience is forced to watch alongside a horrified captive and star of the film, Penny. The film is there to reinforce the monstrousness of its stars and their primitive, animalistic sexuality.

There are further examples of sexual perversion throughout the show most significantly with Jimmy. When the audience first meets him, he is chatting up a waitress at a local Jupiter diner. He is wearing thick leather gloves, concealing his difference, lobster claw or cleft hand syndrome. Elsa taunts him by reminding him that once they see his "monstrous" hands he won't get lucky with the ladies. In stigma theory, Erving Goffman (1963) maintains that *passing* is an important aspect of performing and managing a "spoiled identity" such as a physical disability. Far from the celebrations of the medieval carnival, the person with the stigma attempts to emulate normalcy by concealing, as much as possible, that which signals difference.

However, while Jimmy needs to conceal his difference (after all, why will they pay if they can see it for free?), his difference is further exploited. He makes money on the side by visiting bored suburban housewives. Clothed in chiffon dresses, pumps, and wearing pearls, these women are another sign that there are cracks in the American Dream. Jimmy's monstrous hands bring the bored middle-class housewives of Jupiter to full orgasm, something their husbands apparently cannot. While people with disabilities are routinely represented as being asexual, Jimmy's sub-plot does not dispel the stereotype.

He is there to pleasure *them*. They do not return the sexual favors to Jimmy. They remain fully clothed during the encounter. Jimmy does not have intercourse with them. It is his hands which bring the women to orgasm. Jimmy is a cyborg: both flesh and machine. He is a human dildo. The progeny of the nation is safe.

The inspiration for Jimmy's character comes not from Browning's film but from the real sideshow stage. Grady Stiles, Jr., was born in 1937 and was performing as "Lobster Boy" from a young age up until his murder in 1992 in Gibsonton, Florida, the off-season place for carnival folks. Grady, an alcoholic and abusive husband and father, was found guilty of murdering his daughter's fiancé in 1978, but served no time due to the lack of accessibility in the prison system. He also had another talent that was not represented on the stage and one that serves as the inspiration for Jimmy's aggrandized performance. Grady said: "'Everyone I have sex with wants to have sex with my claws. They love it when I use my claws.' He was proud of the fact. Barbara [his wife], who was sitting across the room, nodded in agreement" (Rosen 1995, 78).

In contrast to Jimmy and Grady, but similar to Chang and Eng's performance, Dot is represented as being asexual and therefore virginal, while Bette is, to use her sister's descriptor, a "slut." This paradox, however, is the contradiction most women face in western society. Ideal beauty for women is wrapped up in this contradiction of being both the "virgin and the whore." Women with disabilities and/or differences are of course excluded from the beauty ideal and are not represented as being attractive nor pure.

The separation of the Brody twins is also included in Dot and Bette's storyline. While living with the man/child, Dandy, the sisters learn about the possibility of surgical separation. In episode six, "Bullseye," Dandy is reading the local Jupiter *Tequesta Inquirer* while the sisters are playing a game of Yahtzee. He reads the headline and looks over at them. He announces that there is an article they might be interested in: "They performed the first surgery separating Siamese twins." The camera shows a full image of the twins as Dandy says the last few words, "separating Siamese twins." Dot asks him for more detail and he proceeds to read the story. The audience is peering over Dandy's shoulder and reading along with him: "Fused in the Womb: Separated by Nations Best Surgeons: Chief of Medicine Declares surgery a 'Triumph.'"

This news gives Dot hope. Hope that she could one day be rid of her parasitic sister. However, Dot and Bette's attachment is rare among conjoined twins. In medical terms, they are dicephalus twins; twins that share a single body but each have a separate neck and head. The Brodie twins were craniopagus twins, joined at the head. Since the camera gives us a peek at Dot and Bette from behind Dandy's newspaper, it is reaffirmed in the audience's minds that both could not survive separation. Drawing on Chang and Eng's mythology, Dot tells Bette, "I would rather one of us truly live, than both of us wither away together."

Separation is a constant theme when representing conjoined twins yet is contradictory to the actual lived experiences of most conjoined siblings. For example, Donny and Ronny Galyon are 64 years old and conjoined at their lower abdomens. Laurie and Reba Schnapple are 55 and are conjoined at the side of their heads. Abigail and Brittany Hensel are 26 years old and, like Dot and Bette, share one body. All live in the United States and all reject the notion of separation (Wallis 1996; Weissbrod 2000). "Don't fix what is not broken," says Laurie Schnapple (Weissbrod 1999).

This paradox in identity is at its most obvious in the twins, but exists in each of the show's characters. Several characters are not only hybrids of good and evil, human and monster; they are also hybrids of characters from other films created by Tod Browning as well as embodying the main historical events from 1952. For example, Elsa is most obviously a combination of both Cleopatra and Madame Tetrallini, the owner of the circus in *Freaks*. Elsa is both good and evil. She is a conjoined twin. Madame Tetrallini refers to her performers as "children," while Elsa calls them "my monsters."

Elsa is a hybrid of parts of these characters with an added twist of another. Elsa conceals the fact that she too is disabled. At the end of the first episode she is sitting in her tent alone, listening to Vera Lynn's 1952 hit *"Auf Wiedasen."* She slowly takes off her silk stockings to reveal that she has two wooden legs. Elsa is one of them, but no one knows this. In Browning's 1927 film *The Unknown*, Lon Chaney plays Alonzo, the armless knife thrower who is in love with his model target. He is a murderer who is hiding from the law and hides his arms to avoid being fingerprinted for murder. Elsa is similarly a knife thrower and maliciously attaches Paul to the spinning board and gravely injures him. Alonzo is pretending to be disabled while Elsa, just like Jimmy, is hiding her disability. She is, however, hiding it not just from the outsiders, but from everyone on the inside. Elsa, is an enemy within. Her paradoxical identity of both good and evil is slowly revealed to Ethel (Kathy Bates) but remains hidden from everyone else.

Elsa is also a hybrid of Christen Jorgensen, the first recipient of transsexual surgery. Both share a similar appearance in the fact that they have Marlene Dietrich as their style icon although Elsa with her inflated ego believes that somehow Marlena stole her career from her. Both also get to follow their dreams and have variety television shows. Interestingly, Christine said the following about her decision to go into show business, the only option that was left for her after her transition, "I decided if they wanted to see me, they had to pay for it" (Jackson et al. 2016, 99).

Life Imitates Art

Dear Diary,
    It was the glorious 3rd of September when I was finally free from the shadows. The future had never seen brighter.... I have seen my future and it is wrapped in silk. I never would have thought that my escape from darkness would be so complete.... Glorious freedom! For the first time in my life I dare to imagine myself surrounded by beauty...

[Bette]

It is fitting to end as we began, with one-half of the story. Bette's diary entry for the 3rd of September sits in grave contrast to the entry of her sister. Back in episode one, Detective Hodges warned the performers that if they went ahead and exhibited people for profit, they would be shut down. In the final episode, Dandy, who purchased the sideshow from Elsa, is informed that he will never be "one of us." He goes on a murderous rampage killing everyone he can find including the remaining characters played by real sideshow performers. One by one, he encounters the performers all doing mundane everyday activities such as hanging up laundry, cooking, and cleaning. These activities framed Browning's film and its backstage community and demonstrated our communal connection to the characters. In *AHS: Freak Show*, however, that connection is not made. The audience has a front row seat to watch Dandy shoot Paul, legless Suzie, Toulouse, and Amazon Eve in the head.

Jimmy returns to the circus grounds at night unaware of the massacre. He returns from recuperating from surgery that removed his claw hands. He now has prosthetic hands similar to Elsa's legs. He discovers the bodies piled up around the main stage in the Big Tent where Dandy positioned them. It is fitting that even in death their bodies are on display. In the end, *all* the actors with disabilities and or differences perform perhaps one of the most pervasive stereotypes that threaten people with disabilities the most: the better-off-dead representation.

While the medical model signaled the end of the golden age of freaks, that model continues to dominate experiences of disability and difference. Today, people with disabilities are still globally denied basic human rights. Institutionalization, violence, poverty, unemployment, are some of the systemic barriers facing people with disabilities. For example, despite being ranked the "Happiest Place to Live" by the *World Happiness Report 2016* (Helliwell et al. 2016), the Danish government announced in 2011 that the nation could be "down syndrome free by 2030" (Lev 2011) through aggressive prenatal testing and a selective termination campaign. This is the era of "newgenics" where eugenics is continuing in the form of prenatal testing, selective abortions, preimplantation genetic diagnosis, and biotechnologies (Parens

2000; Hampton 2005; Tremain 2006). Newgenics has even surpassed the medical arena and has found its way into other aspects of society including systemic barriers to sexuality and reproductive and parental rights (Carlson et al 2000; Aunos and Feldman 2002). People with disabilities are argued to be increasingly at risk for non-consensual termination in countries including Canada and the United States where there exists physician-assisted suicide laws.

In *A Cyborg Manifesto*, Donna Haraway (1991) concludes that understanding cyborg imagery can assist us in challenging the dualisms that construct our identity. If we believe that we are both human *and* cyborg, then we will understand that binaries are not what make us human. By examining freak mythology and the social historical reality surrounding its construction, we can understand what it means to be human. Just as Haraway (1991) insists that the cyborg is made, not born, and that the "machine is us" (180), so too are freaks made, not born. However, the grotesque body that was celebrated has receded into our minds and been forgotten. What is left is the gaze and so therefore we stare.

AHS: Freak Show offers another voyeuristic opportunity to gaze at bodies of difference. Because of this they were successful in duplicating the sideshow experience of awe, wonder, *and* disgust, reaffirming our belief in our own normalcy while condemning the other to a mere object. I want to conclude with what could be considered a contradictory explanation as to why we stare and why we watch. Through a critical reading of *AHS: Freak Show* and identifying the events that lay at its foundation, we can evoke those lost memories and subsequently identify what is truly monstrous about patriarchal, colonial capitalism and the dualisms it reinforces. Once we see the images in a critical way perhaps we can then realize that we are drawn to stare because subconsciously we remember our communal connection to those on display. As Sigmund Freud (2001) maintained, the only way to tap into our subconscious is through our dreams. However, if not done with a critical understanding, what is trapped in the layers of the unconscious will emerge as a "fetish" penchant. As *American Horror Story: Freak Show* has demonstrated, dreams can be paradoxically nightmares.

REFERENCES

Aunos, M., and M.A. Feldman. 2002. "Attitudes Towards Sexuality, Sterilization and Parenting Rights of Persons with Intellectual Disabilities." *Journal of Applied Research in Intellectual Disabilities* 15: 285–296.

Bakhtin, Mikhail. 1984. *Rabelais and His World*. Bloomington: Indiana University Press.

Black, Rhonda, and Lori Pretes. 2007. "Victims and Victors: Representation of Physical Disability on the Silver Screen." *Research & Practice for Persons with Severe Disabilities* 32(1): 66–83.

Bogdan, Robert. 1998. *Freak Show: Presenting Human Oddities for Amusement and Profit*. Chicago: University of Chicago Press.

Browning, Tod. 2004. *Freaks*. 1932. Film. Beverley Hills: Metro Goldwin Mayer. DVD.

Bynum, Jeremy. 2004. *Showdown at High Noon: Witch-Hunts, Critics, and the End of the Western*. Lanham, MD: Scarecrow Press.

Carlson, Glenys, Miriam Taylor, and Jill Wilson. 2002. "Sterilisation, Drugs Which Suppress Sexual Drive, And Young Men Who Have Intellectual Disability." *Journal of Intellectual & Developmental Disability* 25(2): 91–102.

Carroll, Noell. 1990. *The Philosophy of Horror; or, Paradoxes of the Heart*. New York: Routledge.

Chivers, Sally, and Nicole Martoić. 2010. *The Problem Body: Projecting Disability on Film*. Columbus: Ohio State University Press.

Evans, Suzanne E. 2004. *Forgotten Crimes: The Holocaust and People with Disabilities*. Chicago: Ivan R. Dee.

Fiedler, Leslie. 1978. *Freaks: Myths and Images of the Secret Self*. New York: Simon & Schuster.

Fraser, Harry L. 1951. *Chained for Life*. Beverly Hills: Spera Productions. Film.

Freud, Sigmund. 2001. *On Dreams*. New York: Dover.

Garland-Thomson, Rosemarie. 1996. "Introduction: From Wonder to Error—A Genealogy of Freak Discourse in Modernity." In *Freakery: Cultural Spectacles of the Extraordinary Body*, edited by Rosemarie Garland-Thomson, 1–19. New York: New York University Press.

Goffman, Erving. 1963. *Stigma: Notes on the Management of Spoiled Identity*. Englewood Cliffs: Prentice-Hall.

Hall, Stuart. 1997. "The Spectacle of the 'Other.'" In *Representation: Cultural Representations and Signifying Practices*, edited by Stuart Hall, 223–290. London: Sage.

Hampton, Simon. 2005. "Family Eugenics." *Disability & Society* 20(5): 553–561.

Haraway, Donna. 1991. "A Cyborg Manifesto: Science, Technology, and Socialist-Feminism in the Late Twentieth Century." In *Simians, Cyborgs and Women: The Reinvention of Nature*, edited by Donna Haraway, 149–181. New York: Routledge.

Helliwell, John, Layard Richard, and Sachs Jeffery. 2016. *World Happiness Report, 2016*. The Earth Institute, Columbia University; Sustainable Development Solutions Network; Center for Economic Performance; Canadian Institute for Advanced Research.

Jackson, Kathy, Lisa Payne, and Kathy Stoley. 2016. *The Intersection of Star Culture in American and International Medical Tourism*. Lanham, MD: Lexington Books.

Johnson, Carl. 1984. "Cancer Incidence in an Area of Radioactive Fallout Downwind from the Nevada Test Site." *Journal of the American Medical Association* 251(2): 230–236.

Jones, Richard, and Kirstin Lopez. 2006. *Human Reproductive Biology*. Third Edition. Boston: Academic Press.

Lev, Elizabeth. 2011. "Misdirected Wonder at the Miracle of Life: Rottenness in Denmark." *Zenit*. https://zenit.org/articles/misdirected-wonder-at-the-miracle-of-life-rottenness-beyond-denmark/.

Longmore, Paul. 2001. "Screening Stereotypes: Images of Disabled People." *Social Policy* 16: 31–37.

Mangano, Joseph. 1999. *Low Level Radiation and Immune System Damage: An Atomic Era Legacy*. Boca Raton: Lewis.

Markotic, Nicole. 2001. "Disabling the Viewer: Perceptions of Disability in Tod Browning's *Freaks*." In *Screening Disability: Essays on Cinema and Disability*, edited by Christopher Smit, 65–72. Lanham, MD: University Press of America.

Marx, Karl. 1998. *The German Ideology*. New York: Prometheus.

Miles, Daniel. 2013. *Radioactive Clouds of Death Over Utah: Downwinders' Fallout Cancer Epidemic Updated*. Manchester: Trafford.

Miller, Richard. 1986. *Under the Cloud: The Decades of Nuclear Testing*. The Woodlands, TX: Two Sixty Press.

Mulvey, Laura. 1975. "Visual Pleasure and Narrative Cinema." *Screen* 16(3): 22–34.

Murphy, Ryan, and Brad Falchuk. 2014–2015. *American Horror Story: Freak Show*. Los Angeles: 20th Century Television. Television.

Parens, Erik, and Adrienne Asch. 2000. "The Disability Rights Critique of Prenatal Genetic Testing: Reflections and Recommendations." *Prenatal Testing and Disability Rights*, edited by Eric Parens and Adrienne Asch, 3–43. Washington, D.C.: Georgetown University Press.

Rosen, Fred. 1995. *Lobster Boy: The Bizarre Life and Brutal Death of Grady Stiles, Jr.* New York: Open Road.

Smith, Angela. 2011. *Hideous Progeny: Disability, Eugenics, and Classic Horror Cinema.* New York: Columbia University Press.

Smith, Dorothy. 1987. *The Everyday World as Problematic: A Feminist Sociology.* Toronto: University of Toronto Press.

Tremain, Shelley. 2006. "Reproductive Freedom, Self-Regulation, and the Government of Impairment in Utero." *Hypatia* 21(1): 35–53.

Wallis, Claudia. 1996. "The Most Intimate Bond." *Time* 14(13): 60–64.

Weissbrod, Ellen. 1999. *Face to Face: The Story of the Schnappell Twins.* A & E Television. Television. VHS.

Whittington-Walsh, Fiona. 2002. "From Freaks to Savants: Disability and Hegemony from The Hunchback of Notre Dame (1939) to Sling Blade (1997)." *Disability & Society* 17(6): 695–707.

Whittington-Walsh, Fiona. 2007. "Freak Mythology: Ideological Construction of Conjoined Twins." Paper presented at the Somatechnics Conference, panel Enfreakment, Macquarie University, Sydney, Australia. April 21 2007.

Power and Punishment in *Game of Thrones*

MIA HARRISON

The impact HBO's *Game of Thrones* has had on the discussion of disability in pop culture is undeniable. In 2013, the Media Access Awards (an organization honoring "accurate, inclusive, and multi-faceted" depictions of disability) awarded it the Visionary Award for producing "a show that embraces the reality that no one is easily definable" (Winter Is Coming 2013). The various characters with disabilities in the series (notably the "dwarf" Tyrion Lannister) have inspired countless think pieces on disability representation. More importantly, the characters have taught millions of able-bodied viewers that disability need not be confined by two-dimensional plot devices and tropes often found in popular media. The idea of a complex, compelling, ambitious, sexual, intelligent, brave, kind, or cruel character pursuing goals and relationships independent of their disabilities is still an abstract concept for television shows intending to reach broad audiences. Yet, characters such as Tyrion demonstrate that it is possible to create interesting narrative arcs that neither depend upon nor ignore the physical and social realities of disability. With so many writers continuing to exploit stereotypes that essentialize the experiences of people with disabilities, rather than exploring diverse stories and characters, Tyrion's complexity and popularity with audiences is significant (Rodan and Ellis 2016).

Despite the media focus on Tyrion, however, *Game of Thrones* is host to a multitude of characters with disabilities that expose broader trends in popular disability representation. Politicized constructions of the disabled body are more deeply embedded in pop culture than the largely positive reaction to *Game of Thrones* might suggest. *Game of Thrones* does many things well, such as casting actors with disabilities to portray characters such as Tyrion (actor Peter Dinklage was born with achondroplasia) and Maester

Aemon (the late Peter Vaughan was partially blind), but it is not immune to other problematic narrative trends in disability representation. Additionally, the show appears to offer a critique of these narratives, playing on audience preconceptions and exposing biases. Normalized depictions of disability in media are important both for combatting sociocultural stereotyping, and for encouraging positive constructions of self-identity amongst audiences with disabilities (Dahl 1993). Due to the diversity of experiences presented in the show (both positive and problematic), *Game of Thrones* serves as a productive case study for understanding the ways pop culture has the power to subvert or reinforce dominant ableist narratives.

It is easy to overlook problematic notions of disability when they are placed next to celebrated examples such as Tyrion Lannister. Others have written extensively on the complexity of Tyrion's character in both the show and the books that *Game of Thrones* is based on, with notable examples including Massie and Mayer (2014), Lambert (2015), and Ellis (2014). This essay will therefore look beyond the more acclaimed representation of Tyrion, and instead investigate the subtle and normalized ways ableist rhetoric is validated and complicated in *Game of Thrones* holistically beyond any individual character.

Disability as Punishment

The "disability as punishment" trope is one of the oldest disability tropes, with its roots stretching back to biblical and mythological narratives. The trope is frequently used in classical stories where characters are blinded as direct or implied punishment for a wrongdoing such as the biblical Zedekiah and Tobit, Rhoecus and Phineus of Greek mythology, and Peeping Tom in the legend of Lady Godiva (Baskin and Harris 1977). In the fantasy genre, disability generally manifests as a form of cosmic justice rather than a direct punishment, where the villain might lose a limb and therefore be seen to have got what they "deserved." Regardless of the circumstance, the implication of this trope is that disability is inherently a "punishment" for someone who has done something wrong. The audience understands that the situation of the character is now unambiguously worse, and the character is lacking in a fundamental way, thereby producing a subject that is less than fully human.

The pervasiveness of the disability as punishment trope is aided by the persistent assumption in society that if something "bad" happens to an individual, there must be a "good" reason for it. This mentality, known as the "Just World" theory, was studied extensively by psychologist Melvin Lerner (2013), whose experiments suggest that people are unwilling to believe that society is ungoverned by a system of rules that reward and punish behavior.

Lerner claims that people believe entitlements, in a general sense, are based on behavior and attributes, so those who behave badly or are "inferior" are entitled to less. The use of this premise in the disability as punishment trope depends upon normative values of disability. Because disability is normatively considered an "undesirable" and "deviant" state, Lerner's work would suggest that, psychologically, people may believe that people with disabilities must have done something to "deserve" them.

We are introduced to the disability as punishment trope in the first episode of *Game of Thrones* with ten-year-old Bran. Towards the end of the episode, Bran climbs the castle wall of his home, despite having promised his mother that he would not. When he discovers the Queen having sex with her twin brother, the renowned knight Jaime Lannister, Jaime pushes Bran from the window, intending for him to die and the secret of their incest along with him. Though surviving the fall, Bran's spine is injured, resulting in the permanent loss of use of his legs. Thus, Bran's disobedience is punished with the narrative justice of acquiring a disability.

Jaime's own "retribution" with the narrative of disability would follow early in season three. Jaime Lannister is defined throughout the first two seasons by his swordsmanship and his relationship with his sister. Fighting is not simply a skill for Jaime, but a crucial part of his identity. Besides those closest to him, few people know who Jaime is beyond the highly skilled knight who killed the previous king. Thus, when his dominant sword hand is chopped off by his enemies, Jaime must learn to create a new identity for himself. Jaime believes it is his sword hand that makes him a knight, claiming, "I was that hand." As he begins to accept his loss, he must also redefine what it means to be Jaime Lannister. Previously, he had always considered himself a male version of his sister—powerful, attractive, and self-interested. The ridicule and stigma he experiences after his hand is removed allows him to relate more to his other sibling, Tyrion.

The removal of Jaime's hand is the pivotal point of his story arc. Though it is tempting to decide Jaime's past behavior warrants such a "punishment," his development as the series progresses complicates this perspective. Before this event, we know he is guilty of murder, regicide, incest, and general cruelty. His loss teaches him humility. Over the course of season three, Jaime opens up and starts treating his traveling companion, Brienne, with kindness. At one point, he even risks his life to save her. We see that he has true affection for Tyrion, and is perhaps the only person who genuinely loves him. For Jaime, his right hand symbolizes everything he must forfeit to become a better person: his fighting, his masculinity, and his selfishness.

Despite this transformation, a metaphorical analysis of Jaime's arc reveals that he has not quite outgrown the paradigms that govern his society. When Jaime's stump is on display, he is portrayed as broken and raw, yet there is an integrity to his emotions that was never before seen. The moment he returns home, however, he is fitted with an "elegant" prosthesis and is encouraged to act as though he is the same person he was before. For Jaime to pass as "normal," both he and his society must accept his prosthesis as an adequate replacement for his hand, thus restoring his status to the dominant position of normativity, and consequently desirability. Jaime, however, refuses to do this entirely, pointing out that a hook would be more practical than a hand constructed from gold. The prosthesis is clumsy and heavy, limiting its functionality as an instrument. It functions well, however, as a status symbol, ensuring that although Jaime has been lowered in the social hierarchy according to his ability, he still retains the privilege of wealth and political power. Jaime's prosthesis presents an interesting commentary on passing politics in disability studies—that passing is not only made possible by the conscious acts of a person with a disability, but also by the collective repression of society (Siebers 2004). Jaime understands that his life would be physically easier with a hook or no prosthesis at all, but socially it would be made more difficult. By donning a normative appendage—better yet, one that is made of an expensive material that flaunts his higher status—Jaime demonstrates that adhering to social conventions is easier than accepting a disabled identity.

This attitude towards disability provides a complicated approach to the disability as punishment trope. Though presented superficially as a form of cosmic justice, the viewer is encouraged to feel that Jaime is undeserving of his punishment. Despite the difficulties of learning to adjust to the use of one hand, Jaime soon becomes a much more interesting and complex figure in his own right. His story arc surpasses the singular loss of his hand, and instead presents a richly developed character that is much more than simply a one-handed soldier. Jaime becomes a man learning to reconcile a range of varying and often conflicting identities—a knight, a lord's son, a cripple, a Kingslayer, a lover, a brother, a son, a killer, and a protector. It is the interplay of these identities that makes Jaime who he is.

Jaime Lannister highlights an important distinction that should be made when discussing disability representation. While it is problematic to assign disability as the primary denotation of subjecthood, it should not be denied that disability can often form an intrinsic part of identity, and must, therefore, be studied with attention to the experience of being "disabled" in any particular society (Mitchell and Snyder 2000). Jaime's lack of his sword hand does not define him. Rather, it frees him of the self-imposed definitions of identity he had formerly possessed, and allows him to have a new and complex relationship with the society he had previously thought he understood. This transformation is impressive, yet might never have happened without the loss of his hand. In this way, Jaime both resists and conforms to the disability as punishment trope as a character that is in many ways the product of his disability, yet is still able to transgress the traditional expectations of a "disabled character."

Poor Little Things, Brave Little Souls

Social attitudes towards disability are often informed by paradoxical feelings of compassion and distrust (Baskin and Harris 1977). Characters with disabilities regularly function as metaphors for wider social issues. This can be seen in common examples such as the popular blind character who is perceptive of things nobody else can see. This character is one of the many disability tropes that are generally presented to foster sympathy but rarely provide a favorable or complex understanding of disability representation. Characters with disabilities routinely present a specific set of stereotypical traits: they are non-sexual, a burden on those around them, and are often the object of violence or humor (Irwin and Moeller 2010). They are to be pitied, derided, or feared. These characteristics come together to produce what Ayala refers to as "poor little things" and "brave little souls" (2010).

In *Game of Thrones*, Princess Shireen, a young girl left disfigured by a usually fatal disease, is a key example of the "poor little thing" trope. Shireen is despised by her mother and largely neglected by her father. Though regularly featured throughout the series, she is never afforded the opportunity to become a complete character in her own right. In fact, her various interactions with other characters serve to explain their personalities and motivations more than her own. Those who show Shireen compassion are presented as "good," while those who resent her, or seek only to use her for personal gain are "bad." When she is eventually burnt alive as a sacrifice, the camera (rarely shy of visceral deaths) spends most of its time on the faces of Shireen's parents, rather than Shireen herself. It is their different reactions to her death, rather than the death itself, that are important.

Shireen's various appearances throughout *Game of Thrones* highlight the functionality of her disability in the narrative. Her death was widely regarded as one of the most "gut-churning" scenes of the show to date, despite the audience knowing very little of who Shireen is beyond a scaly face and a symbol of innocence (Kornhaber 2015). In fact, it is that very innocence that caused so many to react so strongly to the scene. *The Hollywood Reporter* lamented that her death was so painful because she was "one of the only characters whose innocence hadn't been taken away" (Couch 2015). In a series like *Game of Thrones*, the death of a child is not shocking—there are even articles dedicated to ranking the deaths of children in the show (Jones 2015). As a "poor little thing," however, Shireen functions as a mirror to the morality of those around her. It is not her death that is difficult to cope with, but the understanding that it was socially sanctioned.

The character Hodor similarly fits the "poor little thing" trope. He is unusually large (a result of possible gigantism) with a suggested intellectual disability, and is only able to say one word: "Hodor." Hodor's role in *Game of Thrones* is a particularly problematic example of disability representation, as he literally provides a prosthesis for Bran. Hodor not only carries Bran, but also supplies a body for him to magically possess (known in *Game of Thrones* as "warging"), a feat so unusual it can be assumed that it was only made possible due to Hodor's disability. Here the combination of Hodor's physical ability, and Bran's intellectual ability, combine to create one fully-functioning being, rendering each of them individually less than human.

For most of *Game of Thrones*, the prosthetic and comedic function of Hodor's physical ability and intellectual disability is relatively inconsequential. Hodor helps progress the narrative in a practical fashion, as he literally enables Bran to move through the story. In this way, Hodor could easily be replaced by a horse and specialized saddle, much like the one Tyrion gifts Bran in the first season. He also provides Bran with strength, something which Bran forcibly takes from Hodor when he wargs into his body without consent. Hodor's function as an object of humor and pity, or a tool to be abused by others more "intellectually capable" than him, serves as a troubling reflection of the experiences of individuals with intellectual disabilities (Rapley 2004; Marquis and Jackson 2000; Jahoda et al. 2010). Though treated sympathetically by the narrative, Hodor is ultimately abused or laughed at by most of the show's characters.

It is not until season six when it is revealed Bran inadvertently caused Hodor's disability, and possibly his death (Hodor's fate is unclear at the end of season six), that the implication of Hodor's function as a narrative device is truly appreciated. While *Game of Thrones* is infamous for killing off major characters, the treatment of Hodor and Shireen is especially problematic because their roles as disabled characters allow the writers to substitute superficial sympathy in audiences for genuine empathy. The show can provide a tragic backstory, or present a young, innocent girl who is socially burdened by her disfigurement, as a quick way to elicit emotion without dealing with the complexities of the experience. Given that the writers have proven in characters such as Tyrion that they can develop complex and commendable emotional arcs in characters with disabilities, the trope-heavy shortcuts employed with Hodor and Shireen are all the more troubling.

Conversely, characters such as the cosmetically disfigured antihero Sandor Clegane demonstrate that *Game of Thrones* is well aware of the impact corporeal tropes can have in fantasy media. Physical appearance in fantasy often directly relates to the spiritual "goodness" of a character—heroes and royal figures are beautiful, while villains are malformed and hideous (Lambert 2015). Fictional disability is considered a trope for human suffering and/or corruption, where the disabled character becomes a manifestation of pity or evil, a figure to be sympathized with or feared (Baskin and Harris 1977). In the case of Sandor Clegane, the show complicates this trope by deliberately playing up the grotesqueness of the facial burns he received as a child, while slowly unpacking the psyche of the character. As the series progresses, Clegane's villainy is first explained, then subverted as he makes decisions that increasingly seem to help the show's protagonists. This is further complicated when the young, shallow, and beautiful Sansa Stark appears to be developing suppressed romantic feelings for Clegane. This subversion builds upon the dichotomy of beauty and monstrosity that stories such as *Beauty and the Beast* have relied upon for hundreds of years. Beast-type characters like Clegane present a complex commentary on stigma and social prejudice (Berberi and Berberi 2013). Where the initial pairing of Clegane's physical monstrosity with his callous and cruel behavior appears to conform to broader tropes of disability signifying evil in fiction, *Game of Thrones* manages to destabilize this popular convention. Though sometimes pitiful, and sometimes villainous, Clegane never completely conforms to these stereotypes.

The "poor little things" and "brave little souls" of *Game of Thrones* highlight the broader ways that disability tropes are employed by fantasy writers as substitutes for complex character development. By presenting characters as pitiful, frightening, inspirational, or visually interesting based solely on their physical or intellectual difference, fantasy representations of disability contribute to harmful popular narratives that establish people with disabilities as a cultural "Other." Though *Game of Thrones* does utilize disability tropes in many ways that are problematic, it also displays an understanding of the popularity of these tropes, subverting them to expose the ableist values that disability tropes depend upon for their power. Characters such as Sandor Clegane show how writers can use disability tropes in ways that uncover the undercurrent of ableist ideologies that populate fantasy narratives. By forcing audiences to confront their initial expectations of a disabled character, disability tropes can provide audiences with the opportunity to question the assumptions they make based on cognitive and physical difference.

Supercrips

Another popular disability trope is the "supercrip," a character of incredible talent because, or in spite, of their disability (Siebers 2004). In traditional fantasy narratives, this character rarely accomplishes more than any of the other characters. The assumption is that characters with disabilities are so grievously disadvantaged that seemingly inconsequential feats (in some cases, just being employed, successful, or happy) should be considered a great achievement. Romanticizing characters with disabilities can lead to these characters being praised for achieving tasks a "normal" person would have no difficulty doing (Baskin and Harris 1977). This sentimental approach to disability representation has become especially popular in social media narratives today (commonly referred to as "inspiration porn"), but is still regularly employed in the fantasy genre (Ellis 2015).

The elevation of ordinary characters to "exceptional" or "inspirational" purely based on their disability invites a voyeuristic reading of disability narratives, where physical or cognitive disability is exaggerated to encourage empathy (Siebers 2004). In addition to these exaggerated disabilities, which must be "overcome" (literally or metaphorically) by the end of the narrative, characters with disabilities also regularly possess talents that supersede those of the other characters, as though providing balance for their apparent "lack." This overcompensation takes on an interesting quality in fantasy narratives, where mystical abilities are paired with characters who provide visual interest to the story. Such is the case with the infamous "blind seer" trope popular in fantasy stories (Dahl 1993). This character type, though visually impaired in a physical sense, can metaphorically "see" more than anyone else. A lesser version of this presents itself in *Game of Thrones* through the perceptiveness of the elderly and blind scholar Maester Aemon, who despite being unable to see is always able to tell when a person is speaking the truth. The blind seer trope in fantasy builds upon the binary of the blind and not-blind in fiction, which is generally perceived as a dichotomy between those who can experience truth, and those who cannot (Bolt 2013). Writers usually disqualify blind subjects from experiences such as truth and beauty in narratives, instead dehumanizing them by suggesting that the ability to see is a prerequisite for understanding these values. The blind seer inverts this metaphor, giving blind characters the ability to see more than their sighted fellows. This is an equally problematic disability metaphor because it implies the character only regains the value "lost" through their blindness by acquiring a supernatural ability.

Game of Thrones employs the blind seer trope with Arya Stark, the runaway orphan daughter of the Lord of the North. In an attempt to recreate her identity, Arya accepts blindness as part of a necessary sacrifice in the pursuit of gaining the magical abilities of the "faceless" assassins. In the supercrip trope, disability becomes a form of currency. Arya commodifies her body, trading sight for the opportunity to gain a supernatural talent. This trading of disability for ability is not unique to *Game of Thrones*, with fiction regularly featuring characters who, on their quests for spiritual enlightenment, have their disability manifest as "payment" (Baskin and Harris 1977). When pop culture presents disability in such a way, it reflects the societal perception that pain is noble, and suffering for a greater cause is purifying. Disability is not simply an accident or a fact of life, but a price characters pay for greater power.

Game of Thrones employs the commodification of disability throughout the series in two major and distinct ways: voluntarily and involuntarily. Throughout her training, Arya is constantly offered the opportunity to regain her sight and return to her former life. In each instance, she refuses, understanding that her disability is a temporary "sacrifice" for a noble cause. Conversely, Maester Aemon's blindness is naturally acquired. Though *Game of Thrones* does not directly attribute his perceptiveness to his blindness, the show tries to highlight the irony of a blind man being able to clearly see the true nature of those around him. Arya's younger brother, Bran, similarly acquires his disability involuntarily and (perhaps even more so given his age) his attitude towards disability is vastly different to that of his sister.

When Bran loses his ability to walk he becomes bitter, believing this to be the one real obstacle to his success. Bran's "accident" is seen throughout his homeland as a terrible tragedy, and is considered by most to be worse than death. In fact, it is remarked that his murder would be a "mercy" as he is "dead already." Further still, Jaime Lannister reflects that "even if the boy lives, he'll be a cripple, a grotesque." Though these comments are undoubtedly motivated by self-interest, the mentality is consistent with what society had thus far held for Bran, as one of the younger sons of his family, valued only for the promise of becoming a solider. With this potential now taken away, Bran has entirely lost his value. The only character who seems to believe otherwise is Tyrion, who ("speaking for the grotesques") tells Jaime, "Life is full of possibilities." As someone who has equally been the victim of society's low expectations for people with disabilities, only Tyrion can imagine a life beyond the limited and gendered futures afforded to the able-bodied characters of the world of *Game of Thrones*.

Despite Tyrion's more optimistic outlook on disability, it is only through the acquisition of supernatural abilities that Bran can move past his anger and develop as a character. His ability to warg begins almost immediately after his accident, with the trauma acting as a trigger to unlock his "gift." Warging gives Bran the ability to literally change his skin. He can run as a wolf and is even promised that he will one day fly. These abilities allow Bran's body to become almost irrelevant. Even still, part of him always believes that he will be able to find a way to regain the use of his legs. As the show continues, however, it becomes clear that this is impossible. When he reaches the end of his initial quest in the finale of season four, he is told bluntly that he "will never walk again." By understanding and accepting the permanence of his disability, Bran is able to spend more energy focusing on developing his unique talents.

Here *Game of Thrones* differs from popular fictional works such as *The Secret Garden*, *Pollyanna*, and *What Katy Did*; there is no "magical cure" for Bran (Keith 2001). Yet the magnitude of his new talents are presented as adequate compensation for his loss, which is similarly problematic. Disability becomes a sacrifice, and it is only by acquiring extraordinary and unique gifts that Bran regains his value. Bran is never given the opportunity to prove that he is still valuable and interesting as a boy who cannot walk. He is petulant, resentful of being carried around, and widely regarded as a pitiful "cripple." Without discovering that he possesses talents that far surpass those of almost any of the other character, he might never have transcended that role. As a "supercrip," Bran's status as a cripple is useful only if it allows him access to greater power.

The supercrip trope depends upon the problematic mythology of "disability as an advantage" (Siebers 2001). By establishing disability as a position of desirability, the suffering of individuals who experience pain and stigma are undermined. This mythology manifests itself in popular perceptions of people with disabilities as "cheats" trying to obtain benefits such as welfare payments, better parking spaces, or cuts in line at Disneyland (Hadley 2016). Individuals are constantly called on to perform their disability and to prove that they are actually deserving of their "reward." The transactional nature of Bran's mystical abilities plays into this idea. Rather than working through his pain or reaching out for help, Bran is simply "reimbursed" with extraordinary powers. Thus, disability is symbolically transformed into a sacrifice for something "greater." This, of course, is not a choice given to people with disabilities, and negates the social disadvantage and isolation felt by those who experience this position. As an example of disability representation, Bran is inadequate, as his strength and complexity all come from sources he has no control over. He is never allowed the opportunity to empower himself.

Eunuchs

Where historically difference has been a sign of power, modern society values homogeneity, and privileges the "normal" subject as the most desirable position (Garland-Thomson 1997). The normate is unmarked and valuable for its "neutrality." Hegemonic thought favors a medical perspective of ability, where someone is either able or not, and encourages the invisibility of those who do not adhere to a normative standard of able-bodiedness (McRuer 2006a). Disabled existence is often sidelined in similar ways to queer existence as posited in Adrienne Rich's (1980) famous essay on "Compulsory Heterosexuality," where disabled and queer bodies are both considered at best invisible or alternatively deviant and unnatural. To explore this intersection of the disabled queer experience, the eunuchs of *Game of Thrones* present an interesting subject of analysis, as they regularly challenge notions of gender, able-bodiedness, and sexuality.

The Unsullied are the most normalized example of the eunuch in *Game of Thrones*. Children are sold from a young age to the Unsullied slavemasters, with males being trained as highly obedient soldiers. Their names are taken from them, instead being replaced with that of vermin such as "Red Flea" and "Grey Worm," and their genitals are removed in the final stages of training. They are described as having "absolute obedience, absolute loyalty," with one of the slaves explaining: "They obey, that is all. Once they are yours, they are yours. They will fall on their swords if you command it."

The Unsullied body is systemized into fragments that are categorized as "useful" (the parts of the body that can be used to fight) and "useless" (the parts of the body that cannot). The slave master demonstrates the systemization of the Unsullied body by slicing off the nipple of one of his soldiers while explaining that "men don't need nipples." The Unsullied challenge notions of "able-bodied heterosexuality" by considering the sexual, able body as not simply unnecessary, but an obstacle towards obedience (McRuer 2006a, 302). The Unsullied do not embody a masculine identity—they are not considered men at all. This is not to suggest, however, that the Unsullied should be considered positive examples of non-normative identity representation. Instead, they present a clear idea of what should be considered the "acceptable" queer or disabled body: docile, compliant, and useful only in the service of others.

The eunuchs in *Game of Thrones* might be the perfect pop culture example of Foucault's (1977) studies into the "power of normalization" (208). The eunuch is at once both deviant and submissive. Castration is implemented not only as punishment, but as a method for ensuring good behavior. Yet this behavior is never rewarded. The eunuch is always considered less than a man, and the absence of genitalia is regularly used as the most prominent description for characters who have been castrated. Thus, the word "eunuch" operates in a similar way to the act of castration itself. By defining the eunuch not simply by what it is (a eunuch), but also by what it is not (a "man"), individuals without genitalia are treated categorically, and thus are denied individuality. This essentialist view of the eunuch is consistent with historical and biblical classification, with all eunuchs—as defined by Ulpian in Roman Law: "those by nature, those who are made, … and any other kind"—donning the same name (Kuefler 2001, 33). Furthermore, the categorization of the eunuch disqualifies those who have been castrated from full participation in society because they belong to a group that is fundamentally "Other."

The innate Othering of the eunuch can be seen most clearly in the once arrogant and traitorous young lord, Theon Greyjoy, who becomes ultimately unrecognizable after his castration. After being captured and tortured in season three, his fingers and penis are brutally removed as he undergoes physical and psychological torment. This treatment eventually transforms him into the alter-ego "Reek." Where Theon was proud and cheerful, yet often cruel, Reek is nobody. He is the perfect servant, so fearful of his master that he does not dare disobey him. He abandons his previous identity and instead adopts the only persona he has been permitted by his master. Like the Unsullied, he is a malleable creature, built to obey. On one level, this presents another superficial example of the disability as punishment trope. Theon's past behavior has been appalling: he betrayed his adopted family, murdered two children, and generally acted abhorrently. On another level, it would be simplistic to treat his fate as a form of "justice" because his punishment is so extreme it is difficult to apply the Just World theory to Theon. Even within the disability as punishment trope, the violence he experiences seems too severe for any crime. The torture and castration of Theon becomes more than the simple result of narrative justice—it is a crucial part of the character's formation of selfhood (a.k.a. the assumption of "Reek").

Even once Theon resumes his former identity and returns to his family, he is viewed by those who used to know him as less than a man. His sister, whom he had previously been infuriated to think might replace him as commander of their father's fleet is now seen as the superior of the two. This is further supported by his sister's sexuality: while she is able and eager to have sex with women, Theon—emotionally and physically traumatized by his torture and castration—is not. Even though Theon's sister similarly lacks a penis, her dominant personality and sexual relationships with women afford her an identity of masculinity that Theon no longer possesses. When she puts herself forward as the heir to the Greyjoy family, Theon is her greatest supporter. From an intersectional perspective of disability studies, this new relationship between siblings is bittersweet; while Theon's support for his sister is both progressive and evident of a rejection of traditional notions of masculinity, this rejection has been forced upon Theon through violence. It is also only made possible because of Theon's regressive ideas about disability and what is means to be a "man," as well as the more broadly posited idea in fictional narratives that to be a eunuch is to be sexless (Pugh 2008). Interestingly, the inclusion of Theon's sister's sexuality resists classical ideas about eunuchs—that they disrupt the norm of men as dominant and penetrating in sex, while women are penetrated (Kuefler 2001). By placing Theon's sexlessness next to the non-heteronormative sexuality of his sister, *Game of Thrones* challenges the idea of the eunuch as dangerous to the sexual normativity of society. While Theon presents problematic ideas about disability, gender, and sexuality, the complexity of his representation encourages new ways of thinking about what it means to be a man in an ableist patriarchal society. The most complex and prominent eunuch in *Game of Thrones* is undoubtedly Lord Varys, regularly referred to as simply "the eunuch." For most of the series he sits on the small council as the Master of Whispers, commanding a far-reaching network of child spies that he uses to maneuver himself and those around him politically. He is bald, fat, and effeminate, often dressing in soft velvet robes. Interestingly, Varys never makes attempts to "pass" as an able-bodied heterosexual male, despite the cultural pressures of able-heteroperformativity (McRuer 2006b). Even though it would presumably be easy to hide his castration, Varys instead embraces the gender and sexual ambiguity associated with being a eunuch. He capitalizes on his identity to pursue sex work as a teenager. In season three, he has a "coming-out" scene where he shares the story of his castration with Tyrion and his ascent into his position of power. Though his identity as a eunuch has been no secret, the act of Varys actively entering a political sphere of disability by sharing his experiences mirrors the coming-out narratives of queer communities, where an identity is taken from the medicalized private realm into the political (Garland-Thomson 2002). This complicates the implicit negative associations of his disability by actively denying those around Varys from having the privilege of thinking of him as "normal."

Beyond his role on the council and his identity as a eunuch, Lord Varys is an enigma. The viewer is given very little about his history, his motives, or how he spends most of his time. His temperament is pleasant and steady, yet he proves several times to be capable of murder if it will serve his agenda. Though such skills cannot be directly attributed to his castration, the show regularly links the two:

> CERSEI: Do you know why Varys is so dangerous?
> TYRION: Because he has thousands of spies in his employ. Because he knows everything we do before we do it.
> CERSEI: Because he doesn't have a cock.

Varys' lack of "manhood" affords him a fluidity of identity, and possibly morality, that might not have been attainable were he not a eunuch. Indeed, women and eunuchs are compared explicitly in season one as the kinds of people who choose poison as a murder weapon. Being a eunuch is inextricably entwined with Varys' identity. This frees him from the socially-imposed restrictions of "normalcy." He shares a space with the most dangerous women of the show, acquiring power through political savvy rather than brute force. In being denied the identity of a "man," Varys is paradoxically given the opportunity to choose his own identity.

The exclusion of the eunuch from manhood parallels the exclusion of women with disabilities from traditional roles of femininity. As with Varys, Theon, and the Unsullied, women with disabilities are often considered "genderless" and "asexual," which some have argued can be viewed as freedom from the strictly gendered roles of a patriarchal society (Asch and Fine 1997). By rejecting traditional notions of masculinity, the Unsullied become more disciplined and better warriors. Theon becomes a more supportive brother and compassionate human being, and Varys can occupy a space in society that is usually reserved for women and children, while still retaining elements of his male privilege (i.e., his various positions of high political power throughout the series). Though not considered traditionally "disabled," eunuchs are treated primarily in relation to their physical "deficiency" in the show. The lack of mention of prosthetic use (even in a sexual context) suggests that castration is not a state that is regarded as "remediable," so must therefore be considered innate. Yet, the trauma of their experiences also affects them in profound and difficult ways. Thus, castration proves crucial in the formation of these characters' narrative identities.

Conclusion

Disability representation in popular media still has a long way to go. Shows such as *Game of Thrones* demonstrate an acknowledgment in the television industry of the value of disability narratives in pop culture, and the overwhelmingly positive reception of Tyrion Lannister as a major character provides hope that more writers will follow this example. Yet *Game of Thrones* is also highly indicative of many of the weaknesses of disability story conventions. For a show that is widely regarded to be one of the best examples of disability representation in popular media, the series still perpetuates some of the harmful stereotypes that often dominate stories about disability in pop culture. This, perhaps more than anything else, demonstrates that there is still much work to be done.

Besides Tyrion Lannister, one of the most constructive efforts *Game of Thrones* makes in disability representation is its complication of usually simplistic ableist tropes. Though imperfect, the series stands out as a notable example of the multiplicity of disability in television. It can be tempting to focus on these positive examples of disability representation when considering *Game of Thrones* and thus forgive the exploitation of problematic stereotypes. After all, most shows only avoid this problem by simply not providing any disability representation whatsoever. *Game of Thrones'* successes in disability representation prove that nuanced constructions of disability in characters are not only possible, but also far more compelling than simplistic renditions of overused and problematic tropes.

It is important to consider both the strengths and problems with *Game of Thrones* if we hope to understand the current climate of disability representation in cultural consciousness. Intersectional disability representation is still severely lacking in popular culture, and queer or feminist readings of disabled characters cannot compensate for this inadequacy. While characters such as Theon or Varys might create opportunities for audiences to see themselves reflected in fictional narratives, they are unsatisfactory substitutes for purposeful and complex intersectional representation. There are still few examples of queer, non-male, or non-white characters with disabilities in popular media that explore how these different identities interplay to produce more complex subjects. *Game of Thrones* stands as a tangible example of what pop culture is doing well. Nevertheless, it also indicates what work is left to be done. A more positive future for disability in pop culture will see shows of similar popularity able to entirely forgo simplistic tropes or broadly privileged disability representation in favor of characters that are better able to reflect the diversity of contemporary audiences.

REFERENCES

Asch, Adrienne, and Michelle Fine. 1997. "Nurturance, Sexuality and Women with Disabilities: The Example of Women and Literature." In *The Disability Studies Reader*, edited by Lennard J. Davis, 241–259. New York: Routledge.
Ayala, Emiliano C. 2010. "'Poor Little Things' and 'Brave Little Souls': The Portrayal of Individuals with Disabilities in Children's Literature." *Literacy Research and Instruction* 39(1): 103–117.
Baskin, Barbara H., and Karen H. Harris. 1977. *Notes from a Different Drummer: A Guide to Juvenile Literature Portraying the Handicapped*. New York: R. R. Bowker.
Berberi, Tammy, and Berberi Viktor. 2013. "A Place at the Table: Being Human in the *Beauty and the Beast* Tradition." In *Diversity in Disney Films: Critical Essays on Race, Ethnicity, Gender, Sexuality and Disability*, edited by Johnson Cheu, 195–208. Jefferson: McFarland.
Bolt, David. 2013. "Aesthetic Blindness: Symbolism, Realism, and Reality." *Mosaic: a journal for the interdisciplinary study of literature* 46(3): 93–108.
Couch, Aaron. 2015. "Did "Game of Thrones" Go Too Far with Latest Death?" *The Hollywood Reporter*, June 7, 2015. http://www.hollywoodreporter.com/live-feed/game-thrones-shireen-baratheon-death-800862.
Dahl, Marilyn. 1993. "The Role of the Media in Promoting Images of Disability-Disability as Metaphor: The Evil Crip." *Canadian Journal of Communication* 18(1).
Ellis, Katie. 2014. "Cripples, Bastards and Broken Things: Disability in *Game of Thrones*." *Journal of Media and Culture* 17(5).
_____. 2015. *Disability and Popular Culture: Focusing Passion, Creating Community and Expressing Defiance*. Farnham: Ashgate.
Foucault, Michel. 1977. *Discipline and Punish: The Birth of the Prison*. London: Penguin.
Garland-Thomson, Rosemary. 1997. *Extraordinary Bodies: Figuring Physical Disability in American Culture and Literature*. New York: Columbia University Press.
_____. 2002. "Integrating Disability, Transforming Feminist Theory." *NWSA Journal* 14(3): 1–32.
Hadley, Bree. 2016. "Cheats, Charity Cases and Inspirations: Disrupting the Circulation of Disability-Based Memes Online." *Disability & Society* 31(5): 676–692.
Irwin, Marilyn, and Robin Moeller. 2010. "Seeing Different: Portrayals of Disability in Young Adult Graphic Novels." *School Library Journal* 40(9): 139–42.

Jahoda, Andrew, et al. 2010. "Living with Stigma and the Self-Perceptions of People with Mild Intellectual Disabilities." *Journal of Social Issues* 66(3): 521–534.

Jones, Nate. 2015. "The Saddest Child Deaths on Game of Thrones … Ranked!" *Vulture*, June 8, 2015. http://www.vulture.com/2015/06/saddest-child-deaths-on-game-of-thrones.html.

Keith, Lois. 2001. *Take Up Thy Bed and Walk: Death, Disability and Cure in Classic Fiction for Girls.* London: The Women's Press.

Kornhaber, Spencer. 2015. "The Most Disturbing Thing About *Game of Thrones'* Most Disturbing Scene." *The Atlantic*, June 11, 2015. http://www.theatlantic.com/entertainment/archive/2015/06/game-of-thrones-shireen-human-sacrifice-history/395573.

Kuefler, Mathew 2001. *The Manly Eunuch: Masculinity, Gender Ambiguity, and Christian Ideology in Late Antiquity.* Chicago: University of Chicago Press.

Lambert, Charles. 2015. "A Tender Spot in My Heart: Disability in *A Song of Ice and Fire.*" *Critical Quarterly* 57(1): 20–33.

Lerner, Melvin. 2013. *The Belief in a Just World: A Fundamental Delusion.* Waterloo: Springer Science & Business Media.

Marquis, Ruth, and Robert Jackson. 2000. "Quality of Life and Quality of Service Relationships: Experiences of People with Disabilities." *Disability & Society* 15(3): 411–425.

Massie, Pascall, and Lauren Mayer. 2014. "Bringing Elsewhere Home: *A Song of Ice and Fire's* Ethics of Disability." In *Studies in Medievalism,* edited by Karl Fugelso, 45–59. Cambridge: D. S. Brewer.

McRuer, Robert. 2006a. "Compulsory Able-Bodiedness and Queer/Disabled Existence." In *The Disability Studies Reader,* edited by Lennard J. Davis, 301–309. New York: Routledge

_____. 2006b. *Crip Theory: Cultural Signs of Queerness and Disability.* New York: New York University Press.

Mitchell, David T., and Sharon L. Snyder. 2000. *Narrative Prosthesis: Disability and the Dependencies of Discourse.* Ann Arbor: University of Michigan Press.

_____. 2010. "The Eugenic Atlantic: Race, Disability, and the Making of an International Eugenic Science, 1800–1945." *Disability & Society* 18(7): 843–864.

Pugh, Tison 2008. *Sexuality and Its Queer Discontents in Middle English Literature.* New York: Palgrave Macmillan.

Rapley, Mark. 2004. *The Social Construction of Intellectual Disability.* Cambridge: Cambridge University Press.

Rich, Adrienne. 1980. "Compulsory Heterosexuality and Lesbian Existence." *Signs* 5(4): 631–660.

Rodan, Debbie, and Katie Ellis. 2016. *Disability, Obesity and Ageing: Popular Media Identifications.* London: Routledge.

Siebers, Tobin. 2001. "Disability in Theory: From Social Constructionism to the New Realism of the Body." *American Literary History* 13(4): 737–754.

_____. 2004. "Disability as Masquerade." *Literature and Medicine* 23(1): 1–22.

Winter Is Coming. 2013. "Game of Thrones Wins Award Honoring Disability Awareness." *Winter Is Coming: The Game of Thrones News Source.* http://winteriscoming.net/2013/10/22/game-of-thrones-wins-award-honoring-disability-awareness.

Superheroes in a Silent World

Hawkeye and El Deafo

BILL BEECHLER, JR.

"Truth, Justice, and the American Way!"
—opening to the television program
The Adventures of Superman (1952)

Jerry Siegel and Joe Shuster were two quiet, teen boys growing up in Cleveland, Ohio, in the 1930s. They bonded over a mutual love of science-fiction stories, created their own fan magazines, and dreamed up a character who would become the template for the American superhero. The two sides of their character—Clark Kent and Superman—reflected the two aspects many readers looked for in a hero protagonist in the first half of the 20th century. The Clark Kent side was meant to be their point of identification. Those consuming comics and movies at the time, especially if they were boys, could see a bit of themselves in Clark. He was the smart, nice guy with glasses who loved his family but was often unlucky in love. He was the very definition of a "normal" guy in the imagination of many Americans in 1940 when the population was 90 percent white (U.S. Census 1940) and President Roosevelt often hid his use of a wheelchair from the public (Berish 2016).

However, movements for equality and inclusion in all areas of public life have changed what readers want to see in pop culture. Clark Kent wore glasses, but he didn't need them. Moreover, even with those glasses and his job as a journalist, he did not seem to acknowledge real world issues. There were reasons for this, of course. It is much easier to write a story about super-heroes defeating an invasion of Earth by space aliens than have them fight poverty and discrimination. By the 1970s, the fight to expand the rights of all Americans finally made it to the pages of DC Comics, the home of Super-man. In a story by Denny O'Neil and Neal Adams (1970) from "Green Lantern co-starring Green Arrow," an elderly African American man approaches Green Lantern, a white superhero space cop, and says, "I been readin' about you … how you work for the blue skins … and how on a planet someplace you helped out the orange skins … and you done considerable for the purple skins! Only there's skins you never bothered with! The Black skins! I want to know…. How come?! Answer me that, Mr. Green Lantern!" (6). That moment was considered the beginning of the "relevant comics" movement, which continues to evolve today (Irving 2009).

While recent strides have been made in character representation away from the straight, white, male template, physical and sensory challenges continue to be difficult to find in superhero stories on the page and screen beyond the most tokenistic representations. When they are depicted in stories and characters, it is often by writers and artists who do not have those challenges themselves or do not take the time to get to know the community of fans who do in any meaningful way (Doug T. 2016).

Two recent examples of characters, both well-received by fans with and without deafness, allow for an exploration of the real life experience of being deaf within the comic book medium. The first example is Hawkeye, who is the uber-archer from the Avengers. His tag line is "I'm an orphan raised by carnies fighting with a stick and a string from the Paleolithic era" (Fraction 2012). Most know the Hawkeye character as played by Jeremy Renner from the Joss Whedon films *The Avengers* (2012) and *Avengers: Age of Ultron* (2015) and the Russo Brothers' film *Captain America: Civil War* (2016). Fans are generally surprised to learn that Hawkeye has been a long-running character who has been shown to have deafness on and off through decades in Marvel comics. The first real effort to show what it is like to be a deaf superhero in a world of gods, monsters, and super-science was published in 2014 in the last few issues of the "Hawkeye" series by Matt Fraction and David Aja. The second example is *El Deafo* by Cece Bell. This graphic novel is based on a superhero character Bell created when she was a young child that led to self-empowerment (Bell 2014).

While the stories of Hawkeye and El Deafo are both about characters who are deaf, they are unique pieces of art. Their authors' viewpoints and life experiences, the creative environment in which they were created, and the intended audiences for the works all left their marks. For instance, the creators of Hawkeye are not deaf, but they did seek out fans and non-fans in the deaf community for input in creating Hawkeye. *El Deafo* is the depiction of Cece Bell's real experiences as a deaf child. The issues of Hawkeye by Fraction and Aja were meant for an older teen and adult audience. *El Deafo* is an all-ages story, using cute animals as stand-ins for Bell and the people in her life. "Hawkeye" is a comic series that is one part of the larger universe that makes up Marvel comics, which includes hundreds of titles and thousands of issues since 1961. While Fraction and Aja were the creators of a comic series featuring Hawkeye, which ran from 2012 to 2014, Hawkeye continued and continues to be used as a character in other comic series published by Marvel and the character's main title continued after this creative team left. *El Deafo* is a self-contained, biographical story which is told by Cece Bell and is under her complete control.

Hawkeye and the Erasure of Disability

"My! People come and go so quickly here!"
—Dorothy in *The Wizard of Oz* (1939)

In the Avengers films, there are no indications that Hawkeye is, or ever was, hearing impaired. In fact, for years in the comics it was not a part of his backstory either. Hawkeye was created in 1964 by Stan Lee and Don Heck in "Tales of Suspense" #57 as a foil for Tony Stark's superhero identity, Iron Man. As an orphan, he was raised in a traveling circus and perfected his archery skills there. For a while he played the villainous role but, primarily due to his hero-worship of Captain America, Hawkeye decided to reform and became a member of the team in "The Avengers" #16 in 1965. He and the team of superheroes had years of adventures together but it was not until a 1983 "Hawkeye" miniseries, by Mark Gruenwald and Brett Breeding, that Hawkeye became a deaf superhero. During the miniseries, a villain uses an "ultrasonic" device to make the heroic duo of Hawkeye and Mockingbird attack each other. The villain turns off the device for a few moments to assess the amount of time it takes victims to recover and, during that short time, Hawkeye takes a "hypersonic" arrowhead and places it in his mouth to counteract the "ultrasonic" device. While the science behind it may be a tad unrealistic, in the story it keeps the villainous device from working on Hawkeye, enabling the duo to defeat the villain. The side effect of having the "hypersonic" arrowhead in his mouth is severe damage to his middle ear that causes deafness.

Throughout the Marvel comics of the 1980s, when the writers and artists remembered—which was not often—Hawkeye wore a small hearing aid and at times, struggled to use it. In fact, one of the only times it was mentioned in-story was when the Avengers appeared on the David Letterman show in "The Avengers" #239, by Roger Stern, Al Milgrom, and Joe Sinnott in 1984, where Hawkeye refused to wear his hearing aid since "the fewer people who know that I'm deaf, the safer it'll be for all of us." This implies that villains would be watching the show and use Hawkeye's deafness against him and the team. Hawkeye's sentiment reflected how many Americans at that time perceived disability through the medical model. Under the medical model, the problems associated with deafness are something to fix or cure; they are to be hidden so the individual affected does not seem weak or ineffective in their job (Sullivan 2011). This seems like a convenient, in-story wallpapering of an issue that the creative teams or editorial staff responsible for creating Hawkeye would rather ignore. Not only is Hawkeye, by not wearing his hearing aid, hiding his disability from the comic book villains he faces, he is also hiding it from fans.

Then, as happens every few years, a storyline was created which affected all the superhero titles published by Marvel. One such story event was entitled "Heroes Reborn" and was published in 1996 and 1997. During that event, both the Avengers, including Hawkeye, and the Fantastic Four seem to have been killed. It turned out, though, that Franklin Richards, the powerful mutant son of Reed and Sue Richards from the Fantastic Four, had placed them in a "pocket universe" for safe keeping from the villain of the event, Onslaught. The only relevance that this has for Hawkeye and his deafness is that, at the end of the event, Franklin brings him back to the "real universe" without being deaf. Since Franklin did not know that Hawkeye was ever deaf, the Hawkeye that was brought back had normal hearing. This was all explained, four years after the "Heroes Reborn" event, in the "Avengers Annual" of 2001 by Kurt Busiek, Ian Churchill, and Norm Rapmund because by then the hardcore fans of Marvel began asking why Hawkeye could hear without his hearing aid (Cronan 2016). The fact that it took four years indicates that Hawkeye being a superhero with deafness was not a key part of his character to most of Marvel's editorial and creative teams.

This brings up a spot of apprehension among fans with physical and sensory disabilities. In these large superhero universes, characters may have a disability, but it does not seem to be much of a challenge, as most can be "fixed" almost on a whim. The positive aspects of having a character like Daredevil (blind) or Charles Xavier (wheelchair user) represented in comics are counterbalanced by their superpowers affectively negating the disability. Daredevil can "see" better than everyone around him using his "radar sense," while Xavier can use his telekinesis to move his body and walk. And, due to the superpowers, mutant abilities, future technology, and magic inherent in a superhero universe, characters like Hawkeye and Batgirl/Barbara Gordon (wheelchair user after a spinal injury) can be "cured" over the course of a few comic panels. In the past, readers just took this as part and parcel of reading comics, but increasing awareness and self-advocacy have led to some changes (Hawkins 2014). Between 2012 and 2014, fans reaching out to creators at Marvel, along with disability advocates who had personal connections to Marvel creators, led to the creation of an award-winning story featuring Hawkeye and his deafness.

After the *Avengers* (2012) film directed by Joss Whedon became a hit,

Marvel wanted to feature all the characters from the film in various comic series. Even the main villain, Loki, starred in a series. "Hawkeye" by Matt Fraction and David Aja began in October 2012. Clint Barton, Hawkeye's everyday name, was different from the other Avengers. He did not have superpowers nor was he a super spy. He was just a guy who had become a great marksman with a bow. The series emphasized the everyday aspects of Clint's life away from the adventures with the Avengers. It depicted him as more of an everyman who always tries to look out for those who are bullied. He is constantly being knocked down but refuses to stay down. Even some of the people he saves in his role of superhero call him "Hawkguy" rather than Hawkeye.

In 2012, a couple of things happened, both fan-related. In May, the New Hampshire Union Leader published a story about four-year-old Anthony Smith (Hanson 2012). He was a huge fan of the Marvel superhero characters and had no hearing in his right ear and minimal hearing in his left due to mosaic trisomy 22. Christina D'Allesandro, his mother, had taken to social media to ask friends about superheroes that were deaf because Anthony had stopped wearing his conspicuous blue hearing aid, saying that "superheroes don't wear blue ears." She then sent an email to the Marvel offices in New York, hoping that an answer from the very place Anthony's heroes were created would help. She received an email back from Marvel editorial stating that, yes, Hawkeye of the Avengers had worn a hearing aid at one point. A short time later, the family received a drawing from Marvel artist Nelson Ribeiro of a brand-new superhero, Blue Ear. It was in the style of a comic book cover with Blue Ear standing on a rooftop with his hearing aid in place and radar like waves emanating from it. In a word balloon, he is saying, "Thanks to my Listening Device, I hear someone in trouble" (Morris 2012)! Anthony shared the drawing at his school and it became a trending topic on fan sites and social media, and was then reported on network news (Castillo 2012). The attention led to the Swiss hearing systems company, Phonak, to create a poster campaign based on Anthony's story. In it, Iron Man explains to kids that his armor is just fancy technology, like hearing aids, which allows him to function and do amazing things (Parkin 2013). While this was a nice thing for Marvel to do and it was great publicity, in the comics Hawkeye could still hear just fine.

Around this same time, Clint Nowicke, a blogger about comics on the site popmythology.com, sent a letter to the "Hawkeye" editorial team. Nowicke is deaf and wears a hearing aid. He is also a long-time fan and remembered the stories of Hawkeye struggling with deafness but persevering. Nowicke asked in his letter if that was something that Fraction and Aja might come back to in their new stories. His letter was printed in the third issue of the new series and the editor's response boiled down to—good memory, but no plans to revisit that experience (Nowicke 2012). Nowicke also sent a tweet to actor Clark Gregg, who plays SHIELD agent Coulson in the first *Avengers* film and in the subsequent ABC series *Marvel's Agents of SHIELD*. The tweet was "Can Coulson please know sign language? It would mean a lot to your Deaf fans." Clark Gregg responded with a tweet stating, "Great idea." Even Nowicke wasn't sure that he had much chance in affecting upcoming storylines (Nowicke 2014a). At the time, he didn't know about the influence Leah Coleman and her mother, Rachel Coleman—the creator of the television program *Signing Time*—was having on "Hawkeye" writer, Matt Fraction.

Natalie Crofts published a story in August 2014 on KSL.com (the website of the KSL-FM news radio station in Salt Lake City, Utah), which quoted "Hawkeye" writer Matt Fraction and the Colemans about the reintroduction of Hawkeye's deafness in issue #19 of the series. Rachel Coleman had created *Signing Time* to teach young children and their families about ASL (American Sign Language) after learning that her daughter, Leah, was deaf. The series was picked up and broadcast by many PBS stations and was a favorite of Fraction's as he worked to communicate with his own young child. Rachel Coleman and Fraction met at a 2012 *Signing Time* live concert in Portland, Oregon, where Fraction lived with his family. According to the article, he told Coleman how much he enjoyed the show and they discussed how ASL and comics had much in common as a visual means of communication; how neither depended on a specific written language to convey complex ideas and emotions. Coleman added that they had also talked about Hawkeye, and Fraction had voiced disappointment that the character's deafness had been written-out of Marvel Comics continuity prior to his time writing the "Hawkeye" series. They kept in touch and, in 2013, Fraction told Coleman that he had found the right story to bring Hawkeye's hearing loss back into the book. He also asked her to help him and artist David Aja to bring the experience of ASL onto the page. Issue #19 carried a dedication to "Leah" for Rachel Coleman's daughter as a nod to the help the Colemans gave the team in creating the issue.

The final issue of Matt Fraction's run on "Hawkeye" is #22, so #19 comes very near the end and it is the buildup for the climax of the main storyline that runs through the entire series. Hawkeye has purchased, using money taken from various criminals he has fought, a run-down apartment building in Manhattan. During the series, Hawkeye and the readers get to know the people living in the building and most of them, like Hawkeye, are just holding on but making do. In fact, Hawkeye's con-man brother, Barney, who is a wheelchair user and homeless, has moved in with Hawkeye by issue #19. The building is the final piece of real estate that needs to be bought and demolished so that a large shopping mecca, financed by a multinational group of legitimate and organized crime powerbrokers, can be built. Hawkeye, who has had numerous run-ins with the criminal part of this group during the series, refuses to sell primarily because it would force his newfound friends to move out. Just prior to #19, an assassin is sent to the building and uses two of Hawkeye's arrows to stab him in both ears, causing severe middle ear damage.

Issue #19, entitled "The Stuff What Don't Get Spoke," uses the unique visual communication tools of the comics medium to put the reader in the place of a person with a severe hearing impairment. The first two pages mirror each other. The first page is a flashback to Clint and Barney's childhood, showing Clint, Barney, and their parents sitting in a doctor's office. The word balloons on this page are full of marks, but nothing can be read. The reader is viewing the event from Clint's viewpoint as a young boy sitting on the exam table in the office. While he can hear that the doctor and his parents are talking, he cannot make out any of the words. The four panels at the top of the page show us that the doctor is writing a note stating that Clint's middle ear has been damaged and that he is now partially deaf, but that the doctor hopes that it is a temporary condition. Fraction is creating what is known in comics as retroactive continuity or a "retcon." This is when a creator places new information in the past of a character or the plot which has consequences going forward in the story. Fraction, through the course of his "Hawkeye" run, added to Hawkeye's history that Clint and Barney's father was a violent alcoholic who often physically abused the boys. The strong implication of this first page of #19 is that this abuse led to Clint's initial experience with deafness. This addition is important to the remainder of #19 and the final issues of the series in that it sets up a reason for Clint and Barney to know ASL and can communicate with each other using it.

The second page takes place "now" with Clint again sitting on an exam table while his brother and doctor discuss his injuries. Again, the top four panels are the doctor's notes, now being written on a computer screen, and the word balloons on this page are empty. Clint has no hearing at all now. The two pages are arranged so that Clint as a boy and Clint as a man are literally sitting back to back. The second page is the first in the series to use ASL. Barney initially tries to talk to Clint because, as we find out later, he knows that Clint can also lip-read. When Clint does not respond, he begins to use ASL. Throughout the issue, when ASL is used, it is not translated. Words are spelled out, letter by letter, in separate panels with one hand in each, as "Clint" is on this page, or in numbered panels depicting a full torso and arms with arrows showing the direction of movements of the arms in order to convey more complex communication. These are arranged around panels showing the characters involved and their interactions or actions. The lack of written translations for the ASL communication was on purpose by Fraction and Aja. They wanted the reader to feel, at least a bit, the frustration that the 0.9 percent of the world population who use sign language as their first language experience when trying to communicate with the hearing population (World Federation of the Deaf 2016).

As we go through the next pages, Barney and Clint take a taxi back home and Barney becomes more and more frustrated by Clint's refusal to talk to him. Barney makes sure that Clint is looking at him when he speaks and he begins to use more ASL. As Barney becomes angry at Clint, his emotion is conveyed not only on his face but in changes to how his empty word balloons are drawn. The smooth borders of the balloons switch abruptly to sharp spikes as Clint continues to ignore him. After continuing to try to talk to Clint and being rebuffed, Barney leaves the apartment and goes down the hall to the apartment of a woman he has a relationship with. As soon as he enters her apartment, words and word balloons go back to "normal." As the issue goes on, and the storyline goes back and forth from just after Clint lost his hearing as a boy and the present, Fraction and Aja also depict the difficult skill of lip-reading. When Clint is trying to understand what Barney is saying by reading his lips, the word balloons for Barney are not the usual rounded balloons used for speech in comics but rather stacks of rectangular balloons with a typeface font replacing the more typical hand-lettering. When Barney is talking and doing something else with his mouth, the words are not quite right. This happens in a flashback scene in which the boys are talking about their father. As Barney takes a drink from a whiskey bottle as he is talking, the description of their father becomes "that son of a b(ench)." Ultimately, the brothers air their differences, come to an understanding, and work on rallying the tenants to defeat the villains.

This final storyline was collected in book form as *Hawkeye: Rio Bravo* (2015). There are many allusions to the 1959 film *Rio Bravo* in Fraction and Aja's final issues. In the film, a sheriff bands together with a group of people that are undervalued by society—an alcoholic, an elderly man, and a woman—to stand against a band of outlaws in a small western town. In the same way, Clint and Barney, both men with disabilities, bring together their friends consisting of people of diverse races, ages, and backgrounds to stand against an armed group sent by powerful men. It is not ultimately Clint as Hawkeye that saves the day; it is the community that he built over the entire series. After being injured, Clint had given up but Barney and the others show him that heroism is not a solitary job. Moreover, in Fraction and Aja's (2015) final issue, on the final pages of the story, Hawkeye is depicted wearing prominent purple (his superhero uniform color) bilateral hearing aids. The series had once again made deafness a part of Hawkeye's life.

The issue received much attention and positive write-ups upon release; everyone from general fans to the intelligentsia of the comic form as represented by *The Comics Journal* (Fischer 2015) to more general pop culture media like *The A.V. Club* (Sava 2014) and *The New York Times* (Gustines

2014). Clint Nowicke (2014), the blogger and fan who had sent that letter to the editor of Hawkeye back in issue #3 about bringing back Clint's deafness, wrote "A Deaf Comic Geek's Grateful Review of Hawkeye #19" on popmythology.com soon after issue #19 was released. He wrote, "From a Deaf perspective, there are several things Matt Fraction and David Aja nail down that few writers and artists have been able to do and whether they did so intentionally, I am not sure. Either way, the characterization of Deaf-Clint Barton is genius." He especially appreciated that the issue depicted how difficult lip reading is since he had been frustrated by depictions of it in other media with characters who could "practically lip-read through walls" (Nowicke 2014b). He also praised the creative team for making the issue purposefully difficult to read in order to convey to hearing readers the everyday frustrations of people with hearing impairments.

Unfortunately, what the Marvel universe can give, it can quickly take away. Fraction and Aja moved on to other projects after issue #22 and Marvel began the "All-New Hawkeye" series with a new first issue and a new creative team in March 2015. While the overall story continued to focus on Clint and Barney, one panel in that first issue effectively erased the hope that Hawkeye would continue to be depicted as a superhero with a disability. In that panel, Hawkeye is talking to an ally by a remote communication device and needs something repeated to him. At first, the reader may think that Hawkeye is not wearing his hearing aids or that they are not working properly. Hawkeye's dialog in the panel dispels that "the hearing aids Stark hooked me up with are pretty amazing, actually" (Lemire 2015). So now Hawkeye has super-tech, invisible hearing aids created by Tony Stark which makes him a superhero without deafness again. He has been "normalized" so no one, including the creative teams, must acknowledge his deafness. Sadly, the journey that had started with a PR campaign to help a boy feel better about wearing devices which allowed him to more easily communicate with his world starring Hawkeye and Iron Man ended in a storyline involving those same two characters indicating that Hawkeye hides his devices from the world. The irony of it all was not lost on some fans with deafness. Nowicke (2015) wrote about his disappointment, again on popmythology.com, in an article entitled "All-New Hawkeye, the 'Daredevil Syndrome' and a Step Back for Deaf Readers." Nowicke stated that he worked at a school for the Deaf and the children there often talked about disliking their hearing aids for making them stand-out from peers as different. He was excited to see Hawkeye again wearing hearing aids and had used panels from the Fraction and Aja issues to help the kids, especially the younger ones, to feel better about it. The representation of an Avenger dealing with the same things that they did was powerful. He even included a photo in the article of his office door that was decorated with panels from Hawkeye. He voiced his unhappiness that the direction of the new series, now with Hawkeye's unseen hearing aids, could give a young reader the idea that they, too, needed to be fixed or that their disability should be hidden.

El Deafo, *a Different Type of Hero*

> "Fairy tales do not give the child his first idea of bogey. What fairy tales give the child is his first clear idea of the possible defeat of bogey. The baby has known the dragon intimately ever since he had an imagination. What the fairy tale provides for him is a St. George to kill the dragon."
> —G.K. Chesterton in *The Red Angel*
> in *Tremendous Trifles*

So maybe kids need a different type of hero. One that isn't tied to the whims of Marvel. And maybe that hero could also be a bunny. To this end, in the same year that issue #19 of "Hawkeye" hit comic shop shelves, another comic story featuring a young hero who struggles with hearing impairment and feeling different due to wearing hearing aids was published. *El Deafo* by writer and artist Cece Bell was a popular and critical hit, even becoming a Newbery Honor Book. By 2014, the genre of autobiographical or semi-fictionalized biography in graphic novel form had been placed in the spotlight by the work of creators like Raina Telgemeier who had published, at that time, three novel-length comics for young readers which grossed $4.6 million in sales in that year alone (Asselin 2015). The first, in 2010, was *Smile* which chronicled the years after an accident which caused severe dental trauma. It was an honest depiction of the injury and the multiple orthodontic procedures required to treat it but it was also about Telgemeier's inner life and her struggles with being bullied and feeling alone. *El Deafo* is also an autobiographical work which, while still all-ages appropriate, tries to be honest about being angry, sad, and lonely when you are "different." Bell wants the readers who are deaf to know that they not alone. But she also wants to emphasize to every reader that the inner lives of all kids are similar, and to grow that recognition into empathy and understanding.

During a 2015 podcast interview with the Anti-Defamation League, Bell was asked why she wrote *El Deafo*. She stated,

A couple of things inspired me to write it. The first was a personal exchange that I had in a grocery store with a very rude cashier. It was a moment where … what I should have said was "I can't hear very well. Let's start over." But I couldn't because all of my life I had been pretending that I didn't have this problem. That exchange left me so upset and frustrated that I thought to myself, "I am going to write a book that explains to people what I need from them." I was finally ready to speak out and say yes, I do have trouble hearing and it's not a big deal. It becomes a big deal when I don't say it. That was the personal thing that happened; I wanted to create this manual for hearing people to better understand what it was like for deaf people.

The second inspiration, as she stated in that same podcast, had been her reading of Telgemeier's *Smile* and realizing that the graphic novel format was the perfect way to tell her personal story.

Bell, like Fraction and Aja, uses the medium of comics to convey life as a person with hearing impairment, both internally and externally, in ways only a silent, completely visual medium can. She depicts problems with hearing and lip-reading by, like Aja, altering the text in the word balloons or allowing us to read the character's thoughts. And in the medium of comics, she can populate her world with people who look like rabbits but live normal human lives without it seeming weird or off-putting. Bell can also tell her story in a way that could never be done with an established superhero character in an ongoing comic book universe.

Importantly, this is *her* story. Bell, even as a rabbit, is the protagonist and is not part of a giant narrative where she plays a small or supporting role. And, by authoring her own story, she avoids the "inspiration porn" problem which sullies many depictions of people with disabilities, especially children, in the media. As author and disability activist Stella Young (2012) wrote on her blog *Ramp Up*, "inspiration porn is an image of a person with a disability, often a kid, doing something completely ordinary—like playing, or talking, or running, or drawing a picture, or hitting a tennis ball—carrying a caption like 'your excuse is invalid' or 'before you quit, try.' In this way, these modified images exceptionalise and objectify those of us they claim to represent. It's no coincidence that these genuinely adorable kids in these images are never named: it doesn't matter what their names are, they're just there as objects of inspiration." Bell does not want to be an inspiration for readers who can hear, she is trying to convey that her experiences growing up were the same as all kids. As stated above, to her, the hearing loss was "not a big deal" but it was something that caused problems when it was not owned as one part of herself.

By writing an autobiography, Bell can also comment on American culture and the types of media she consumed as a child. She uses superhero and disability tropes from comics and TV in her thoughts and fantasy life to process and deal with her real-life issues. Clint Barton/Hawkeye is trapped in his comic book universe. He cannot float above his narrative and critique how his hearing loss is perceived and how it appears and disappears on the whims of his writers, artists, and editors. By being a small cog in the monthly comic publishing machine, Hawkeye can never have an ending. Bell, on the other hand, is in total control of this story of her childhood. It is self-contained and she is able to build to a satisfying conclusion.

Every character in *El Deafo* is a rabbit. Bell is using a well-established conceit of children's literature and other media. By making the characters animals, the societal barriers which can keep the reader from identifying with them can be eliminated. Bell is already reaching out to readers through the main character with a disability most of them will not have experienced and, by using anthropomorphism, she makes that task a bit easier. Her choice of animal was not random. In an interview with the School Library Journal, she stated, "Bunnies have giant ears and excellent hearing. My portrayal as the one rabbit whose giant ears did not work—that's kind of the way it felt. Exaggerated? Sure. But I wanted to convey the feeling of really standing out when I didn't want to stand out at all. I'm finding out now that the whole bunny-instead-of-human thing helps the book resonate with kids of all ethnicities, too. I love that" (Parrott 2014).

The book opens with Cece losing her hearing because of severe meningitis as a young child. As this occurs over the first few pages, the text in the word balloons begins to fade until only empty balloons are left. Her thought balloons continue with normal text, acting as a contrast. Louder voices and sounds, which she still cannot hear early in the book, are depicted by using larger empty balloons. When she receives her first hearing aid, the text fades back in except, when a speaker speaks quickly, the text is gibberish. Bell wants the reader to understand that sounds and voices, although a hearing aid can amplify them, can still sound muffled or unclear to the person wearing it. In a clever use of the medium, Bell relates an experience at a friend's house where the friend asks, "Do you want something to drink? We have cherry pop, juice, or a coke." To Cece it sounds like and is written in the word balloon as "Doo yoo wan sumding do dring? We haff Jerry's mop, shoes, or a goat." In Cece's thought balloons, we see cute pictures showing a mop with a gift tag for Jerry, shoes, and a goat in a glass (2014, 25).

In scenes from her year in kindergarten, Bell explains the difficulties associated with lip-reading, drawing close-ups of how mouths can look the same when saying certain similar but different sounds. Her character becomes clothed in classic Sherlock Holmes attire as she learns to use context, visual, and gestural clues to assist in understanding while lip-reading. Through a series of panels where Cece holds signs just for the reader, breaking the "fourth wall" of comics, she explains the basic complicating factors of lip-reading such as group conversations, facial hair, and poor lighting (2014, 29–32). Barriers for lip-readers, ones that would not occur to most hearing individuals, are explained by using nonsense text in balloons. Some of young Cece's frustrations include: television shows which cut away from the actor talking to show the facial reactions of the other actors, animated mouths in cartoons not being synced with the dialog, and friends expecting you to understand audio recordings. Sleepover parties are frustrating for Cece as her friends like to talk after the lights are off and she cannot follow the conversations. These frustrations ultimately lead to a superheroic rebirth in the comic.

The addition of the superhero aspect of *El Deafo* is what ultimately elevates the work to something beyond a simple autobiography for children. Bell's stated objective for creating the story was to produce a "manual for hearing people to better understand what it was like for deaf people" (Bell 2015). But by describing through words and images how she used fiction and imagination in her life for comfort, to safely sort through her feelings, and to finally accept and advocate for who she is as a person, she created a guidebook for her readers to do the same in their lives.

While fantasy stories can be escapes from reality, they can also empower. For children, princesses and superheroes are often their first exposure to characters who are adults. They populate children's books, films, and toy aisles. As a child, you have next to no power but by pretending to be Elsa or Spider-Man using action figures, costumes, or just your imagination, you can do anything. For children who feel different, these characters can be a comfort and even a friend. Author and teacher Christina Blanch (2016) wrote about this in an article shortly after Carrie Fisher's death:

> It got me starting to think about why I am so attached to these people and the characters they represent. I think it's because when I was growing up, and even now to some degree, I never felt like I fit in. That's not an easy thing to admit to people, but it's true. I always feel like I'm on the outside of things, just not quite belonging. But when watching these people on television and in the movies or reading about them in books and comics, they became my friends. Bilbo Baggins has always been a dear friend of mine. And everyone in Star Wars was, and still is, my friend.

Throughout *El Deafo*, Bell shows herself as being a fan of Batman. In various scenes, she is watching the Adam West *Batman* television series, reading Batman comic books, or drawing Batman during art class at school. When stressful or unusual things happen to her, she uses Batman and his story as means to cope with them. When she begins first grade, she is given a Phonic Ear® device which, when paired with a microphone that her teacher wears, allows Cece to more clearly hear what is said in the classroom. The device is introduced into the story in a full-page schematic reminiscent of the way superhero comics reveal all the features of items like Batman's utility belt. Since it is worn under her clothing, Bell even adds that we are experiencing the device by "x-ray view" in a nod to Superman's x-ray vision (2014, 38–39). Cece is amazed at how well she can understand her teacher with the new device. However, she is even more excited when she realizes that, when her teacher forgets to take off the microphone, she can hear her teacher's conversations in the lounge and, to her shock/delight, the sounds of her urinating in the restroom. At that moment, Cece's thought balloon fills with various

Batman technology—his belt, his batarang, his communication devices—and she thinks, "I have amazing abilities unknown to anyone! Just like Bruce Wayne uses all that crazy technology to turn himself into Batman on TV" (2014, 43). With this feeling of joy and power, Cece's image of herself improves markedly and, when she pictures herself in her own mind, she now sports a red superhero cape.

Batman is not Cece's hero only due to his gadgets, though. Two key aspects of the Batman story are his feelings of isolation/loss and his resilience to overcome all obstacles. For many Batman fans those are the primary touchstones and they draw strength from them. The words of Bruce Wayne's father in Christopher Nolan's film *Batman Begins* (2005), "And why do we fall, Bruce? So we can learn to pick ourselves up," have become a mantra. They have become especially powerful for those in the disability community. In the documentary film, *Legends of the Knight* (2013), Jill Pantozzi, a writer and disability advocate with muscular dystrophy, describes what it was like for her as a child looking for fantasy role models without "magical powers" and ultimately drawing strength from the non-superpowered character, Batman. In *El Deafo*, Bell shows Cece utilizing Batman in her imagination in multiple ways. Just when she becomes excited about her Phonic Ear® device, how it provides her with a superpower, a fellow student disrupts her reverie by tactlessly asking if Cece is deaf. Immediately we see her imagine Batman, head down and alone, slinking back to the Batcave. "Superheroes might be awesome, but they are also different," Cece thinks (2014, 46). Batman is an inspiration, but also a comfort. She feels alone sometimes, but so does Batman. Cece begins to make friends, but one friend in particular, Laura, constantly directs their activities and becomes jealous when Cece tries to make other friends. When Cece becomes frustrated with the friendship, Batman returns to her imagination and urges her to stand up for herself, to "push back." She then imagines using the wires of her Phonic Ear® device to tie up Laura and hypnotize her with the feedback from the ear buds (2014, 58).

As the character of Cece ages and matures through the book, Bell brings us through the next evolutionary phase of being both an artist and a budding self-advocate. She begins to take Batman and the other parts of pop culture surrounding her and create new inner narratives that allow her to grow as a person. Just like a painter begins to find their style by first copying works of art that speak to them or musicians learn to write original songs by starting a cover band, we see Bell's first steps toward being an author and artist when she takes pieces of superhero stories and merges them with her real life experiences and disappointments. In fact, the thing that sparks her imagination to create the character which ultimately becomes the focus of her most popular work to date is a low-budget TV movie.

This final step toward creating and, in her young mind, being El Deafo occurs while watching an *ABC Afterschool Special* with her siblings. In the movie, Cece sees an actor playing a deaf teenager wearing a similar hearing aid device to hers. She's fascinated as this is the first time she has ever seen someone "like her" depicted in a movie or on television. During a bullying scene, Cece asks her sister what the bully called the character who is deaf. Her sister hesitates, but tells her, "Um … the one kid called the other kid–ahem–'deafo.'" At first, Cece is angry but quickly decides that if kids like her are going to be called "deafo," she will turn that into a strength. She will use it herself and own the name so that others cannot use it against her. The superhero persona that she has been developing in her head over the past few months now has a name—El Deafo. Cece didn't have the benefit of witnessing a heroic character like her in popular media, so she created one.

Bell's story acts as an almost perfect antidote to the "Tiny Tim" and "supercrip" stereotypes that unfortunately are still prominent in all types of media. The "Tiny Tim" concept is ancient. He or she is never the hero, or even the protagonist, of the story. They are simply there to pity and provide a character for the hero to save or "cure." And, as law student and disability rights blogger Claire Stanley (2015) writes, "supercrip is this stereotype that has formed around many people with disabilities. People look at us as these inspirational models. Wow, look at Claire, she is blind but she still went to law school. That's amazing! One of the bar prep professors this summer announced in front of everyone that she was impressed that I had went to law school and was studying for the bar. People see us as these inspirational stories to gawk at." Bell's depiction of herself as a young child and her superhero creation, El Deafo, are both front and center in the narrative. While she uses a hearing device, Cece never dwells on wanting to be "fixed" so much as just accepted and understood. And one of the final scenes of the book felt like an actual roundhouse punch to the nose of the "supercrip" stereotype.

The key aspect of the "supercrip" stereotype is that a person with a disability is super heroic by completing what would be an everyday task for someone without that disability. Examples would be Ms. Stanley's antidote above or a woman who uses a wheelchair and utilizes city public transportation being called "brave" in a newspaper story. Bell has been building Cece's superhero identity throughout *El Deafo* but this has just been for her, she never shares it or her superpower—being able to hear what her teacher is saying and doing outside of the classroom thanks to her hearing device. When she sees her classmates, including close friends, continuously getting into trouble as they are caught in horseplay whenever their teacher returns to the classroom after a break, she decides to rescue them. As Cece hears the teacher returning, she shouts out a warning which allows the students to return to their desks and appear to be working quietly. When she does this, the El Deafo of her imagination takes off her cape and places it on Cece's back (2014,

218). It feels like a graduation as Cece has the power now and, with that power, she finally feels comfortable with who she is as a complete person. It is this Cece Bell, wearing that cape, who will grow into the woman telling this story and, hopefully, will spark the imagination of the reader to start the process again.

When we feel different, for whatever reason, encountering a character in a comic, a novel, a film, or a television program that reflects our perceptions of being "other" is powerful. Screenwriter William Nicholson wrote, "We read to know we're not alone," and this applies to young children like Anthony Smith as well as to adults like Clint Nowicke and Christina Blanch. Matt Fraction and David Aja's stint on "Hawkeye" and Cece Bell's stand-alone graphic novel *El Deafo* are works which resonated with readers with and without hearing impairment. A major difference remains, though. Hawkeye's disability, and thus its impact, was fleeting. And for many fans with hearing impairment, that is disappointing. The power of *El Deafo* lies in the fact that the superhero, El Deafo, still lives within a real person. Cece Bell has an online presence at cecebell.wordpress.com and answers questions from readers there. She posts art and stories from fans. Bell personifies the need for creators of all backgrounds to tell their own stories, stand up for themselves, and be superheroes.

REFERENCES

Asselin, Janelle. 2015. "Bookscan: Women and Children Were the Big Comics Moneymakers in 2014." *Comics Alliance* (online), March 3. http://comicsalliance.com/bookscan-sales-figures-2014
Bell, Cece. 2014. *El Deafo*. New York: Amulet Books.
Bell, Cece, and Jinnie Spiegler. 2015. Cece Bell, children's book author and illustrator—Anti-Defamation League Podcast. http://podcast.adl.org/podcast/cece-bell.
Berish, Amy. 2016. "FDR and Polio." FDRlibrary.org. https://fdrlibrary.org/polio.
Blanch, Christina. 2016. "Carrie Fisher: The Hero Worth Meeting." 13thdimension.com, December 27. http://13thdimension.com/carrie-fisher-the-hero-worth-meeting.
Busiek, Kurt, Ian Churchill, and Norm Rapmund. 2001. "House Cleaning." The Avengers Annual 2001, September.
Castillo, Michelle. 2012. "Marvel Team Creates Deaf Superhero Called Blue Ear in Honor of Boy." *CBS News.com*, May 27. http://www.cbsnews.com/news/marvel-team-creates-deaf-superhero-called-blue-ear-in-honor-of-boy.
Crofts, Natalie. 2014. "Utah Girl Inspires Marvel Comic Featuring Deaf Hero." KSL.com, August 29. http://www.ksl.com/index.php?sid=31334353&nid=1205&title=utah-girl-inspires-marvel-comic-featuring-deaf-hero.
Cronan, Brian. 2016. "The Abandoned an' Forsaked—What's the Deal with Hawkeye's Hearing?" CBR.com, July 16. http://www.cbr.com/the-abandoned-an-forsaked-whats-the-deal-with-hawkeyes-hearing.
Doug T. 2016. "Hey Comic Book Writers! Stop "Curing" Our Disabled Heroes!" *Pop Culture Uncovered*, March 3. https://popcultureuncovered.com/2016/03/14/hey-comic-book-writers-stop-curing-our-disabled-heroes.
Fischer, Craig. 2015. "Hawkeye Supercut." *The Comics Journal* (online), July 1. www.tcj.com/hawkeye-supercut.
Fraction, Matt, and David Aja. 2012. "Lucky: A Clint Barton / Hawkeye Adventure." *Hawkeye*, October.

_____. 2014. "The Stuff What Don't Get Spoke." *Hawkeye*, July.

_____. 2015. *Hawkeye: Rio Bravo.* New York: Marvel.

Gruenwald, Mark, and Brett Breeding. 1983. *Hawkeye* (mini-series), September–December.

Gustines, George Gene. 2014. "One of Marvel's Avengers Turns to Sign Language." *New York Times*, July 24. http://artsbeat.blogs.nytimes.com/2014/07/24/one-of-marvels-avengers-turns-to-sign-language/?_r=1.

Hanson, Julie. 2012. "Superheroes Do Wear Blue Ears, Thanks to NH Boy." *New Hampshire Union Leader* (Manchester), May 26.

Hawkins, Kathleen. 2014. "With Great Power Comes Great Disability." *BBC News—Ouch Blog*, June 24. http://www.bbc.com/news/blogs-ouch-27883836.

"Historical Census Statistics on Population Totals by Race, 1790 to 1990, and by Hispanic Origin, 1970 to 1990, For the United States, Regions, Divisions, and States" (PDF). Census.gov. https://www.census.gov/population/www/documentation/twps0076/twps0076.pdf.

Irving, Christopher. 2009. "The Political Evolution of Denny O'Neil." *Graphic NYC* (blog), April 27, 2009. http://graphicnyc.blogspot.com/2009/04/political-evolution-of-denny-oneil.html.

Lemire, Jeff, and Ramon Perez. 2015. "Wunderkammer: Part One of Five." *All-New Hawkeye*, March.

Morris, Steve. 2012. "Marvel Creates New Superhero for a Hearing-Impaired Fan." *The Beat*, May 23. http://www.comicsbeat.com/marvel-creates-new-superhero-for-a-hearing-impaired-fan.

Nowicke, Clint. 2012. "Letter to the Editor." *Hawkeye*, October.

_____. 2014a. "Hawkeye, Blue Ear, Why We Need a Deaf Superhero and Why I'm Still Waiting." Popmythology.com, June 27. https://www.popmythology.com/hawkeye-blue-ear-why-we-need-a-deaf-superhero-and-why-im-still-waiting

_____. 2014b. "A Deaf Comic Geek's Grateful Review of Hawkeye #19." Popmythology.com, August 4. https://www.popmythology.com/a-deaf-comic-geeks-grateful-review-of-hawkeye-19/

_____. 2015. "All-New Hawkeye, The 'Daredevil Syndrome' and a Step Back for Deaf Readers." Popmythology.com, March 6. https://www.popmythology.com/all-new-hawkeye-daredevil-syndrome/.

O'Neil, Denny, and Neal Adams. 1970. "No Evil Shall Escape My Sight!" *Green Lantern Co-Starring Green Arrow*, April.

Parkin, John. 2013. "Iron Man and Blue Ear Debut Poster Campaign for Hearing-Impaired Kids." CBR.com, March 3. http://www.cbr.com/iron-man-and-blue-ear-debut-poster-campaign-for-hearing-impaired-kids.

Parrot, Kiera. 2014. "SLJ Chats with Cece Bell About Her Graphic Novel Memoir 'El Deafo.'" SLJ.com, December 8. http://www.slj.com/2014/12/interviews/up-close/slj-chats-with-cece-bell-about-her-graphic-novel-memoir-el-deafo-up-close.

Sava, Oliver. 2014. "Hawkeye #19 Uses Deafness to Help a Broken Clint Barton Find His Voice." *A.V. Club* (online), August 1. http://www.avclub.com/article/hawkeye-19-uses-deafness-help-broken-clint-barton—207612.

Stanley, Claire. 2015. "What I Want You to Understand About the 'Supercrip' Stereotype." themighty.com, December 22. https://themighty.com/2015/12/challenging-the-supercrip-stereotype-of-people-with-disabilities.

Stern, Roger, Al Milgrom, and Joe Sinnott. 1984. "Late Night of the Super-Stars." *The Avengers*, January.

Sullivan, Kathryn. 2011. "The Prevalence of the Medical Model of Disability in Society." *AHS Capstone Projects.* Paper 13. http://digitalcommons.olin.edu/ahs_capstone_2011/13.

World Federation of the Deaf. 2016. "Sign Language." *WFDEAF.org.* https://wfdeaf.org/human-rights/crpd/sign-language.

Young, Stella. 2012. "We're not here for your inspiration." *Ramp Up—Disability, Discussion, Debate: Content from Across the ABC Blog*, July 2. http://www.abc.net.au/rampup/articles/2012/07/02/3537035.htm.

Jimmy's Resistance, or Killing the Joy of Cruel Optimism in *South Park*

SARA BETH BROOKS *and* TYLER SNELLING

We'll fight until you're PC black and blue! Woo-woo!
We are language police fighting bigotry!
Hurtful words can suck our turds, 'cause it's PC for me!
And you! Woo-woo!
        —PC Bros, "Stunning and Brave"

To date, 20 seasons of Trey Stone and Matt Parker's television show *South Park* have aired on Comedy Central since August 1997. The animated series portrays the struggles of people living in a small town in Colorado with the same name as the show. Alison Halsall (2008) claims that "the program interweaves levels of parody and satire to mock many of the figures and symbols that are iconic of American culture" (23). Since the introduction of Timmy and Jimmy in seasons four and five, several scholars have noted that the show uses these strategies of humor to interrogate themes about ableism and life as a disabled person (White 2005; Reid-Hresko and Reid 2005; Chermers and Karamanos 2012).

In season 19, Stone and Parker introduce a set of characters called the PC Bros, which sparks a conflict about "politically correct" values. From the introduction of an art district to a new Whole Foods supermarket store, the city South Park is culturally portrayed as becoming more "progressive." PC Principal's replacement of Principal Victoria at South Park Elementary School comes with sweeping changes about what is considered acceptable language.

61

The PC Delta Fraternity forms when the PC Bros connect with each other upon arriving to the city. As the epigraph at the beginning of this essay suggests, the new principle guides the group to share and enforce their linguistic expectations with violence. Although the full season offers multiple opportunities for valuable cultural critique, "Sponsored Content" emphasizes a conflict between the hegemon—PC Principal—and a disabled resistor—Jimmy. With an audience of over one million people on the day of release alone, this episode serves as a case study to uncover the transmission of strategies of control and dissent in representations on television (Porter 2015). Analyzing this content is warranted because media has transformed how subjectivity is constituted since it both requires and produces "new forms of social organization and new modes of perception" (DeLuca and Peeple 2002, 131). Scripts, themes, ideologies, and feelings are constantly distributed and reinforced via television, which affects how people come to see themselves and others (Medina 2013).

Although rhetorical criticism is often associated with uncovering a "deeper" or "intended" meaning of the text, the nature and medium of *South Park* warrant a different framework. Instead, we should approach the series as a postmodern text and urge scholars towards critical inquiry. To this end, Brian Ott (2008) contends that the inconsistent development of characters and plot paired with pushing linguistic boundaries creates a fragmented narrative (39–40). Hence, critics should find "counterhegemonic pleasures" by analyzing how the show "speaks directly to the body" (Ott 2008, 40–41). Ott (2008) concluded that scholars act "as 'cultural teachers,' who do the invaluable work of assisting individuals to live more meaningful and fulfilling lives within a media culture" (52). Consequently, we read queer, feminist, and disability theory into this episode of *South Park* to share an interpretation of how the show espouses prominent themes related to the experiences of disabled people and women. A framework for the struggle between PC Principal and Jimmy emerges from this close reading of the text instead of an *a priori* selection (Jasinski 2001, 256). The possibility for counterhegemonic activity lies within the drama of progressive culture, which can exist uninterrupted or face complications from resistance. Jimmy's tactics disrupt the PC Bros' ideology and raise awareness about their paternalism and sexual objectification.

Call Out Culture Comes to South Park

The episode "Sponsored Content" opens with the bellowing voice of PC Principal threatening to break the legs of the person responsible for printing the word "retarded" in the school newspaper. In the first episode of the season,

PC Principal explicitly denounced this word at an assembly before many students, including Jimmy. The PC Bros commitment to language policing dramatizes what Asam Ahmad (2015) terms "call-out culture" or a "tendency among progressives, radicals, activists, and community organizers to publicly name instances or patterns of oppressive behavior and language use by others" (para. 3). The PC Bros repeatedly enact this strategy through their commitment to politically correct culture by using shame and physical violence. While the residents of South Park do not stop saying politically incorrect things, the PC Bros continue to congratulate themselves on improving the world by enforcing decorum. However, skepticism of this approach is warranted. This form of "call-out culture" as a tactic "mirrors what the prison industrial complex teaches us about crime and punishment," which is to blame, segregate, and discipline (Ahmad 2015, para. 1). This strategy ensures the continuation of hegemonic politics by asserting dominance instead of finding mutual encounters for dialogue or redress. The PC Bros take their call-out culture to the violent extreme while congratulating one another on advocating for oppressed populations.

The satisfaction of appearing to alleviate oppression despite the ensuing violence stimulates the PC Bros' attachment to their politics. The mood felt by the Bros is the key to unpacking how their politically correct agenda appears desirable. We follow Zizi Papacharissi (2015) to study affect "as the sum of—often discordant—feelings about affairs, public and private," which "is examined as the energy that drives, neutralizes or entraps networked publics" (7). The PC Bros are *energized* both by and for enforcing political correctness. One can imagine the Bros experiencing a tingling sensation approaching excitement when prompted with the opportunity to enforce their ideology. Lauren Berlant's (2008) theory of "cruel optimism" accounts for how the PC Bros are tricked into pursuing a politics contradictory with their stated desires of justice. Berlant (2008) explains that a "relation of cruel optimism exists when something you desire is actually an obstacle to your flourishing" (1). Understood in this way, concepts such as voting and legislative reforms become objects of the good life even though each only prolongs the legitimacy of corrupt structures (Berlant 2008, 226–228). Amanda Lashaw's (2013) ethnographic analysis of an unnamed nonprofit organization in Oakland, California, supports why progressive ideology and strategies similar to the PC Bros warrant considering the attachment to these objects as cruel optimism. The research noted how member's satisfaction from change "was not so much the fuel of the movement as a valued end in itself," which prevented a broader focus on resistance (Lashaw 2013, 19). In other words, creating systematic change became a secondary goal to the self-congratulatory feelings that ensued after agitating for political correctness.

PC Principal's explanation of what being PC involves very closely resembles this theme: "It means you love nothin' more than beer, workin' out, and that feelin' you get when you rhetorically defend a marginalized community from systems of oppression." The PC Bros' feel good for calling people out, and that good feeling is what sustains their commitment to the cause. Participation depends upon being recognized as helping a minority group. This politic is clear from examining the initiation rituals for joining PC Delta Fraternity, which stipulate to "go out there and check someone's privilege." As Jimmy's confrontation over PC values illustrates, "the continuity of its form provides something of the continuity of the subject's sense of what it means to keep on living on" (Berlant 2008, 24). Ultimately, the antagonism in this episode stresses how PC Bros "keep on living on" due to their politics, which is already obvious because their name dramatizes the entanglement between their sense of self and being politically correct. A "good life" involves aggressively checking people's privilege as well as the principles that are often found within the stereotype of a fraternity house.

Disability scholars extended Berlant's work on "cruel optimism" to suggest how images of the good life reify ablenormativity (Fritsch 2013; Kolorova 2015; Runswick-Cole and Goodley 2015; Shildrick 2015). Kelly Fritsch (2013) argued that the International Symbol of Access (ISA) is an object of cruel optimism since it projects an exclusive image of what disabilities are included. Importantly, she illuminates how the commitment towards progressive values actually obstructs change. The excitement created by the feelings of a better society develops a subject complicit with their own oppression: "That the ISA has persisted over 40 years after its original design is not due to a lack of alternative symbols, but rather because the sign *does* something for disabled people.... Participating in the affective happiness of wanting the ISA to work is a way of reinvesting in the neoliberal individual who ensures their own self-care through market relations. Simply put, the ISA is an affectively happy object, and an object of cruel optimism" (Fritsch 2013, 146). The resilience of symbolic inclusion for disabled people suggests a need to document how attachments to those symbols are more than just rational commitments. Rather, they are lodged somewhere in our affect, emotions, and bodies. The examples of cruel optimism discussed here illustrate both how the violence inflicted by the PC Bros precludes their desire for a progressive culture even though it provides them the satisfaction of feeling correct, and hence, why noting the affective nature of hegemonic violence is valuable.

Within moments of PC Principal's initial outburst and threat to break the legs of the student responsible, it is revealed that Jimmy—who uses crutches for mobility—is the editor of the newspaper. When faced with a disabled person using a word that historically marginalizes people with cognitive impairments, PC Principal stares wordlessly with his mouth agape. It is immediately apparent that the administrator has never met Jimmy before, as he introduces himself during the next scene in the office. It is also quickly revealed that Jimmy intends to defend his decision as editor of the newspaper. When PC Principal asserts that "retarded" is a bad word, Jimmy responds, "Says who?" The principal insists that he "doesn't want to get angry." Rather than give up, Jimmy carefully probes further, "Why? Are you uncomfortable around disabled people?" This direct questioning exposes the paternalism of PC Principal's linguistic intercession. When the principal shields himself from critical interrogation by asserting that he "know[s] a thing or two about the rights of people with disabilities," Jimmy defends his choice not to alter the newspaper by explaining that he did not "want people to be afraid of words if it stops them from having a dialog." Rather than listen to Jimmy, PC Principal asserts power by banning distribution of the newspaper within South Park Elementary School unless approved beforehand. Multiple shots of PC Principal's face in stunned silence during this scene indicate that Jimmy's resistance disrupted his grip on how reality works. Jimmy's response forces reflection, which provokes PC Principal's backlash because it is easier than reconcile being wrong. Jimmy's strategy during this dialogue extends throughout the episode. He resists the PC Bros by probing through questions, printing subversive content, and, ultimately, risking discipline from his unabashed questioning of PC Principal's logic.

Killing PC Principal's Joy

Jimmy is not simply engaging in a childish game of questioning, but radically counters the attachment to abstract values of political correctness. This strategy resembles Sara Ahmed's project of killing joy. A "killjoy" was once a patriarchal epithet developed to stigmatize women who complain, pester, or nag. In Ahmed's (2010a) reclamation, the killjoy becomes a symbol of empowerment and an intersectional feminist worldview. Disabled people face a similar delegitimization of their claims to oppression. Those who "nag" are often ignored by labeling their complaints as selfish, self-serving, and narcissistic (Siebers 2002). Yet, the killjoy resists dismissing these concerns and "disturb[s] the very fantasy that happiness can be found" through ignoring the oppressed (Ahmed 2010a, 66). This requires the will "to go against a social order, which is protected as a moral order" (Ahmed 2010b, para. 12). Jimmy's tactics disrupt the object of happiness that sustains the PC Bros' worldview. To borrow Ahmed's (2017) language, Jimmy embodies feminism by "asking ethical questions about how to live better in an unjust and unequal world" (1). Reading Ahmed's theory of the killjoy into the confrontation of PC Principal's paternalism infuses disability into feminist politics, which

Rosemarie Garland-Thomson (2002) argued can "strengthen the critique that is feminism" (28). Although Ahmed does not explicitly tie disability to her theorization of the killjoy, she started questioning ability privilege in a way that other scholars readily applied to disability studies at large (Fritsch 2013). Ahmed (2017) discusses experiences with temporary disability from rat race fracturing her pelvis and helping her disabled mother, quotes several disability studies scholars, and concludes that using crip to describe oneself or politics is a reclamation. In "Queer Fragility," Ahmed (2016) aligns crips and queers with women as groups that have been identified as vulnerable and in need of paternalistic protection.

Jimmy's resistance to the PC Bros can be read along Robert McRuer's (2006) subversive reclaiming of the slur "cripple," which demonized physical impairment. In reclamation, cripping is a politics that exposes the hegemonic impulse to absorb disability or eradicate it from existence. *Living a Feminist Life* elaborates further on ableism by evaluating the system of power as a privilege: "I began to think more about my able-bodied privilege, which is not to say that I have thought about it enough: I have not. It is easy for me to forget to think about it, which is what makes a privilege a privilege: the experiences you are protected from having; the thoughts you do not have to think" (Ahmed 2017, 181–182). Consequently, the feminist killjoy as a strategy to resist inequalities must attend to hegemonic ableism since, as Garland-Thompson (2002) contends, "[d]isability, like gender and race, is everywhere, once we know how to look for it" (28). The killjoy who speaks truth to white patriarchy can also be the killjoy who speaks truth to ableist paternalism.

At the same time, it is important to note that Jimmy critiques sexism and ableism but not racism. He is aware of the lack of people of color in South Park, which is evident when he remarks in the episode "Krazy Kripples" that "there's not one crippled colored person in South Park." Even in previous episodes which revolve completely around disabled students Timmy, Jimmy, and Nathan, such as "Krazy Kripples" or "Crippled Summer," there has been little representation of black disabled people or disabled people of color. Except for Chef in the first several seasons, Token has fulfilled the role of highlighting underrepresentation of black people on television. *South Park* has done a poor job developing black people and people of color as complex characters in the way that they have developed white characters. Jimmy, Timmy, and Nathan participate in storylines where they were not the only disabled person and displayed a wide range of emotions, motives, values, and beliefs. Other scholars have also examined the ways that *South Park* critiqued whiteness (Chaney 2004; Binder 2014). The lack of development of characters who are not white continues to be a problem and a critical reading of the episode is incomplete without situating the different experiences of disabled people based on race. Disability Studies has long been criticized for focusing on representations and experiences of white authors and white people. Recently there has been a racial turn in disability scholarship that is starting to fill in the gaps, but there is certainly more work to be done (Erevelles 2011; Grech 2015).

Nevertheless, Jimmy refuses the politically correct fantasies that sustain PC Principal. Instead, he smiles and defies them. His clever response to banning distribution of the school is to ride his toy train through town delivering *Super School News* to private residences. Cheerful music accompanies the smile on his face, signifying enjoyment. Jimmy still distributes the news while avoiding PC Principal's ban on passing out the newspaper at school. The meaningfulness or the embodied dimension of this agency is further captured by examining the scene showing him toss the paper onto PC Delta Fraternity's doorstep. The headline reads "PC Principal's Retarded Policy: by Jimmy Valmer." The camera pans back to Jimmy flipping PC Principal off and gleefully remarking, "S-s-s-suck my dick, PC Principal!" as he rides off. The incorporation of public shame into Jimmy's resistance mimics the tactics used by the PC Bros. Jimmy's newspaper creates the opportunity for him to publicly challenge PC Principal's hegemonic control of language. This strikes a critical chord as PC Principal gathers his PC Bros, complaining, "I said one microaggression to him, OK? One little microaggression, but that doesn't mean I have an unconscious bias towards people with disabilities!" This is hardly the only time that the PC Bros insulate each other from criticism and reinforce their existing beliefs about what politically correctness means. Ahmed (2014) warns that progressivism shields non-oppressed people from responsibility for their involvement in structures of power. It becomes the defining reason for why they cannot harbor prejudice. Progressives simply "cannot see how they are implicated in the problem" (Ahmed 2014, para. 10). Politically correct culture empowers supposedly well-meaning people to act and deflect any subsequent criticism, creating a hiding place that permits the disavowal of responsibility for systematic injustice.

The illusion of radical change and affective attachment to progress leads PC Principal to conclude that it is his job to show Jimmy how he is being an "Uncle Able." This problematic phrasing is appropriated from black communities where it pejoratively refers to someone who assimilates to white society (Spingarn 2010). In addition to appropriation, the phrase indicates confusion about Jimmy's strategy. Rather than assimilate to politically correct norms, Jimmy's defense of "retarded" and the ensuing conflict scrutinizes the lack of critical thinking inherent to PC culture. The PC Bros investment in enforcing politically correct culture through violence demonstrates that something they desire prevents them from accomplishing their goal (Berlant 2008). Cruel optimism theorizes these paradoxical or contradictory commitments made to push for a better society while seeking personal reward. The "cruelty" of this attachment manifests in the violence done to others by the PC Bros despite being interested in social justice. Their desire for a politically correct world can never be fulfilled while they use violence to achieve their goals. Yet, it is the illusion and allure of these goals that energizes their enforcement.

The newspaper headline lands Jimmy back in the principal's office, thereby illustrating how the commitment to progressive values shields violence. The interaction starts with PC Principal pathologizing Jimmy by asserting that he is confused about their previous conversation. When Jimmy protests, PC Principal reasserts his position with notable annoyance since he expects to arbitrate what is and is not true. But Jimmy refuses to be agreeable. This interaction dramatizes how hegemons escalate their control when disabled people resist. In *Nothing About Us Without Us: Disability Oppression and Empowerment*, James I. Charlton (1989) documents repeated injustices from people speaking for or in place of disabled people (3–5). Similar to how the International Symbol of Access serves as a cruel optimism, seemingly benign media from progressive groups can reinforce oppression for disabled people. Examining Autism Speaks generates an anecdote that represents one of these organizations. *Autism Every Day* and *I Am Autism*, two of their sponsored films, demonstrate a cruel optimism towards change by reaffirming the social conditions for disempowering autistic people. The films represent autism as a problem to be solved because of its burden on society or cost to parents (Adams 2008; Wallis 2009; Nicolaidis 2012). Jimmy's tactics for frustrating PC Principal is reminiscent of the 26 disability activist organizations that aligned to kill Autism Speaks' joy. They used media to create trouble by publishing an open letter with numerous examples of how the progressive organization hurts autistic people (Autistic Self Advocacy Network 2014). This letter contends that the paternalistic nature of these films stems from autistic people not working within the organization's leadership. As will be discussed in the next section, the solution is not as simple as including autistic people. Rather, the assumptions concerning why disability needs repair or a cure require examination. Even though this is only one example, disabled people's relationship with the Americans with Disability Act, their caretakers, and the educational systems are additional cases of why the conflict between the PC Bros and Jimmy reaches far beyond an episode of television (Campbell 2012; Hughes 2012).

PC Principal attempts to begin from the epistemology of a disabled person by including Nathan in the meeting. This decision reflects how hegemons play disabled people against one another as a form of control. Nathan represents PC Principal's "oppressed friend." Background from the show reveals why this cannot be interpreted as a neutral decision. For instance, Nathan tried to sabotage Jimmy from winning a summer camp competition in season

14 and from raising money for the camp in season 18. When PC Principal asks Nathan to describe his reaction to the word "retarded," he remarks tautologically, "it hurts my feelings because I feel bad." A clearly frustrated Jimmy returns to direct questioning by saying, "Are you *serious* right now?" Detecting the challenge, PC Principal casually prompts a response by saying, "You feel bad, right. You feel like that's a no-no word, right?" Nathan's quip emphasizes the comical and critical nature of this scene: "That word makes my heart piss its pants." Rather than referencing the history of the term's violence based on its use for isolating and shaming people with cognitive impairments, this scene illuminates that the PC Bros care more about being right than actually helping. Jimmy is not deterred and returns to his "killjoy survival kit" by asking a damning direct question (Ahmed 2017, 255–256). He critically integrates the premise of the entire situation with his inquiry, "Do you want to ask him what he means by that, or are you just pandering because you're uncomfortable around disabled people?" This question forces PC Principal to justify his position, which he cannot do. In a frustrated flurry of sputtering, he calls for another PC Bro to help him. A PC Bro appears from the hallway, stammering that "retarded" is "derogatory hate speech which fosters isolation and loneliness and being part of a voice to stop the R word is not only right, but extremely important!" As we previously learned from examining PC Delta's values, the Bros care more about their stats and satisfaction than resistance. The prioritization of belonging to a group exemplifies how the PC Bros' affective attachments animate their politics. Ultimately, the good feelings experienced from defending marginalized communities poison the possibilities for resistance by sustaining a power hierarchy where non-oppressed people determine the course of action.

From Allies to Victims

In response to bad press, the PC Bros throw a party showing their support for disabled people. Despite only inviting disabled children, the setting of a fraternity house creates an awkward climate for minors. Several disabled children stand together in a line while typical rituals of a frat party—beer pong, dancing, drinking out of red plastic cups—happen around them. Everybody at the party, disabled students included, are white. The party is an attempt to resolve Jimmy's criticism by appearing inclusive of disabled people. David T. Mitchell and Sharon L. Snyder (2015) describe inclusionary politics as "an embrace of diversity-based practices by which we include those who look, act, function, and feel different; yet our contention here is that inclusionism obscures at least as much as it reveals" (4). While disabled children are physically present—included—nothing is done to assist them or challenge ableism as a structure. This illusion of allyship reproduces violence, as Fiona Campbell (2009) argues, "For whilst claiming 'inclusion,' ableism simultaneously always restates and enshrines itself. On the one hand, discourses of equality promote 'inclusion' by way of promoting positive attitudes ... and yet on the other hand, ableist discourses proclaim quite emphatically that disability is inherently negative, ontologically intolerable and in the end, a dispensable remnant" (12). The presence of disabled children signifies diversity, but they quickly become dispensable props to achieve other desires. Although a PC Bro does start a conversation with Jimmy, he abruptly disengages when a woman walks by. A different, unnamed PC member mentions how "it just bugs me when people refer to persons with disabilities as 'handicapped.' When I hear that word I wanna fuckin' punch them in the fuckin' face." After the woman comments, "Wow, you're really progressive," the PC bro responds, "No other way to be. So uh, listen. I think you're really pretty and interesting, and I'd kinda like to take you upstairs and totally crush your pussy. Would that be acceptable to you?" This gesture of consent is padded with sexual objectification by framing the vagina as the only valuable part of a woman. Sexual objectification reduces a person to their genitals and assumes that those genitals can sum up a whole person (Kozee et al. 2007). The PC Bro exploits sympathy for oppressed people to have sex.

The party scenes make clear that the violence used by the PC Bros does not stop at physical violence. Although their identity hinges upon equality and social justice, their actions paternalize disabled people, sexually objectify women, and rely on an assumption of liberal inclusion. At the party, the commitment to disabled students is exposed as a vehicle for objectification—an act of violence which reduces another person to "relative or instrumental value" (Papadaki 2007, 340). The next morning, we learn that many PC Bros had sex after the party as PC Principal collects signed consent forms. Despite disabled children and women being guests at the party, both become objectified by the PC Bros: disabled people as tokens of their progressivism and women as objects for their consumption. The party itself intends to absolve the PC Bros from responsibility for ableism but ultimately reproduces patriarchal violence by using progressive values as social capital. More materially, it produces a politically correct culture of sexual objectification and then celebrates that culture as having done something beneficial.

When an unnamed PC Bro uses his progressive values as flirtation for sex, Jimmy looks on with horror. Writing for *Super School News* facilitates his resistance. The morning headline reads: "PC Stands for Pussy Crushing." This article prompts an immediate response. The PC Bros turn inward, as we witness an emergency meeting only composed of fraternity members:

UNNAMED PC BRO: Bro, that little kid wrote that our tolerant views and fight for social justice is just a way for us to crush puss!

PC PRINCIPAL: That's not true!!
UNNAMED PC BRO: I know, bro!! We're being totally victimized!
PC PRINCIPAL: That little fucker, dude!

After the PC Bros agree they were victimized by Jimmy, one member suggests "like … that makes us pretty cool." Another agrees by saying, "yeah, I bet now we can get a lot more puss." Alternatively, one member returns to violence by expressing his desire to "rip that dude apart and then go home and totally smash some puss, bro." These responses illustrate the insularity of progressivism. To "cope" with being victimized, the group barricaded themselves within their house by hanging yellow police tape that says "Do Not Cross: Safe Space." The cooption of safe spaces is another tactic of liberalism employed by the PC Bros. Although the PC Bros never state their identities, we learn that they have not been victimized until Jimmy shames them for objectifying women. The organization appears to be exclusively able white cismen, which illustrates a connection with Men's Rights Activists (MRAs). Both groups deploy the rhetoric of being victimized when criticized for their privilege or behavior. The ignorance of MRAs and the PC Bros stems from a failure to recognize how systems produce violence rather than isolated acts of discrimination. The PC Bros' politics resembles Bethany Coston and Michael Kimmel's (2013) criticism of MRAs as "competitive me-first*ism* that can only take without giving anything back" (384). The PC Bros' connection between being victimized and having more sexual intercourse reveals how their commitment to hegemonic politics hinges upon a self-centered interest in personal gratification. Their political ideology reduces violent structures of power to mere status politics, which makes it difficult to conceptualize how the ideology could become transgressive. After being victimized, their response is to destroy the one criticizing them or look for more sex, which provides a clear moment drawing together the episode's dramatization of violence inflicted by progressives.

Until confronted by Jimmy, PC Principal is happily able to impose social and moral order across South Park. The PC Bros emphasize that a "good life" involves drinking, working out, and policing potentially hurtful language. By reading Berlant's cruel optimism and Ahmed's killjoy into the conflict between the PC Bros and Jimmy, *South Park* illustrates how progressivism becomes a cruel optimism resisted by the killjoy. Ahmed (2010a) argues that the "feminist killjoy 'spoils' the happiness of others; she is a spoilsport because she refuses to convene, to assemble, or to meet up over happiness" (Ahmed 2010a, 65). Jimmy refuses acquiescence to this PC culture in two ways: asking direct questions that probe at its ideological justifications and creating trouble for the PC Bros by using their own tactic of public shame against them. His disobedience is neither generic nor nagging, but calculated to provoke and critique hegemonic control. Instead of lobbying within the school as a liberal activist, he directly resists the dominant paradigm. Jimmy rejects inclusion as a failed project and creates a new strategy for achieving his goal to spread the news. The killjoy enacts sustained criticism designed to neutralize the advancement of progressive values and rob the feeling of joy from those who uphold those values without warrant. Jimmy forces internal reflection, killing the PC Bros' joy by demanding justification for their actions. As a killjoy, he is always already in opposition to the dominant paradigm.

Conclusion

Our analysis of "Sponsored Content" seeks out the counterhegemonic pleasure or the affective possibilities for resistance within Jimmy's response to the progressive yet hegemonic politics of PC culture. The PC Bros' obsession with political correctness convinces them that only one valid interpretation of decorum, language use, and enforcement is possible. Instead of reflecting from criticism, they take personal offense and assume victimhood. This underscores the affective commitment made to their politics despite misidentifying the problem, misrepresenting the solution, and perpetuating violence. The PC Bros' attachment to these values shields them from being culpable for any wrongdoings and, hence, becomes a cruel optimism towards those who are oppressed. Yet, Jimmy's resistance is relentless. His direct questions and public shaming forces PC Principal to reexamine his intentions and beliefs. He does not stop at issues of ability. He challenges the PC Bros on their sexual objectification of women. As a crip feminist killjoy, Jimmy attacks the symbolic foundation of PC Bro culture.

While Jimmy does meaningfully attack sexism and ableism throughout the episode, one cannot forget his social privileges. As a white person who lives in the suburbs and edits *Super School News*, Jimmy accesses cultural and social resources that permit his resistance. One can imagine that Jimmy's discipline would have been harsher had he been black or brown. Within their analysis of inclusionism, Mitchell and Snyder (2015) theoretically ground why this privilege operates by stating, "those occupying peripheral embodiments cannot be adequately accommodated even under the most liberal, fluid, and flexible diversity doctrine given the in-built limits of community infrastructure, reasonable tolerance, limited economic resources, and traditional historical expectations about who will share the rapidly dwindling commonwealth represented by public and private spaces" (14). These features of an inaccessible public sphere contextualize why Jimmy's tactics may not be useful for people of color. The creators of *South Park* should have representations of black disabled people since the consequences of the medium demonstrate why these white representations matter even if they are criticized. Although this assessment challenges the accessibility of Jimmy's agency, critically reading the episode combats the invisibility of whiteness and injects new meaning into discussions about *South Park*.

Postmodern texts invite numerous readings without an essence to discern which is "true" or "false." Our essay criticizes the episode to work against two unethical interpretations. First, one could not critically notice disability. Max Nicholson (2015) and Chris Longo (2015) commented on Jimmy's success defusing PC Principal, but disability remained absent from both reviews. One may recall Ahmed's (2017) writings on privilege discussed earlier. This invisibility obscures the advantages and consequences that hinge upon someone's ability. Alternatively, Dan Caffrey (2015) descriptively mentioned disability as a character trait in relation to the show, but neglected to account for how Jimmy frustrated hegemonic power. If the battle between PC Principal and Jimmy is an allegory for larger conflicts, then these reviews of the episode stifle the lessons about resistance that are learned by using a critical framework. Second, Milo Yiannopoulos (2015), a clear critic of "politically correct" culture, interprets the criticism of PC Bros throughout the series as support for the pejorative use of "social justice warrior." Jimmy's resistance demonstrates the difficult work activists and organizers face from calling out sexist behavior—when the PC Bros "crush puss"—without stifling critical conversations by censoring language. To suggest these two readings are "wrong" in an interpretive sense is misplaced since text lacks a single meaning. However, they are unethical and prone to neutralize the value of disability representation or ignore a critique of broader hegemonic structures.

Aside from the substance of *South Park* being transgressive, the medium used to narrate the story creates new "public screens" for engagement. DeLuca and Peeples developed this concept with regards to the online activism that emerged after the 1999 World Trade Organization protests in Seattle. This concept does not replace the public sphere, but accounts for the consequences of technology transforming our channels for deliberating about politics and social issues. Hence, "media are not mere means of communicating in a public sphere[;] … media produce[s] the public sphere and public screen as primal scenes of Being. Particular configurations of media … open the spaces from which epistemologies and ontologies emerge" (Deluca and Peeples 2002, 132). Katie Ellis and Gerard Goggi (2015) note the importance of media for disabled people by describing it as "the *great organ* of the social" since the "media is paramount for awareness-raising, attitude formation, circulation of ideas, personal expression, social identity, and cultural currency" (6). Consequently, representations in the media need analysis since they participate in constructing how society conceives of disability.

South Park's depictions of disability help to constitute the "social imaginary" people are enmeshed within. This term encompasses the shared repertoire of texts, images, and representations that structure our social and political world. Medina (2013) connects the importance of the imaginary to resistance by suggesting that "[i]magination is not a luxury or a privilege, but a necessity. Individuals as well as groups cannot have any sort of identity and agency without the capacity to imagine themselves, their worlds, and those who inhabit them" (268). In the abstract, this passage sounds like liberal cognitive expectations, but Medina (2013) continues by saying that the "social imagination is inscribed in our habitual ways of thinking, acting, and feeling" (269–270). Our interpretation of *South Park*—as a form of play within the social imaginary—activates the potential to redraw the social coordinates that require compulsory ableism. Situating rhetorical critics as cultural teachers create moments for understanding how people are taught, conditioned, and learn these norms. The failure of media to develop complex disabled characters reveals why acts of imagination are vital to resistance by creating a world outside of compulsory ableism. As Campbell (2012) suggests, "[a]bleism is founded on utopian hermeneutics of the desirable and the disgusting and therefore it is, as Halberstam … puts it, necessary to inculcate alternative political imaginaries" (224). *South Park* develops these alternative texts and representations through their synthesis of cultural critique and open engagement with non-normative perspectives.

References

Adams, Sam. 2008. "Three Documentaries Put Faces on Autism." *Los Angeles Times*, March 25. http://www.latimes.com/entertainment/la-et-autism25mar25-story.html.

Ahmad, Asam. 2015. "A Note on Call-Out Culture." *Briarpatch Magazine*, March 2. https://briarpatchmagazine.com/articles/view/a-note-on-call-out-culture.

Ahmed, Sara. 2010a. *The Promise of Happiness*. Durham: Duke University Press.

_____. 2010b. "Feminist Killjoys and Other Willful Subjects." *The Scholar and Feminist Online* 8(3): par. 12.

_____. 2014. "Living the Consequences." *feministkilljoys*, January 3. https://feministkilljoys.com/2014/01/03/living-the-consequences/.

_____. 2016. "Queer Fragility. *feministkilljoys*, April 21. https://feministkilljoys.com/2016/04/21/queer-fragility/.

_____. 2017. *Living a Feminist Life*. Durham: Duke University Press.

Autistic Self Advocacy Network. 2014. Joint Letter to the Sponsors of Autism Speaks. http://autisticadvocacy.org/2014/07/2013-joint-letter-to-the-sponsors-of-autism-speaks/.

Berlant, Lauren. 2008. *Cruel Optimism*. Durham: Duke University Press.

Binder, Nicole. 2014. "The Portrayal of White Anxiety in South Park's 'With Apologies to Jesse Jackson.'" *Aspeers Journal of American Studies* 7: 41–65.

Caffrey, Dan. 2015. "'Sponsored Content' Works as Both Ruthless Satire and Riveting Sci-Fi." *A.V. Club*, November 19. http://www.avclub.com/tvclub/sponsored-content-works-both-ruthless-satire-and-r-228638.

Campbell, Fiona K. 2009. *Contours of Ableism: The Production of Disability and Ableness*. New York: Palgrave Macmillan.

_____. 2012. "Stalking Ableism: Using Disability to Expose 'Abled' Narcissism." In *Disability and Social Theory: New Developments and Directions*, edited by Dan Goodley, Bill Hughes, and Lennard Davis. New York: Palgrave Macmillan.

Chaney, Michael A. 2004. "Coloring Whiteness and Blackvoice Minstrelsy: Representations of Race and Place in Static Shock, King of the Hill, and South Park." *Journal of Popular Film and Television* 31 (4).

Charlton, James I. 1989. *Nothing About Us Without Us: Disability Oppression and Empowerment.* Berkeley: University of California Press.

Chermers, Michael M., and Hioni Karamanos. 2012. "'I'm Not Special?' Timmy, Jimmy, and the Double-Move of Disability Parody in *South Park.*" In *Deconstructing South Park: Critical Examinations of Animated Transgression,* edited by Brian Cogen. Lanham, MD: Lexington Books.

Coston, Bethany M., and Michael Kimmel. 2013. "White Men as the New Victims: Reverse Discrimination Cases and the Men's Rights Movement." *Nevada Law Journal* 13(2): 368–385.

Deluca, Kevin M., and Jennifer Peeples. 2002. "From Public Sphere to Public Screen: Democracy, Activism, and the 'Violence' of Seattle." *Critical Studies in Media Communication* 19(2): 131.

Ellis, Katie, and Gerard Goggi. 2015. *Disability and the Media.* London: Palgrave Macmillan.

Erevelles, Nirmala. 2011. *Disability and Difference in Global Contexts: Enabling a Transformative Body Politic.* New York: Palgrave Macmillan.

Fritsch, Kelly. 2013. "The Neoliberal Circulation of Affects; Happiness, Accessibility, and the Capacitation of Disability as Wheelchair." *Health, Culture, and Society* 5(1): 135–149.

_____. 2015. "The Neoliberal Biopolitics of Disability: Towards Emergent Intracorporeal Practices." Dissertation. York University.

Garland-Thompson, Rosmarie. 2002. "Integrating Disability, Transforming Feminist Theory." *National Women's Studies Association Journal* 14(3): 1–32.

Gretch, Shaun. 2015. "Decolonising Eurocentric Disability Studies: Why Colonialism Matters in the Disability and Global South Debate." *Social Identities* 21(1): 6–21.

Halsall, Alison. 2008. "'Bigger Longer & Uncut' *South Park* and the Carnivalesque." In *Taking South Park Seriously,* edited by Jeffrey Andrew Weinstock. Albany: State University of New York Press.

Hughes, Bill. 2012. "Civilising Modernity and the Ontological Invalidation of Disabled People." In *Disability and Social Theory: New Developments and Directions,* edited by Lennard J. Davis, Dan Goodley, and Bill Hughes. New York: Palgrave Macmillan.

Jasinksi, James. 2001. "The Status of Theory and Method in Rhetorical Criticism." *Western Journal of Communication* 65(3): 249–270.

Kolářová, Kateřina. 2014. "The Inarticulate Post-Socialist Crip: On the Cruel Optimism of Neoliberal Transformations in the Czech Republic." *Journal of Literary and Cultural Disability Studies* 8(3): 257–274.

Kozee, Holly B., Tracy L. Tylka, Casey L. Augustus-Horvath, and Angela Denchik. 2007. "Development and Psychometric Evaluation of the Interpersonal Sexual Objectification Scale." *Psychology of Women Quarterly* 31(2): 176–189.

Lashaw, Amanda. 2013. "How Progressive Culture Resists Critique: The Impasse of NGO Studies." *Ethnography* 14(4): 501–522.

Longo, Chris. 2015. "*South Park*: 'Sponsored Content' Review." *Den of Geek,* November 19, 2015. http://www.denofgeek.com/us/tv/south-park/250728/south-park-sponsored-content-review.

McRuer, Robert. 2002. *Crip Theory: Cultural Signs of Queerness and Disability.* New York: New York University Press.

Medina, Jose. 2012. *The Epistemology of Resistance.* New York: Oxford University Press.

Mitchell, David T., and Sharon L. Snyder. 2015. *The Biopolitics of Disability.* Ann Arbor: University of Michigan Press.

Nicholson, Max. 2015. "*South Park*: 'Sponsored Content' Review." *Imaginary Games Network,* November 15, 2015. http://www.ign.com/articles/2015/11/19/south-park-sponsored-content-review.

Nicolaidis, Christina. 2012. "What Can Physicians Learn from the Neurodiversity Movement?" *American Medical Association Journal of Ethics* 14(6): 504–505.

Ott, Brian L. 2008. "The Pleasures of South Park: An Experiment in Media Erotics." In *Taking*

South Park Seriously, edited by Jeffrey Andrew Weinstock. Albany: State University of New York Press.

Papacharissi, Zizi. 2015. *Affective Publics: Sentiment, Technology, and Politics*. Oxford: Oxford University Press.

Papadaki, Evangelia. 2007. "Sexual Objectification: From Kant to Contemporary Feminism." *Contemporary Political Theory* 6(6): 340.

Porter, Rick. 2015. "Wednesday Cable Ratings: 'AHS: Hotel' Stable, 'South Park' Down Slightly." *TV By the Numbers*, November 15, 2015. http://tvbythenumbers.zap2it.com/2015/11/19/wednesday-cable-ratings-nov-18–2015/.

Reid-Hresko, John, and Kim Reid. 2005. "Deconstructing Disability: Three Episodes of *South Park*." *Disability Studies Quarterly* 25(4).

Runswick-Cole, Katherine, and Daniel Goodley. 2015. "Disability, Austerity and Cruel Optimism in Big Society: Resistance and 'The Disability Commons.'" *Canadian Journal of Disability Studies* 4 (2): 163.

Shildrick, Margrit. 2015. "Living on; Not Getting Better." *Feminist Review* 111(1).

Siebers, Tobin. 2002. "Tender Organs, Identity Politics, and Narcissism." *Disability Studies: Enabling the Humanities*, edited by Sharon L. Snyder, Brenda Jo Brueggemann, and Rosemarie Garland Thompson. New York: Modern Language Association of America.

Spingarn, Adena. 2010. "When 'Uncle Tom' Became an Insult." *The Root*, May 17. www.theroot.com/articles/politics/2010/05/uncle_tom_from_compliment_to_insult.

Wallis, Claudia. 2009. "'I Am Autism': An Advocacy Video Sparks Protest." *Time*, November 6. http://content.time.com/time/health/article/0,8599,1935959,00.html.

White, Julia. 2005. "'Krazy Kripples': Using South Park to Talk about Disability." In *Building Pedagogical Curb Cutes: Incorporating Disability in the University Classroom and Curriculum*, edited by Liat Ben-Moshe, Rebecca C. Cory, Mia Feldbaum, and Ken Sagendorf. Syracuse: Syracuse University Graduate School.

Yates, Al, and Anne Bartley. 2012. *Progressive Thinking: A Synthesis of American Progressive Values, Beliefs, and Positions*. Denver: American Values Project.

Yiannopoulous, Milo. 2015. "South Park Just Declared Open Season on Social Justice Warriors." *Breitbart*, September 17. http://www.breitbart.com/big-journalism/2015/09/17/south-park-just-declared-open-season-on-social-justice-warriors.

Disabling Masculinity

Masculine Fragility and the Discourses of Disability in AMC's Breaking Bad

JL SCHATZ

AMC's hit television show *Breaking Bad* "will not only be remembered as a TV drama that went out on top—creatively, and in terms of popularity—but possibly as a game-changer for underdog TV shows … [with] 10.3 million viewers" tuning in for the show's finale (Hibberd 2013). Critics applauded *Breaking Bad* for casting an actor with cerebral palsy (CP) in the role of Walter Junior, whose character has CP but whose CP was never the major focus of his existence or something for him to overcome (Rush 2013). After the show's conclusion, RJ Mitte, the actor who played Junior, has been continually active in promoting the need for Hollywood to cast more actors with disabilities (Roshanian 2016). At the same time, *Breaking Bad* has much more to say about disability than the mere politics of inclusion that calls for more actors with disabilities to appear on the screen. No doubt, the show's very premise is based on the notion of disability and what it means to live a "good life." The show's plot is propelled into existence by Walter White's diagnosis with cancer that prompted him to give up his life as a high school chemistry teacher and cook meth to provide for his family. Beyond this fact, numerous characters have or experience disability during the show including addiction in the case of Jesse Pinkman and many of his friends, physical immobility and PTSD in the case of Hank Schrader, among many others. Put simply, this essay argues that disability, as an ever-present reality for *Breaking Bad*, is a trope for understanding how these various characters relate to their sense of masculinity in a way that mirrors society's understanding of being disabled. This analysis of the show will deconstruct ableist stereotypes that linger within the real-world constructions of masculinity as it relates to the experience of disability in the United States.

Given the general lack of positive representations of disability in the media, it is imperative to analyze *Breaking Bad* as a cultural artifact given its continual popularity. The intersections between disability and masculinity demonstrates how the stigmas surrounding disability do not simply occur in a vacuum, but rather overlap with other social identities within matrixes of domination such as gender. As stated by Diane Herndl (2013),

> Feminist disability politics builds on disability politics to recognize the ways that gender can intersect with disability, from specific expectations about male and female bodies to expectations about gender norms regarding sexual orientation, gender identity, the right to engage in sexuality, and the roles that women are expected to fulfill in terms of caretaking. Feminist disability studies['] ... goal is to achieve an ideology of bodies and modalities that does not limit people's potential simply because they function differently than the so-called norm [188].

Breaking Bad serves as a platform for investigating disability that can expose how the normative expectations of the body and health are complicated by the gendered expectations of the characters. Therefore, it is not merely Walt's diagnosis with cancer that causes him to produce meth but it is also the gendered expectation that he must provide for his family—especially for his disabled son, and a newborn baby on the way. Paying attention to these interconnections are a necessary part of critically interrogating and unraveling the way ableism is foundational to patriarchal representations within popular culture.

While it is likely apparent to most readers of this book why focusing on disability representations in the media is important, it is still worth restating. "The media creates walls between its ideals and the people it views as Others, such as when the media views people with autism as 'abnormal mysteries' ... [and] perpetuate this negative view" (Brown 2011). These beliefs then tangibly influence the way parents treat their children, and how children treat their peers. However, what may be less apparent, but still foundational to this essay, is analyzing the gendered expectations of the body in relation to disability in the media. To this end,

> each narrator's story of being a physically disabled male emerges intertwined with cultural understandings of embodiment and deeply engrained understandings of hegemonic masculinities.... As Hatfield (2010) explains this perpetuated argument materializes in an intricate web of cultural performance: Hegemonic masculinity identifies the hegemonic position of males within many Western cultures and argues that men's multiple performed masculinities grapple for power along a continuum ... to determine status (528).... Living through bodies culturally categorized as "atypical" ... continually evoke the attention of others, ... crystallizing the multifaceted constitution of hegemonic masculinity in daily performances of embodied personal identity [Scott 2014].

Put simply, disability cannot be understood absent embodiment because what constitutes able-bodiedness goes beyond one's individual biology alone. The gendered expectations that give way to what "typical" men or women should do, or be, is instrumental in formulating one's identity in relation to disability. Thus, the media's influence in shaping how disability is stigmatized, and its ability to be reclaimed positively through critical analysis, is largely constituted by its gendered expectations. This is why the championing of *Breaking Bad*'s decision to cast RJ as Junior is tied up with his ability to "grow ... an army of female fans" despite his CP (Rush 2013). In what follows, my essay will demonstrate how this tying of hegemonic masculinity to able-bodied expectations is uniquely toxic both within and beyond the screen.

Chemo, Meth or Death: Are You a Pussy or a Man?

As mentioned previously, *Breaking Bad*'s main protagonist, Walter White, was initially inspired to live a secret life as a methamphetamine manufacturer due to his diagnosis with terminal cancer. Within the first two episodes of season one, it is revealed not only that Walt has less than a year to live but also that should he pursue treatment he would undoubtedly bankrupt his family, which were living a middle-class life at the time of his diagnosis. The early twist is that, not only does Walt take up meth production to leave a savings for his family, but also that he wants to forego chemotherapy in its entirety. In episode four, he explains to his wife, Skyler, "And we spend all that money, am I supposed to leave you with all that debt? I just don't want emotions ruling us. Maybe treatment isn't the way to go." It is worth noting that throughout *Breaking Bad*, Walt uses reason and the claim that others are acting emotionally to manipulate the situation to get his way, or at least have the last word. This is significant insofar as "objectivity ... has long been seen by feminists as gendered, structuring what counts as knowledge[,] ... which is how it has been defined by particular kinds of people who are male, white, and middle class" (Swan 2010). In the following episode, at an intervention with his entire family, Walt calmly delivers a detailed monologue to explain his reasoning. He states, "What I want. What I need is choice." While I will return to the rest of the monologue in a moment, Walt's desire for choice in regards to cancer treatment directly stems from his ability to objectively determine the outcome and what he needs to do to care for his family. However, "'autonomy' is itself, prior to any application to persons with disabilities, saturated with ableist norms" (Braswell 2011). And, as *Breaking Bad* demonstrates over its five seasons, Walt's objective analysis is often fraught with mistakes that sends him and others continually spiraling downward into more death and destruction.

Walter's imagination of what chemotherapy might be like, along with his fears of disability, circulate around his concept of autonomy, rationality, and breadwinning. In the bulk of his monologue, Walt's reason for refusing treatment is based on the fear that disabled lives are not worth living. He explains,

Skyler, you've read the statistics. These doctors talking about surviving. One year, two years, like it's the only thing that matters. But what good is it, to just survive if I am too sick to work, to enjoy a meal, to make love? For what time I have left, I want to live in my own house. I want to sleep in my own bed. I don't wanna choke down 30 or 40 pills every single day, lose my hair, and lie around, too tired to get up and so nauseated that I can't even move my head. And you cleaning up after me? Me, with some dead man, some artificially alive, just marking time? No. No. And that's how you would remember me. That's the worst part. So that is my thought process, Skyler. I'm sorry. I just, I choose not to do it.

As one fan website summarized, Walt wanted "to die honorably instead of suffering the indignities of chemotherapy side-effects" (Fandom 2017). This belief in "the right to die with dignity" is one of the core distortions made possible by ableism that encourages individuals who can't enjoy the "good stuff" in life to use their end-of-life autonomy to kill themselves (McGaughey 2010). More troubling still, "because of public images that disability is 'a fate worse than death,' legalized assisted suicide threatens to create a 'two-tiered system,'" and has empirically resulted in insurance companies turning down the cost of treatment to those deemed unworthy (Golden and Zoanni 2010, 18). This returns to the question of autonomy because not everyone has the same access to the choice Walt does to turn down treatment. No doubt, many don't even have the choice for chemo in the first place, and not everyone is willing to produce meth.

The fear of losing autonomy and becoming disabled is directly connected with masculinity for Walt. Moments before Walt's monologue, Marie, Skyler's sister explains, "I x-ray people in treatment every day. Some of them are absolutely miserable." Upon hearing this, Marie's husband Hank, proclaims, "I agree with Marie on that.… Maybe Walt wants to die like a man." Naturally, Skyler disagrees insisting this isn't "debate club," which ultimately culminates in Walt's monologue before the scene ends. Even more telling, and perhaps the reason why Walt ultimately decides to go through chemo in the end, is his son's earlier monologue where Junior says, "I'm pissed off, 'cause you're being … a pussy. You're, like, ready to give up.… What if you gave up on me, huh? This here? All the stuff I've been through, and you're scared of a little chemotherapy?" In one sense, Junior is telling his dad to tough it out and fight for his life. In another sense, it directly reflects the emasculation that can occur because of disability and for those who don't want to fight. It is clear that to Junior for his dad to be a man he must fight to overcome his disability and not give up. When Walt wakes up the morning after the interchange in bed with Skyler, in the very next lines after his monologue, Walt tells her, "All right.... I'll do the treatment." He then immediately reassures Skyler that he will take care of all the details coordinating payment between the hospital and his millionaire college friends, who offered to pay for Walt's treatment. At the end of the episode, it is revealed Walt turned down his friends' help because he had already decided to produce meth instead of risking being dependent upon another man and his wife. In short, for Walt to be the man he imagined his son wanted him to be, he needed to not just fight to overcome his terminal illness but to do so on his own terms while providing for his family, regardless of the consequences that continually worsen over the course of five seasons.

Undoubtedly, some will take "issue with the application of 'end-of-life autonomy' to persons with disabilities," and will therefore disagree with equating Walter's terminal illness as equal to Junior's CP (Braswell 2011). However,

> by narrowing the "end-of-life" to terminal illness, disability rights advocates create their own double standard between the "terminally ill" and the other members of the population ... [that] gives the terminally ill the impression that their lives are less valuable ... [and] potentially inciting the terminally ill to take their own lives. The implication ... is that the very concept of "end-of-life autonomy" is an oxymoron: By singling out certain groups as the recipients of "autonomy," their autonomy to decide freely is compromised.... Such concerns indicate that the problem with "end-of-life autonomy" is deeper than whether or not the concept is applied to the "correct" population [Braswell 2011].

At the same time, it is less about the way either CP or cancer survivors are independently represented, as it is about the way masculinity and the ability to decide one's fate is ensnared within a discourse of disability. "Thus, it will be necessary to move from a discussion of 'end-of-life autonomy' to a more general consideration of the problems with 'autonomy's' role as a key conception of subjectivity in liberal democratic society" (Braswell 2011). To this end, while Junior and Walt's disabilities are different, their desire to be autonomous and not be perceived of as a "pussy" is the same. In both cases, a hegemonic masculinity of able-bodiedness shapes the social circumstances around which lives are worth living in the first place.

More directly, the hegemonic masculinity of able-bodiedness normalizes certain embodiments and abilities at the same time it keeps what counts as having a disability elusive. In fact, "both disability and fatness are terms without consistent definitions, either in terms of social or medical understandings. This is illustrated by the open-ended wording of the Americans with Disabilities Act [ADA] and the continually expansive way it has been legally applied to include categories such as drug and alcohol addiction" (Schalk 2013). No doubt, this is a large part of the reason why the ADA often fails to protect individuals who seek help for various drug addictions because whether addiction is a disability is debatable (Hill 2007). From this viewpoint, the entirety of *Breaking Bad* can be understood as a story about disability because central to its theme is the impact on, and the addiction of, meth and other drug users. Addiction can be seen in Walt's business partner, Jesse Pinkman, in Jesse's friends and girlfriend, who dies from an overdose of heroin toward the end of season two, and the occasional glimpse of individual meth users on the street. At the same time, there is a certain desire by many to not consider drug use, or obesity for that matter, a disability because it is understood as an issue of autonomy and choice. While it is beyond the scope of this essay to review the literature demonstrating how there are both physiological and mental components to drug addiction and obesity, there are two other implications of this objection to understanding addiction as a disability that are immediately relevant to this essay. Firstly, it once again returns to the question of choice and autonomy as the litmus test for able-bodiedness, which ignores the conflicting societal pressures of being able to freely choose in the first place. Certainly, many of the reasons people end up addicted to heavy drug use is because of social inequality as well as other social and structural conditions (Room 2005). Secondly, "previous research has shown that people labeled with drug addiction are viewed as more blameworthy and dangerous compared to individuals labeled with mental illness who, in turn, are viewed more harshly than those with physical disabilities" (Corrigan et al. 2009). In turn, disability and the associated social stigma correlate with a negative perception based upon how readily an individual can be recognized as disabled or fully able-bodied. Therefore, while a mobility-impaired CP character is championed for living a "normal life" in *Breaking Bad*, and addicts like Jesse who struggle with addiction garnish sympathy, the average drug-user on the show is entirely disregarded and represented as your stereotypical meth-head junkie.

This relationship to addiction within the show should not be understated because, as much as *Breaking Bad* attempts to positively represent disability, it still directly stigmatizes both drug users and the drug industry at large. Understanding these connections are crucial because research has "shown that public attitudes about groups of people affected by health and social problems are strongly influenced by depictions in the news media, popular media, and elsewhere [that] ... may be an important contributor to public attitudes about these conditions" (McGinty et al. 2015, 74). In other words,

stigma ... represents a significant barrier to mental health. Recent meta-analyses demonstrate associations between experiences of stigma with increased rates of mental illness and psychological distress as well as decreased well-being ... among people living with a variety of devalued marks and attributes. Stigma associated with drug addiction and use is strong and often structurally reinforced by government policies that contribute to its widespread acceptability. For example, ... [the] "war on drugs" within the United States contributes to the "socio-cultural stigmatization of drug users and view of drug use and users as 'criminals' and 'junkies'" [Earnshaw et al. 2012].

Thus, the stigma surrounding drug use and addiction often helps perpetuate a cycle that forecloses other options for help. Furthermore, the stigma associated with disability and other socio-economic factors can drive people into addiction, thereby perpetuating the stigmas associated with disability (Room 2005). Sadly, while "portrayals of persons with ... mental illness occur frequently in the mass media[,] ... the majority of individuals ... depicted in the media exhibit deviant or abnormal behavior" (McGinty et al. 2015, 74). Again, given the popularity of *Breaking Bad*, interrogating these representations is crucial because "stigma shapes the way that individuals who are not drug users feel toward, think about, and treat people with a known or assumed history of drug addiction" (Earnshaw et al. 2012). By unraveling the connection between stigma, addiction, and the diversity of disabilities it can be possible to move beyond merely demonizing drug use and forge a path toward a more complete form of justice for all.

In this regard, while *Breaking Bad* surely has numerous departures from reality, one of the most troubling aspects is "its occasional depiction of meth users as largely disconnected from society and utterly desperate. That's not always true. There are 'functional' addicts, especially working mothers, who rely upon strong stimulants like meth to juggle their sundry responsibilities" (Matthews 2013). This flawed perspective of meth users legitimizes the war on drugs based on the overstated violence of the drug market, which is often heightened by the stigma and criminalization of drugs and disability. This skewed perspective is explicitly reinforced when Hank takes Junior to the Crossroads Motel in episode three of season one. He tells his nephew, "This here's what we call the Crystal Palace. Now you know who lives in the palace? Meth-heads. Nasty, skeevy, meth-heads who'd sell their grandma's coochie for a hit.... Every last one of these miserable wastes of skin got started how?... Dollars to doughnuts, and I shit you not, that gateway drug was marijuana." Naturally, it makes sense that Hank would connect meth with marijuana, given his employment as a DEA agent and his distaste for the Mexican cartel. However, the criminalization of marijuana grew out of racist sentiments toward Mexicans, who Hank openly calls racial names throughout the show. And, while it is beyond the scope of this essay to fully debunk the gateway hypothesis, it will suffice to say that there is virtually no credible studies that confirm it as a matter of causation (Boeri 2015). More importantly to note, these negative representations of drug use reproduce the stigmatization of addiction so that the socio-economic conditions of individual drug users are forgotten, thereby demonizing addicts as responsible for their own demise.

This is precisely why studies do confirm some correlation between marijuana use and other drugs due to "a person's social environment" (National Institute for Drug Abuse 2017).

Immediately after this personal interchange between Hank and Junior, Hank calls over the Crossroads Motel's resident sex worker to the car and asks, "How much you charge for a windy, Wendy?" The implication of what's happening quickly becomes clear as Hank continues to parade her as an example of the danger of drugs to Junior, even after Wendy objects, "I ain't doing him. He's a kid." The hope for Hank, at the request of sister-in-law, is to scare Junior "straight" by showing him that if he starts using marijuana then he'll get involved with meth, and ultimately be the one giving blowjobs instead of receiving them. In short, it is through threatening Junior's masculinity that he hopes to convince his nephew to stay drug-free. The connection between this and disability becomes apparent when Wendy eventually notices Junior's crutches and asks, "What are you, like, handicapped?" Without giving Junior a chance to answer, Hank steps in saying, "He broke his leg playing football. He's a QB. Got an arm like a howitzer.... Hoof it. Get lost." Not only does the speed at which Hank wraps up this encounter reveal how uncomfortable he is with disability but also how important it is for him to attach a normative form of masculinity onto Junior in order to compensate. This incessant need to assert a hegemonic masculinity, and to pass as able-bodied when threatened with disability, ignores how in reality "the socio-economic exclusion of people with disabilities ... put them at [more] risk for exploitation along with, and as sex workers, who may experience exploitation by those who 'purchase' sex and by those who exploit sex workers" (DAWN 2013). Thus, whether one agrees with the decriminalization of sex work or not, the continuation of a patriarchal form of ableism ensures that those who have the least ability to find other employment will also be the ones most likely to experience the worst abuse of the sex and drug industries. Ultimately, the resulting stigmatization prevents addressing the realities of drug use, as well as the needs of people living with addiction, because of the overemphasis on emasculating drug users through ableist tropes.

It is worth repeating how the criminalization of drugs in general is caught up within a xenophobic form of racism. "The War on Drugs is ... a kind of 'informal American cultural colonization,'" where the desire to stop the flow of drugs from Latin America is connected to a desire to prevent the flow of Mexican and Hispanic culture (Campos 2014). According to Dean Norris, the actor who played Hank's character in *Breaking Bad*, "Hank was a little more racist in the audition piece, which never made it into the show. He still makes some 'beaner' remarks to his partner [Steve Gomez], but it was even worse. It's a tough-guy business" (Tannenbaum 2013). Once again, masculinity is quintessential to Hank's self-expression, given that part of how he overcompensates for his insecurities is through his racialized humor. This becomes apparent in the second season, after Hank has been promoted to the El Paso Task Force, and is chastised by his comrades for not speaking Spanish or knowing Mexican culture. In episode three of season two, after his racial jokes result in silence, and being sidelined in their interrogation of an informant, Hank asserts himself, "How about you stop jerking us off here? Where's the meet? When's it going down?… White boy's gonna kick your ass, you don't stop wasting time." When the informant calmly responds to Hank's insults, "My name's Tortuga. You know what that means?" Hank answers, "Well, if I had to guess, I'd say that's Spanish for 'asshole.'" In short, to make up for what Hank lacked in skill, cultural-sensitivity, and his disability of not speaking Spanish he doubled down on the "tough-guy business" Dean Norris described as essential to his character. Given how *Breaking Bad* continually portrays the Mexican cartel as mad men bent on violence for the sake of violence, it is not surprising that Hank feels the way he does about Mexicans, especially when juxtaposed against the logic and reason his brother-in-law Walt uses. In fact, it is likely that Hank doesn't suspect Walt of manufacturing meth for so long, despite all the evidence, because Walt doesn't live up to his preconceived notion of what a drug dealer looks like.

Of course, Hank's assertion of masculinity fails tragically when, at the end of the episode, Tortuga is reduced to a severed head that explodes when recovered by the El Paso Task Force, killing Hank's El Paso partners and triggering his PTSD that began after a shootout in the finale of season one. Once Hank returns to Albuquerque, he claims it's solely to tie up loose ends in order to find the source of Walt's blue meth, and downplays any trauma over his experience at the border. When his partner, Steve Gomez, is promoted to take Hank's place in El Paso, while being congratulatory Hank can't help but to also work in a few racialized jokes about his friend. In fact, despite numerous episodes having close-ups of Hank as he struggles to breathe and calm down when his PTSD flares up, he continues to mostly keep these incidents to himself, which is a common result of the medical model of disability that teaches people to just tough it out and overcome. Further, it is this attempt to deny his own frailty that best exposes how "the psychological origins of hostility toward disabled people … [comes from] the tendency of nondisabled people to 'deny their vulnerability and frailty and mortality, and to project these uncomfortable issues onto disabled people, who they can subsequently oppress and exclude and ignore'" (Mackey 2009). As such, the whitened version of masculinity Hank puts forward is part of a "collective fantasy … [of] the projected threat of the loss of physical capabilities … [and] the fear of others whose traits are perceived as disturbing" (Mackey 2009). Therefore, Hank assumes driving by the Crossroads Motel would be enough to keep Junior away from drugs. Sadly, "this devaluation is itself enmeshed with social structures that exclude impaired people from public and economic venues, which in turn prevent individual validation through social activity and paid work" (Mackey 2009). Thus, it is not inconsequential that both the sex worker meth-head, and the illegal Mexican immigrant, are used as mirrors in *Breaking Bad* to reflect Hank's own insecurities surrounding his numerous professional inabilities and personal shortcomings.

Hank's insecurity surrounding disability becomes even more explicit in season three after he loses use of his legs as a result of a shootout with two Mexican cartel members, at the end of the eighth episode. His forthcoming disability is foreshadowed earlier in the episode when he tells his wife, Marie, "I freeze…. I can't breathe…. I panic. Ever since that Salamanca thing…. It changed me. And I can't seem to control it…. I'm just not the man I thought I was. I think I'm done as a cop." In this rare admission of PTSD, Hank takes his disability as proof that he lacks the manhood necessary to be a cop because he's no longer in control. Thus, instead of accepting the need for others as a condition for meaningful autonomy, Hank is ready to admit defeat at the mere possibility of something being beyond his control in a way that makes him think about himself as less of a man. This is why Hank is so willing in subsequent episodes to throw in the towel, turn down physical therapy, and continually chastise Marie after the diminished use of his legs. Even by episode 12 in season three, Hank is unwilling to leave the hospital and continues to angrily retort Marie whenever she brings up the fact that the doctor's say he can be discharged. On a family visit, Hank snaps at Junior when he asks if he's well enough, "Jesus, kid, you, too? Do I look well enough? I'm shitting in pants, peeing in pitchers. Can't move my legs." Visibly and audibly upset, Junior responds, "So people in wheelchairs should be in hospitals? What about people on crutches? Maybe I should be in here, too." While this tempers Hank, it doesn't convince him that he's well enough to leave since being compared to someone with CP was proof enough that part of his masculinity was lost. In fact, Hank only checks out toward the end of the episode after losing a bet with Marie that she can't give him an erection in order to prove, in her words, "you're not completely hopeless." Ultimately, even though Hank lives up to his end and goes home, his feelings of emasculation continue in future episodes even though he can get an erection because he remains disabled, and dependent on Marie for day-to-day assistance.

It is worth returning to the question of end-of-life autonomy here, given how apparent it is that Hank believes that his life is one not worth living. In fact, Hank's worries over his ability to be a man and his desire to live at home echoes Walt's initial desires to not seek chemotherapy. Meanwhile, in reality,

this fear of disability typically underlies assisted suicide. Janet Good, an assisted suicide advocate who worked with Jack Kevorkian, was clear about this: Pain is not the main reason we want to die. It's the inability to get out of bed or get onto the toilet….

But as many thousands of people with disabilities who rely on personal assistance have learned, needing help is not undignified, and death is not better than reliance on assistance.... The legalization of assisted suicide would occur "within the context of a health care system and a society pervaded with prejudice and discrimination against people with disabilities" ... [that will] play out in life-threatening ways [Golden and Zoanni 2010, 18].

While Hank is not openly suicidal, the show's emphasis on his recovery in connection with masculinity reinforces an ableist worldview that falsely links disability with emasculinization and the value of life with autonomy, which is coded as masculine. Again, the ability to choose in the first place is one that is uniquely privileged given the reality of health care and socio-economic inequalities that make choice in relation to health and death impossible (Coleman 2014; Enns 2013). No doubt, the only reason why Hank can pay for physical therapy in the first place is because Skyler offered to cover the cost of treatment with the money that Walt was making by cooking meth. For both characters, the fear of being dependent was more threatening than death even though their ability to have a choice in the first place is intimately connected to their suburban middle-class lifestyles. And, despite Junior's ongoing reminder that life with a disability is worth living, both Hank and Walt seem continually unwilling to ever consider this a possibility for themselves since their individual autonomy is too important to their sense of self.

Importantly, the way both Hank and Walt treat their wives is similar insofar as both use their reason and intelligence to belittle Marie and Skyler into submission. For Hank it happens throughout his recovery in physical therapy from simple things like yelling at Marie for bringing back Fritos instead of Cheetos in season four, episode three, as well as in numerous episodes where he criticizes her for not knowing the difference between a rock and a mineral. For Walt it happens every time Skyler tries to object to his meth production, and he rationalizes his continual involvement. This reaches its height in the fourth episode of season five, where to get her children out of the house Skyler resorts to walking into her swimming pool fully clothed and faking a mental breakdown so that Hank and Marie will take the kids. When Walt challenges her on her next move, and Skyler threatens to hurt herself to buy more time, Walt threatens, "So maybe next time, I have you committed. Put you in some inpatient facility while I take care of the kids myself. Is that what you want?" When she threatens to show up with bruises, claiming abuse, Walt responds, "Oh, well, that'll be fun bringing the police up to speed on all of that. But not as much fun as telling your 16-year-old son that his father is a wife-beater." Triumphantly Walt declares, while moving in on Skyler who is increasingly backing away from him and who is becoming increasingly upset, "You wanna take me on? You wanna take away my children? What's the plan?" It's worth noting the historical accuracy of women being institutionalized by their husbands or fathers for disobeying them, as well as the accuracy of how the criminal justice system repeatedly fails survivors of domestic abuse, and the subsequent fallout that families endure (Tasca et al. 2012; Jeltson 2016). Ultimately, through reason and his traditional position of dominance, Walt uses his control over Skyler to affirm his manhood even if things are falling apart all around him. Of course, Skyler, is not ignorant of her position and snaps back with the last words of the scene, "This is the best I could come up with, okay?... But you're right. It's a bad plan.... I don't know what to do. I'm a coward. I can't go to the police. I can't stop laundering your money. I can't keep you out of this house. I can't even keep you out of my bed. All I can do is wait … [f]or the cancer to come back."

Three things can be noted from the above interchange. First, rationality and intelligence remains the center of Walt's masculinity, which he uses to verbally abuse Skyler and put her in life-threatening conditions for the sake of her family. This posing of rationality in opposition to the emotional response of Skyler, which culminates in her use of a mental breakdown to resist, is telling. To this end, "when people define themselves in terms of reason, they place themselves in opposition with everything nonrational, … [which is] seen as antithetical to the self. People who define themselves strictly in terms of reason will invariably cause environmental damage and seek to exploit 'people'—including non-human people—who supposedly aren't rational" (Checkett 2001). Secondly, Walt's belief that Skyler's mental breakdown was fake, because he thought it was a semi-rationally planned strategy to get the children out of the house, ignores the relational pressures Skyler was experiencing and the presence of invisible disabilities, which are often heavily stigmatized as is the case with addiction.

> To pursue such a discussion, however, it is necessary to first explore in more detail what exactly is meant by "real" and "fake" disability in film, where actual bodies enact impairment in order to convey disability's social meanings, with or without the audience's knowledge or complicity.... This dynamic becomes even more complicated when we consider how images of real and fake disability are mapped onto actors' bodies, which themselves are always already constructed according to social understandings of ability and deviance. The fantasy of verifiable and authentic disability as a deserving social category is tested and contested through these filmic portrayals in the deployment of multiple and overlapping categories of realness and falsehood [Samuels 2014, 67].

Thirdly, the control Walt uses in discerning what he will do with the perception of Skyler's breakdown through institutionalization, accurately reflects a world where hegemonic conceptions of masculinity are a privileged place of power (Roth and Lerner 1974). From here, it is all too obvious how the constant clinging to normative able-bodiedness allows for a shifting goalpost where the rationality of some are maintained through the discriminatory violence enacted upon anyone other than the self. Therefore, in season two, episode three, Walt can justify faking a mental breakdown himself to hide his lie about where he was to Skyler without seeing himself as irrational, despite Jesse raising many of the same objections. It is also why Walt can repeatedly justify killing other people to save himself throughout the show since there is a logic to his calculations.

By the end of the show, Walt's drive to affirm his masculinity as a means to overcome his disability and vulnerability has disastrous consequences for himself and his family. Even though twice during the show, the DEA believed they had caught who had been making the blue meth, Walt steers Hank back into investigating further by convincing Hank there is a bigger mastermind out there. This happens as both characters are deployed thematically as Junior's male role models in the show. While in earlier seasons, Walt's assertion of dominance only results in his son throwing up after drinking too much against Hank's protests and Walt's encouragement, in season five it ultimately leads to a face-off between the two characters that results in both of their deaths. The destructiveness of this ableist hegemonic masculinity extends beyond *Breaking Bad* and the fictitious deaths of countless characters over its airtime. "Ableisms historically have been used and still are used by various social groups to justify their elevated level of rights and status in relation to other social groups, other species and the environment…. An ability lens is essential for examining equity and equality discourses" (Wolbring 2012). Fortunately, this does not need to be the case. In short, "ableist culture sustains and perpetuates itself via rhetoric; the ways of interpreting disability and assumptions about bodies that produce ableism are learned. The previous generation teaches it to the next and cultures spread it to each other through modes of intercultural exchange. Adopting a rhetorical perspective to the problem of ableism thus exposes the social systems that keep it alive" (Cherney 2011). The constant presence of these features within *Breaking Bad*, alongside its ongoing popularity, enables a point of entry into educating people through media in order to better understand the necessity for moving away from an ableist worldview. Examining how these notions of gender and disability interplay within media is the perfect starting point to challenge how hegemonic masculinity shapes the everyday ableisms beyond the show.

In fact, in the show's finale there is a hint at an alternative when Walt comes to realize that, despite all his careful calculations, he has gone disastrously wrong. This admission happens when Walt reaches out to Skylar, despite being a fugitive, to try and explain his actions. She cuts him off saying, "If I have to hear one more time that you did this for the family." Walt responds, "I did it for me. I liked it. I was good at it. And I was, really, I was alive." In this admission Walt concedes that everything he did under the patriarchal ideal of breadwinning was not actually for the good of the family, but for his own feelings of pride and self-worth. In short, Walt admits that his most tragic failure was his mistaking of what counted as a life worth living within the confined parameters of a patriarchal ableism. It was his belief that he needed to be a good father—independent and able-bodied—that resulted in his inability to take care of his family. Had this admission happened in season one, Walt would have realized that the best way he could have taken care of his family would have been to refuse to be a "man," instead of responding to Junior's call to not be a "pussy." This idea of failure can be understood as

> crip success [that] is, paradoxically, to fail to become normate. In *The Queer Art of Failure* Halberstam advocates a concept of "failure [that] allows us [crip/queer people] to escape the punishing norms that discipline behavior and manage human development with the goal of delivering us from unruly childhoods to orderly and predictable adulthoods" (3). This queer studies inversion of ways to read non-normative lives as failing standards of heteronormative expectations enables crip/queer people to pursue other modes of existence as alternates to sanctioned social roles.... By applying this crip/queer deployment of "failure," curricular cripistemologies undertake pedagogical practices suppressed (or, at least, devalued) by normative neoliberal educational contexts [Mitchell et al 2014].

Ultimately, by disentangling the ableism bound up with gendered expectations, it is possible to embrace the failures of meeting such expectations in order to overcome the traditional rationality that informs decision-making. Only then can the choices individuals make in relation to disability be understood with the necessary relational autonomy that doesn't diminish one's value because of a reliance on others. We are all relationally reliant. Embracing where we individually fail is a necessary precondition for a more liberatory framework where others are not violently left behind.

References

Boeri, Miriam. 2015. "Marijuana Is Not, Repeat Not, a Gateway Drug." *Newsweek*, April 25. http://www.newsweek.com/marijuana-not-gateway-drug-325358.

Braswell, Harold. 2011. "Can There Be a Disability Studies Theory of 'End-of-Life Autonomy?'" *Disability Studies Quarterly.* http://dsq-sds.org/article/view/1704/1754.

Brown, Rebecca. 2011. "'Screw Normal': Resisting the Myth of Normal by Questioning Media's Depiction of People with Autism and Their Families." *Minnesota Symposium in Disability Studies.*

Campos, Isaac. 2014. *Home Grown: Marijuana and the Origins of Mexico's War on Drugs.* Chapel Hill: University of North Carolina Press.

Checkett, John. 2001. *The Green Goddess Returns: Batman's Poison Ivy as a Symbol of Emerging Ecofeminist Consciousness.* Boca Raton: Florida Atlantic University.

Cherney, James. 2011. "The Rhetoric of Ableism." *Disability Studies Quarterly.* http://dsq-sds.org/article/view/1665/1606.

Coleman, Diane. 2014. "Assisted Suicide and Disability." *Disability Rights and Education Defense Fund.* http://dredf.org/public-policy/assisted-suicide/assisted-suicide-and-disability/.

Corrigan, Patrick, Sachiko Kuwabara, and John O'Shaughnessy. 2009. "The Public Stigma of Mental Illness and Drug Addiction." *Journal of Social Work* 9(2).

DAWN. 2013. "Disability, Sexuality, and the Legalization of Prostitution." July 21. http://www.dawncanada.net/en-news/myths-about-people-with-disabilities-and-sexuality-should-not/.

Earnshaw, Valerie, Laramie Smith, and Michael Copenhaver. 2012. "Drug Addiction Stigma in the Context of Methadone Maintenance Therapy: An Investigation into Understudied Sources of Stigma." *The International Journal of Mental Health Addiction* 11(1): 110–122. https://www.ncbi.nlm.nih.gov/pmc/articles/PMC3743126/.

Enns, Ruth. 2013. "Assisted Suicide Would Jeopardize People with Disabilities." *CBC News*, April 22. http://www.cbc.ca/news/canada/manitoba/assisted-suicide-would-jeopardize-people-with-disabilities-1.1364767

Fandom. 2017. "Walter White." http://breakingbad.wikia.com/wiki/Walter_White.

Golden, Marilyn, and Tyler Zoanni. 2010. "Killing Us Softly: The Dangers of Legalizing Assisted Suicide." *Disability and Health Journal* 3: 16–30. http://dredf.org/PIIS1.pdf.

Herndl, Diane. 2013. "Politics and Sympathy: Recognition and Action in Feminist Literary Disability Studies." *Legacy: A Journal of American Women Writers* 30(1): 187–198.

Hibberd, James. 2013. "'Breaking Bad' Series Finale Ratings Smash All Records." *Entertainment Weekly*, September 30. http://ew.com/article/2013/09/30/breaking-bad-series-finale-ratings/.

Hill, Samantha. 2007. "The ADA's Failure to Protect Drug Addicted Employees Who Want to Seek Help and Rehabilitation." *University of Pennsylvania Journal of Labor and Employment Law* 4: 973–989. http://scholarship.law.upenn.edu/cgi/viewcontent.cgi?article=1291&context=jbl

Jeltson, Melissa. 2016. "This Is How a Domestic Violence Victim Falls Through the Cracks." Huffington Post, March 3. http://www.huffingtonpost.com/2014/06/16/domestic-violence_n_5474177.html.

Mackey, Peter. 2009. "Crip Utopia and the Future of Disability." *Critical Disability Discourses* 1. http://cdd.journals.yorku.ca/index.php/cdd/article/view/23383.

Matthews, Dylan. 2013. "Here's What 'Breaking Bad' Gets Right, and Wrong, about the Meth Business." *Washington Post*, August 15. https://www.washingtonpost.com/news/wonk/wp/2013/08/15/heres-what-breaking-bad-gets-right-and-wrong-about-the-meth-business/?utm_term=.6604cc625c6c.

McGaughey, James. 2010. "Why Do So Many Disability Groups Oppose Physician Assisted Suicide?" *Office of Protection and Advocacy for Persons with Disabilities*. http://www.ct.gov/opapd/cwp/view.asp?Q=519546&A=3683.

McGinty, Emma, Howard Goldman, Bernice Pescosolido, and Colleen Barry. 2015. "Portraying Mental Illness and Drug Addiction as Treatable Health Conditions: Effects of a Randomized Experiment on Stigma and Discrimination." *Social Science & Medicine* 126: 73–85. https://www.researchgate.net/profile/Emma_Mcginty/publication/269876426_Portraying_mental_illness_and_drug_addiction_as_treatable_health_conditions_Effects_of_a_randomized_experiment_on_stigma_and_discrimination/links/5630d53a08ae13bc6c352f1d.pdf.

Michelle, David, Sharon Snyder, and Linda Ware. 2014. "[Every] Child Left Behind: Curricular Cripistemologies and the Crip/Queer Art of Failure." *Journal of Literary and Cultural Disability Studies* 8(3): 295–313.

National Institute of Drug Abuse. 2017. "Is Marijuana a Gateway Drug?" https://www.drugabuse.gov/publications/research-reports/marijuana/marijuana-gateway-drug.

Room, R. 2005. "Stigma, Social Inequality and Alcohol and Drug Use." *Drug and Alcohol Review* 24(2): 143–155.

Roshanian, Arya. 2016. "'Breaking Bad' Actor RJ Mitte: We Need More Disabled People Working in TV." *Variety*, August 25. http://variety.com/2016/tv/news/breaking-bad-rj-mitte-disabled-actors-tv-television-1201844774/.

Roth, Robert, and Judith Lerner. 1974. "Sex-Based Discrimination in the Mental Institutionalization of Women." *California Law Review* 62(3): 798–815.

Rush, George. 2013. "It's Not an Act." *Daily Mail*, July 6. http://www.dailymail.co.uk/health/

article-2357324/Its-act--I-really-cerebral-palsy-says-young-star-Breaking-Bad--unlike-character-R-J-Mitte-cope-crutches-disability-growing-army-female-fans.html

Samuels, Ellen. 2014. *Fantasies of Identification: Disability, Gender, Race.* New York: New York University Press.

Schalk, Sami. 2013. "Coming to Claim Crip: Disidentification with/in Disability Studies." *Disability Studies Quarterly.* http://dsq-sds.org/article/view/3705/3240.

Scott, Julie-Ann. 2014. "Illuminating the Vulnerability of Hegemonic Masculinity through a Performance Analysis of Physically Disabled Men's Personal Narratives." *Disability Studies Quarterly.* http://dsq-sds.org/article/view/3570/3526.

Swan, Elaine. 2010. "States of White Ignorance, and Audit Masculinity in English Higher Education." *Social Politics: International Studies in Gender, State, and Society* 17(4): 477–506.

Tannenbaum, Rob. 2013. "Dean Norris Explains Hank's Moral Code on 'Breaking Bad.'" *Rolling Stone,* September 12. http://www.rollingstone.com/tv/news/dean-norris-explains-hanks-moral-code-on-breaking-bad-20130912.

Tasca, Cecilia, Mariangela Rapetti, Mauro Giovanni Carta, and Bianca Fadda. 2012. "Women and Hysteria in the History of Mental Health." *Clin Pract Epidemiol Ment Health* 8: 110–119.

Wolbring, Gregor. 2012. "Ableism, Disability, and the Academy." http://fedcan.ca/fr/blog/ableism-disability-studies-and-academy.

Deviant Sexuality

The Hypersexualization of Women
with Bipolar Disorder
in Film and Television

HAILEE M. YOSHIZAKI-GIBBONS
and MEGHANN E. O'LEARY

Dominant societal discourses frequently assert the view that people with disabilities are non-sexual. Hahn (1988) referred to the phenomenon of viewing disabled people's sexuality as non-existent or inappropriate as "asexual objectification." Garland-Thomson (2002) similarly noted that the identities of disabled and sexual cannot co-exist; one identity must be denied for the other identity to be believable and acceptable. While some disabled people identify as asexual (Lebowitz 2015), the stereotype of asexuality or non-sexuality is harmful because it prevents disabled people from defining and enacting their own sexuality (Garland-Thomson, 2002). Thus, the asexual objectification of disabled people is a concern for disability rights. However, feminist disability studies has called for scholars and activists to engage in intersectional approaches that consider how gender, disability, and other identities intertwine to influence how society views and attends to the sexuality of disabled women. Intersectionality, which emerged from the work of black feminists, illustrates how identities interact in shaping personal, structural, political, and cultural aspects of lived experience and oppression (Crenshaw 1991). For disabled women, their experiences of sexuality are often paradoxical. As Garland-Thomson (2002) notes, the asexual objectification of disabled women is complex, as the disabled woman "escapes ... sexual objectification at the potential cost of losing her sense of identity and power as a feminine sexual being" (18). Therefore, many disabled women are not sexually objectified in the ways that non-disabled women are, but consequently are prevented from expressing sexuality in meaningful and empowering ways.

Yet, Garland-Thomson's theory is primarily focused on visibly and physically disabled women; discourses about the sexualization of women with psychiatric disabilities are less frequently discussed in feminist disability studies and related fields. Some psychiatric diagnoses, such as depression, classify lack of interest in sex as a symptom, which may contribute to the perception of people with psychiatric disabilities as non-sexual. However, other psychiatric diagnoses, such as bipolar disorder, pathologize people as hypersexual. According to the DSM-V, diagnoses for bipolar disorder, type I and type II, hinge on the experience of a manic or hypomanic episode, which may be marked by an "increase in goal-directed activity," and "excessive involvement in pleasurable activities that have a high potential for painful consequences." Increased sexual desire and sexual activity are included under both symptoms. As Mazza et al. (2011) noted, "In patients with bipolar disorder, excessive involvement in pleasurable activities including hypersexuality is a criterion for the diagnosis" (364). Consequently, hypersexuality has become a defining sign of bipolar disorder in the medical industrial complex (Ehrenreich & Ehrenreich 1971).

These medical discourses have influenced cultural discourses, and have resulted in numerous media representations of hypersexualized bipolar women, which in turn impact public perception of bipolar women and their sexuality (Bipolar Lives 2016; Dolmage 2014). As bipolar women, we have personally experienced the effects of these cultural discourses in our interactions with others, our relationships, and our medical care. In this essay, we analyze multiple television shows and films to demonstrate the ways in which hypersexualized bipolar women characters serve as a metaphor for the dangers of female sexuality and thereby promote normative sexuality. Using intersectionality as a framework, we examine how these film and television representations of hypersexualized bipolar women are intertwined with discourses of gender, racialization, and disablement. We argue that these representations of bipolar disorder reinscribe the dangers of sexuality on women's bodies in new ways by employing disability as a justification for oppression (Baynton 2001). Specifically, our intersectional analysis of television and film portrayals demonstrated that bipolar women are often depicted as having excessive sexuality. The characters are out of control, insatiable, irrational, seductive, and dangerous—to themselves and others. Consequently, bipolar women characters become metaphorical devices for the stereotypical dangers assumed to be inherent in the sexuality of women (Mitchell and Snyder 2001). Hence, hypersexuality is framed as a symptom that indicates lack of control, instability, volatility, and even vulnerability. These representations typically resolve the "problem" of hypersexuality and bipolar disorder through psychiatric treatment, or more frequently, through the support of a strong, stable, and rational heterosexual male figure. The continual juxtaposition of the dangerous, hypersexual woman and the sane male savior contributes to sexist ideology, which has been used to justify men's control and power over women.

Furthermore, we contend these representations are racialized since the vast majority of bipolar women characters are white, which renders bipolar women of color invisible. One of the reasons for this invisibility may be because women of color are often hypersexualized due to racial stereotypes. (Hartman 1996; Shimizu 2007; West 1995). Thus, the hypersexuality of women characters of color is perceived as inherent, and the assignment of disability is not needed. Conversely, for white women to be hypersexualized, they must be cast as deviant in some other way, such as bipolar. By portraying hypersexuality in white women as a "symptom" of an "illness" that requires "treatment," hypersexuality in white women is represented as fixable, whereas it is constructed as innate for women of color due to the long history of colonization, enslavement, and racialized gender oppression. Thus, hypersexuality, as a tool of gendered oppression in media representations, is embedded in narratives of racialization and disablement.

To contextualize this argument, we first discuss the power of media representations and the ways in which the media produces cultural knowledge about disability (Dolmage 2014). Then, we explore various media representations of bipolar women in film and television, and analyze these depictions using disability studies perspectives and frameworks. Lastly, we consider the role of hypersexuality as a tool of oppression and the impact these representations have on public perceptions of bipolar women and their sexuality.

Media Representations of Bipolar Women

For many people, film and television is often considered to reflect reality (Dolmage 2014; Gamson et al. 1992). For disability specifically, media representations fill a gap in knowledge about the disability experience, as the very organization of society makes disability unknowable to many non-disabled people. Disabled people are frequently isolated and excluded from mainstream society. As Erevelles (2001) observes, "Despite their insistence that they possess 'livable' bodies, people with disabilities have lived through a history of segregational practices (in schools, workplaces, residences, communities, etc.) that have constructed them on the outside limits of intelligibility" (97). Thus, disability is situated as a phenomenon beyond non-disabled people's understanding because disabled people are rendered invisible due to lack of access, attitudinal and environmental barriers, and structures such as special education, institutionalization, and sheltered workshops (Erevelles 2001; Linton 1998).

In the case of psychiatric disability, we are pressured to pass as nondisabled in order to avoid stigma, prejudice, and discrimination. This results in many people with psychiatric disabilities not disclosing or divulging their experiences of disability. Even when people with psychiatric disabilities do share their perspectives or stories, we are assumed to lack rhetoricity because we are perceived as irrational and nonsensical (Prendergast 2003). Margaret Price (2011) further conceptualizes this lack of rhetoricity as "the ability to be received as a valid human subject" (26). In other words, people with psychiatric disabilities fail to "make sense" and thus we are not considered reliable authorities on the experience of psychiatric disability. Consequently, due to a lack of diverse first-person narratives from people with psychiatric disabilities, the media becomes a powerful means through which to understand the disabled experience (Safran 1998).

The view that these representations reflect reality can have significant consequences for disabled people. According to Hyler, Gabbard, and Schneider (1991), "While filmmakers do not intend to paint reality, these images ultimately help shape the everyday obstacles formed by public perceptions. Movie imagery, therefore, translates into a political agenda and may create negative outcomes for persons with disabilities" (1044). Furthermore, media and culture mutually reinforce understandings of disability. As Dolmage (2014) writes, "Rhetorical schemes or myths tell familiar stories about disability from an ableist perspective. The use of all of these myths in discourse then both borrows from and shapes cultural beliefs about disability in the everyday" (32). Hence, since people with psychiatric disabilities are denied the opportunity to frame their own experiences, the media uses oppressive psychiatric discourses and ableist conceptualizations to generate representations of psychiatric disability, which in turn influences the non-disabled public's understanding of psychiatric disabilities. In the case of film depictions of women with bipolar disorder, the common portrayal of hypersexuality reinforces negative stereotypes about these women's sexual expression, pathologizing their sexuality as a deviant symptom indicative of an underlying "illness" which must be fixed or cured, often with the assistance of a strong, rational male savior.

Analyses of Media Representations of Bipolar Women

Depictions of people with bipolar disorder in television and film have evolved significantly over time. First, the number of representations has increased. According to Hill (2015), television is giving more screen time than ever to issues related to psychiatric disabilities in general. Second, characters with bipolar disorder are receiving more explicit labels in some series and movies. Earlier depictions of bipolar characters do not reveal their specific diagnoses, but rather present stereotypical symptoms and behaviors commonly associated with bipolar disorder, including mood swings, emotional volatility, impulsivity, and unpredictability. Quite a few films, such as *Blue Sky* (1994) and *Splendor in the Grass* (1961), never mention bipolar disorder or any other diagnosis. Nevertheless, reports from screenwriters, directors, and viewers suggest that the audience is meant to implicitly assume the characters are bipolar based on their depictions (Bipolar Lives 2014; Coleman 2014; Clark 2016). Conversely, in more recent characterizations, such as the television series *Homeland* (2011) and *Shameless* (2011), the diagnosis of bipolar is explicitly provided for the audience. Third, our analysis revealed that there are more instances of bipolar characters serving as primary characters. However, the majority continue to serve as secondary characters that support the development of a non-disabled protagonist. Overall, despite the evolution of these representations, many early and more recent films and television shows depicting bipolar characters share the same characteristics and themes.

The television shows and films included in this intersectional analysis were selected due to their inclusion in multiple online articles and blogs focused on bipolar disorder that listed television and film representations of women with bipolar disorder. We selected the following television shows and films that are well known or popular, and from a range of years: *Splendor in the Grass* (1961), *Blue Sky* (1994), *Crazy/Beautiful* (2001), *Homeland* (2011), *Shameless* (2011), *Friday Night Lights* (2006), and *Silver Linings Playbook* (2012). In the following descriptions of these shows and films, we briefly discuss how bipolar women are conveyed to the audience. These descriptions are interspersed with our analysis of these representations, drawing from disability studies, feminist, and queer theory.

In each of the television and film portrayals analyzed, bipolar disorder serves as a key narrative device central to the development of the plot. Mitchell and Snyder (2001) argue that disability is used as a narrative device in two ways: as a feature of characterization and a metaphorical device. As a feature of characterization, "disability lends a distinctive idiosyncrasy to any character that differentiates the character from the anonymous background of the norm" (Mitchell and Snyder 2001, 47). As a symbol, "disability also serves as a metaphorical signifier of social and individual collapse" (Mitchell and Snyder 2001, 47). To be clear, our focus on plot as distinct from character is to highlight that bipolar disorder is rarely used to "develop" characters. Rather, disabled characters serve as a device to further the development of non-disabled protagonists and the plot.

These television and film portrayals depict bipolar women as having excessive sexuality. The characters are out of control, insatiable, irrational, seductive, and dangerous—to themselves and others. *Blue Sky* (1994) and *Crazy/Beautiful* (2001) both construct the bipolar women's hypersexuality as dangerous, reckless, and threatening to other characters. For instance, in *Blue Sky* (1994), the character Carly Marshall is portrayed as emotionally volatile and sexually seductive. Married to a major in the army, the first scene of the film shows her bathing topless on the beaches of Hawaii, where her husband is stationed. Her multiple extramarital affairs are implicitly and explicitly highlighted throughout the film, and her provocative clothing and dancing establishes her as hypersexual and threatening to other military wives, lest she seduce their husbands. Her hypersexuality becomes particularly dangerous for her husband, when she welcomes the sexual advances of his superior officer, threatening his career and reputation. In *Crazy/Beautiful* (2001), Nicole is a "troubled" high school student. Her hypersexuality, as well as her drinking and drug use, frame Nicole as "crazy" and, as her father notes to her boyfriend Carlos, beyond the help of psychiatrists and prone to suicide attempts. Nicole is portrayed as reckless and impulsive through actions such as dressing and dancing provocatively, making aggressive sexual advances towards the demurer Carlos, and dismissing the necessity of using a condom during sex until Carlos insists. Carlos' relationship with Nicole jeopardizes his excellent academic and athletic status, and he receives several warnings from family members that his deepening involvement with Nicole may result in the loss of future opportunities. Thus, in both films, the bipolar women endanger the status, success, and well-being of their husband and boyfriend.

Conversely, other depictions frame hypersexuality as problematic for the disabled character. For instance, in *Splendor in the Grass* (1961), Deanie's hypersexuality places her at risk for victimization; after she begs her ex-boyfriend Bud to have sex with her and tries to seduce him in a car, she is almost raped by another male character. This near victimization is depicted as the direct result of her wild and out of control sexual behavior. In *Homeland* (2011), Carrie Mathison is framed as out of control, as she engages in high-risk sexual encounters with a variety of partners. In the main plot line of the first season of the show, Carrie's hypersexuality becomes particularly problematic when she is investigating a terrorist suspect. In her determination to expose the suspect, who is a returned American prisoner of war, she develops a sexual relationship with him, breaking codes of conduct as a CIA agent and risking her job. Hence, unlike the prior representations, these film and television shows depict bipolar disorder as a liability and threat to the bipolar character's safety and security.

Whether hypersexualization is constructed as dangerous and problematic for other characters or for the character with bipolar disorder, these film and television representations portray bipolar women as at fault for various obstacles and dilemmas due to their hypersexuality. As oversexual, insatiable, and out-of-control women, they are characterized as responsible for their sexual objectification and sexual assault, their lack of success in academics and employment, and any personal or professional failings experienced by their sane, male partners. Such representations reinforce the sexual objectification of women, rape culture, and sexist ideology and discourse (Projansky, 2001; van Zoonen, 1994).

In addition to these problematic characterizations, bipolar disorder also serves as a metaphor in these films (Mitchell and Snyder 2001). By depicting the bipolar women as "bad girls" who are separate from the good, respectable, moral, and romantically-oriented woman, bipolar disorder comes to symbolize the peril and dangers inherent in the excessive sexuality of women. There is a significant body of scholarship that analyzes how female sexuality has always been constructed as dichotomous: either innocent, pure, moral, and in need of protection, or unpredictable, dangerous, and frightening (Conboy, Medina, and Stanbury 1997). The production and reinforcement of such a dichotomy strictly categorizes women, limits their sexual expression and agency, and justifies either overprotection or punishment, both of which contribute to women's oppression. This dichotomy also simplifies women's sexuality, which contributes to a denial of women's humanity. Furthermore, the hypersexualization of women in film and television has been long documented and continues to persist. However, the increased use of bipolar women characters who are represented as hypersexual reinscribes the danger of sexuality on the body of women in new ways by employing disability as a justification for oppression (Baynton 2001).

As Mitchell and Snyder (2001) note, when disability serves as a signifier of individual or social disintegration, the "problem" of disability must be resolved in some way. In the films and television shows we have discussed, hypersexuality is characterized as a dangerous and threatening symptom that indicates a lack of control, instability, volatility, and even victimization. Characters are "treated" by receiving the attention and support of a strong, stable, and rational male figure. For example, the character Carly's husband, Hank Marshall, serves as the levelheaded, eternally faithful, and stable counterpoint to Carly's volatile emotional outbursts and exorbitant sexuality. Upon the family's move from Hawaii to Alabama, Carly reacts dramatically to the family's new housing situation, screaming, crying and flinging clothes around the house, before driving carelessly to a fabric store. Her husband Hank follows her and attempts to calm her down, soothing her delusional accusations that his work for the Army as a nuclear physicist has made him toxic and dangerous. In *Crazy/Beautiful* (2001), Carlos convinces Nicole to regulate her sexuality and emotions through actions such as insisting on safe and normative, private sex and persuades Nicole to reconcile with her father. As a result, Nicole frequently credits Carlos with her "recovery."

Furthermore, in some depictions, the strong, rational male figure not only serves as a catalyst to "cure" bipolar disorder, but also to restore heteronormativity and uphold the sanctity of the nuclear family. As queer theorists have observed, normative constructions of family that define them as heteronormative (i.e., a traditional monogamous relationship between a heterosexual cisgender man and woman who fulfill stereotypical gender roles) are limiting and oppressive to people marginalized by gender and sexual orientation (Rich 1980; Warner 1991). Thus, these representations promote compulsory able-bodiedness and compulsory heterosexuality. Rich (1980) coined the term "compulsory heterosexuality" to describe the assumed male right of access to women sexually, emotionally, and economically. As males benefit from this access to females, this system centers heterosexuality and casts other forms of sexuality as deviant. Compulsory able-bodiedness operates similarly. As Kafer (2003) explains, "Able-bodiedness has been cast as separate from politics, as a universal ideal and a normal way of life, in much the same way as heterosexuality" (79). Thus, compulsory heterosexuality and compulsory able-bodiedness are intersecting hegemonic ideological systems that hold heterosexuality and able-bodiedness as natural, normal, and desirable. McRuer (2006) further argues that compulsory heterosexuality and compulsory able-bodiedness are intertwined and mutually produced, in order to create, conflate, and regulate queerness and disability. As an example, McRuer (2006) points to the film *As Good as It Gets* (1997) to argue, "heteronormative epiphanies are repeatedly, and often necessarily, able-bodied ones" (13). Drawing on the plot of *As Good as It Gets*, McRuer observes that the protagonist, Melvin, a man with obsessive-compulsive disorder, is essentially cured through a love affair with a cisgender, heterosexual woman, Carol. He writes, "During the film, in short, Melvin's identity flexibly contracts and expands. Able-bodied status is achieved in direct proportion to his increasing awareness of, and need for, (heterosexual) romance" (24). McRuer further argued that heteronormative, able-bodied epiphanies could only occur if disability or queerness are located elsewhere, such as in the case of Simon, Melvin's gay neighbor who acquires a disability after a hate crime.

The depictions of bipolar women as hypersexual allow for characters that locate multiple forms of deviance—gender, sexuality, and disability—within a single "mentally ill" character. Hence, queerness is not a legitimate identity for these characters, but a consequence of hypersexuality, which in turn is a symptom of bipolar disorder—thus allowing the "problems" of both queerness and disability to be solved through a medical or social cure. For example, in *Silver Linings Playbook* (2012), Tiffany's reputation as sexually promiscuous is hinted at throughout the beginning of the film, while the protagonist Pat even refers to her as a "slut." Later in the film, Tiffany reveals that following the death of her husband, amid a crisis, she had sex with multiple partners, both men and women, and people of varying ages, including a woman much older than her. The consequence for her promiscuous and deviant sexual behavior is therapy and medication as well as a living situation in her parents' coach house, under their watchful eyes. Although Tiffany's hypersexuality is treated lightly in the film and she admits to her potential partner Pat that part of her will always be "messy and dirty" and she likes that about herself, the film makes it clear that Tiffany no longer engages in hypersexual behaviors and can thus now find love and healing through a normative relationship with Pat. Therefore, Tiffany's queerness is suggested to be part of her madness. The problem of her disability/queerness is solved through her finding heterosexual, monogamous love with Pat.

Likewise, in *Shameless* (2011), the absent mother figure of Monica Gallagher initially comes back into her husband and her children's lives at the end of the first season, with her Black lesbian partner Roberta. She wreaks havoc on the family's life when she and Roberta threaten to take Liam, one of the children, away. She reappears again in the second season, and claims to want to reunite with her family permanently. However, she then quits taking her medication, and subsequently experiences a manic episode followed by a depressive episode. During mania, she rearranges furniture, takes the children on a shopping spree, and purchases a car. However, after falling into a depression, she attempts suicide by slitting her wrists during the family's Thanksgiving dinner, and is institutionalized in a psychiatric hospital. Monica breaks out of the hospital, but instead of returning to her family, chooses to remain noncompliant with treatment and flees with her new lover, a fellow woman psychiatric patient, which marks her character's departure from the series. In this representation, Monica's ability to be a mother and wife in a heterosexual relationship with her husband is tied to her compliance with medical treatment. When she refuses medication and escapes hospitalization, her bipolar symptoms escalate and she is portrayed in queer relationships. In this case, the problem of Monica's disability/queerness is solved through the character's erasure. Her disappearance was also marked as a consequence of her "noncompliance" with treatment, suggesting that the nuclear family could now "move on" from the destruction caused by Monica's disability/ queerness. Thus, the evolution of these characters from queer/disabled subjects to heterosexual/cured subjects (in the case of *Silver Linings Playbook*) or erased subjects (in the case of *Shameless*) allow for a "picture perfect (heterosexual, able-bodied) ending" in which compulsory heterosexuality and compulsory able-bodiedness are produced and reinforced (McRuer 2006, 25).

Although these portrayals of bipolar women as hypersexual are highly problematic, an intersectional analysis reveals who is not represented. In *Homeland* (2011), *Blue Sky* (1994), *Splendor in the Grass* (1961), *Crazy/Beautiful* (2001), *Shameless* (2011), and *Silver Linings Playbook* (2012), all of the bipolar women characters are white—none are women of color. The only exception to this rule is Waverly Grady in *Friday Night Lights* (2006), a secondary character who is so insignificant that she disappears from the show without an explanation. In her article "Don't We Hurt Like You: Examining the Lack of Portrayals of African American Women and Mental Health," Junior (2015) observes, "Women of color—specifically African American women—are not afforded the same type of humanity on screen, if they're even represented at all. Of the limited shows and films that feature African American women protagonists, only a few have characters with mental illnesses" (para. 3). One of the reasons for why black women with mental health conditions are invisible may be because Black women are hypersexualized due to their race and gender. The Jezebel stereotype demonstrates this phenomenon. During the Antebellum Period, slave owners cast the black female body as hypersexual, claiming it made black women insatiable, promiscuous, and seductive. According to Saidiya Hartman (1996), black female slaves were characterized as having "immoderate and overabundant sexuality, bestial appetites, and capacities which were most often linked to the orangutan, and an untiring readiness that was only to be outstripped by her willingness" (544). This hypersexualization—the foundation of the Jezebel stereotype—was used to rationalize white slave owners completely controlling black female slaves sexually, using rape as a form of domination, and overseeing all aspects of their reproduction (Hartman 1996; West 1995). Additionally, Latina women have also been subject to stereotypes of hypersexuality. "The eroticization of 'brownness' embodies the general objectifying perceptions of 'hypersexualized' bodies as understood by the power of the colonizing gaze" (Arrizón 2008, 191). Similarly, stereotypes of Asian-American women, such as the passive, submissive, and hyperfeminine "lotus blossom" or the dangerous and seductive "dragon lady," also deem Asian-American women as hypersexual (Shimizu 2007).

These stereotypes, rooted in slavery, colonialism, and racism, persist today, and may work in tandem with other stereotypes to influence the lack of cultural representations of bipolar women of color. In other words, due to racialized hypersexuality, the "excessive" sexuality of women of color is inherent, and thus the assignment of disability is not needed. Conversely, for white women to be hypersexualized, they must be cast as deviant in some other way, such as bipolar. Furthermore, by casting hypersexuality in white women as a "symptom" of an "illness" that requires "treatment, hypersexuality in white women is represented as fixable, whereas it is constructed as innate for women of color due to the long history of colonization, enslavement, and racialized gender oppression." Thus, in media representations, hypersexuality, as a tool of gendered oppression, is intertwined with discourses of racialization and disablement.

Conclusion

In this essay, we analyze numerous representations of bipolar women in popular films and television series, and connected our intersectional analysis to wider cultural discourses regarding the hypersexualization of bipolar women. Garland-Thomson (1997) notes, "Seeing disability as a representational system engages several premises of current critical theory: that representation structures reality, that the margins constitute the center, that human identity is multiple and unstable, and that all analysis and evaluation has political implications" (Garland-Thomson 1997, 19). Women have experienced hypersexualization in various forms throughout history. "Hypersexuality is a common stereotypical representation of many marginalized groups, such as people of color, ethnic minorities, women, religious minorities, poor or working-class people, and sexual minorities" (Zemsky 1998, 259). Presently, in the cultural imagination, hypersexuality in women is equated with: nymphomania, sluttiness, queerness, and general deviance. Thus, as a result of the media characterization of bipolar women as hypersexual, women with bipolar disorder are stereotyped as maniacs who engage in impulsive, high risk, and promiscuous sexual behavior. The consequences of this hypersexualization may include shame, prejudice, lack of access to sexual and reproductive healthcare, justification of violence against women, and criminalization, and this is particularly true for bipolar women who also have other marginalized identities, such as women oppressed due to their class, sexuality, gender, race, and ethnicity (Center for Reproductive Rights 2014; Erevelles and Minear 2010; Holmes 2016). Cultural representations in media of women with bipolar disorder produce and reinforce these stereotypes.

As we argued in this essay, television and film depictions of bipolar women use bipolar disorder as a metaphor for the dangers of female sexuality and to promote normative sexuality. We contend the implications of such characterizations are twofold. First, they imply that women, particularly those viewed as hypersexual, must be identified, categorized, and controlled. In other words, women who express their sexuality without acknowledging the constraints imposed by society, may be labeled with a psychiatric diagnosis, or at least subjected to psychiatric treatment, which can then be used to survey, police, and punish their behavior. Second, it pathologizes the sexuality of women who are labeled with a diagnosis such as bipolar disorder. Thus, sexuality in bipolar women becomes viewed as a "symptom" of an "illness" that needs to be "cured," or a problem that needs to be fixed. This rhetoric limits the possibilities for bipolar women to express diverse sexualities, and to assert sexuality in ways that are meaningful and empowering to us.

Throughout this media analysis, we have critiqued women with bipolar disorder's hypersexual objectification, and demonstrated how the implications of these portrayals influence public perception, and the subsequent treatment of bipolar women in society. It is our hope that this analysis will promote dialogue amongst scholars, activists, and producers of media, and prompt them to consider how people with diverse impairments, including psychiatric disabilities, are represented and viewed in regards to sexuality, and disability, more generally. We also call on these groups to consider the ways in which representations of psychiatric disability are gendered, racialized, and queered, and the impact such cultural depictions have on bipolar women with multiple marginalized positionalities. As this essay illustrates, it is essential for disability studies, media studies, and related fields to consider how the sexualities of people with different impairment types, including psychiatric disabilities, are represented in media in diverse ways that contribute to unique intersectional forms of oppression.

References

Arrizón, Alicia. 2008. "Latina Subjectivity, Sexuality, and Sensuality." *Women & Performance: A Journal of Feminist Theory* 18(3): 189–198.

As Good as It Gets. 1998. Directed by James L. Brooks. Culver City: Sony Pictures Studios. DVD.

Baynton, Douglas. 2001. "Disability and the Justification of Inequality in American History." In *The New Disability History: American Perspectives*, edited by Paul K. Longmore, and Lauri Umanksy, 33–57. New York: New York University Press.

Bipolar Lives. 2016. "Movies about Bipolar Disorder." December 30. http://www.bipolar-lives.com/movies-about-bipolar-disorder.html.

Blue Sky. 1994. Directed by Tony Richardson. Beverly Hills: MGM. DVD.

Center for Reproductive Rights. 2017. "Rights of Women and Girls with Disabilities to be Free from Violence & Abuse and to Exercise their Sexual & Reproductive Rights." August 30. https://www.reproductiverights.org/sites/crr.civicactions.net/files/documents/Women%20w%20Disabilities%20UPR%20Fact%20Sheet_FINAL.pdf.

Clark, Michelle. 2016. "Movies and TV Shows with Bipolar Disorder Characters." *Bipolar Bandit*, April 18. https://bipolarbandit.wordpress.com/2016/04/18/hollywood-bipolar-disorder/.

Colman, David. 2014. *The Bipolar Express: Manic Depression and the Movies.* Lanham, MD: Rowman & Littlefield.

Conboy, Katie, Nadia Medina, and Sarah Stanbury. 1997. *Writing on the Body: Female Embodiment and Feminist Theory.* New York: Columbia University Press.

Crazy/Beautiful. 2001. Directed by John Stockwell. Burbank: Touchstone Home Entertainment. DVD.

Crenshaw, Kimberlé. 1991. "Mapping the Margins: Intersectionality, Identity Politics, and Violence against Women of Color." *Stanford Law Review* 43: 1241–1299.

Dolmage, Jay. 2014. *Disability Rhetoric.* Syracuse: Syracuse University Press.

Ehrenreich, Barbara, and James Ehrenreich. 1971. *The American Health Empire: Power, Profits, and Powers.* New York: Vintage.

Erevelles, Nirmala. 2001. "In Search of the Disabled Subject." In *Embodied Rhetorics: Disability* in *Language and Culture*, edited by James C. Wilson, and Cynthia Lewiecki-Wilson, 92–111. Carbondale: Southern Illinois University Press.

Erevelles, Nirmala, and Andrea Minear. 2010. "Unspeakable Offenses: Untangling Race and Disability in Discourses of Intersectionality." *Journal of Literary and Cultural Disability Studies* 4(2): 127–145.

Friday Night Lights. 2006. Directed by Various. Universal City: Universal Studios. DVD.

Gamson, William A., David Croteau, William Hoynes, and Theodore Sasson. 1992. "Media Images and The Social Construction of Reality." *Annual Review of Sociology* 18: 373–393.

Garland-Thomson, Rose Marie. 1997. *Extraordinary Bodies: Figuring Physical Disability in American Culture and Literature*. New York: Columbia University Press.

_____. 2002. "Integrating Disability: Transforming Feminist Theory." *NWSA Journal* 14(3): 1–32.

Hahn, Harlan. 1988. "The Politics of Physical Differences: Disability and Discrimination." *Journal of Social Issues* 44(1): 39–47.

Hartman, Saidiya. 1996. "Seduction and the Ruses of Power." *Callaloo* 19(2): 537–560.

Hill, Libby. 2015. "'You're the Worst' Does What Few Other Shows Can—Makes Depression Comprehensible." *Los Angeles Times*, September 9. http://www.latimes.com/entertain ment/tv/la-et-st-fxx-the-worst-depression-on-tv-20151209-story.html.

Holmes, Lindsay. 2016. "Let's Call Mental Health Stigma What It Really Is: Discrimination." *Huffington Post*, September 27. http://www.huffingtonpost.com/entry/mental-health-discrimination_us_57e55d07e4b0e28b2b53a896.

Homeland. 2011. Directed by Various. New York: Showtime. DVD.

Hyler, Steven E., Glen O. Gabbard, and Ian Schneider. 1991. "Homicidal Maniacs and Narcissistic Parasites: Stigmatization of Mentally Ill Persons in the Movies." *Hospital and Community Psychiatry* 42(10): 1044–1048.

Junior, Nyasha. "Don't We Hurt Like You? Examining the Lack of Portrayals of African American Women and Mental Health." *Bitch Magazine*, May 26. https://bitchmedia.org/arti cle/dont-we-hurt-like-you-black-women-mental-health-depression-representations.

Kafer, Alison. 2003. "Compulsory Bodies: Reflections on Heterosexuality and Able-Bodiedness." *Journal of Women's History* 15(3): 77–89.

Liebowitz, Cara. 2015. "Bringing (A)sexy Back: Exploring Disability and Asexuality." Presentation at the Breaking Silences Conference, Dayton, OH, November 4–6.

Linton, Simi. 1998. *Claiming Disability: Knowledge and Identity*. New York: New York University Press.

Mazza, Marianna, Desiree Harnic, Valeria Catalano, Marco Di Nicola, Angelo Bruschi, Pietro Bria, Antonio Daneile, and Salvatore Mazzo. 2011. "Sexual Behavior in Women with Bipolar Disorder." *Journal of Affective Disorders* 131: 364–367.

McRuer, Robert. 2006. *Crip Theory: Cultural Signs of Queerness and Disability*. New York: New York University Press.

Mitchell, David T., and Sharon Synder. 2001. *Narrative Prosthesis: Disability and the Dependence of Discourse*. Ann Arbor: University of Michigan Press.

Prendergast, Catherine. 2003. "On the Rhetorics of Mental Disability." In *Towards a Rhetoric of Everyday Life: New Directions in Research on Writing, Text, and Discourse*, edited by Martin Nystand, and John Duffy, 189–206. Madison: University of Wisconsin Press.

Price, Margaret. 2011. *Mad at School*. Ann Arbor: University of Michigan Press.

_____. 2015. "The Bodymind Problem and the Possibilities of Pain." *Hypatia* 30(1): 268–284.

Projansky, Sarah. 2001. *Watching Rape: Film and Television in Postfeminist Culture*. New York: New York University Press.

Rich, Adrienne. 1980. "Compulsory Heterosexuality and Lesbian Existence." *Signs* 5(4): 631–660.

Safran, Stephen. P. 1998. "The First Century of Disability Portrayal in Film: An Analysis of the Literature." *The Journal of Special Education* 31(4): 467–479.

Shameless. 2011. Directed by Various. New York: Showtime. DVD.

Shimizu, Celine P. 2007. *The Hypersexuality of Race: Performing Asian/American Women on Screen and Scene*. Durham: Duke University Press.

Silver Linings Playbook. 2012. Directed by David O. Russell. Ontario: TWC. DVD.

Splendor in the Grass. 1961. Directed by Elia Kazan. Burbank: Warner Home Video. DVD.

van Zoonen, Liesbet. 1994. *Feminist Media Studies.* Thousand Oaks: Sage.

Warner, Michael. 1991. "Introduction: Fear of a Queer Planet." *Social Text* 29: 3–17.

West, Carolyn M. 1995. "Mammy, Sapphire, and Jezebel: Historical Images of Black Women and their Implications for Psychotherapy." *Psychotherapy* 32(3): 458–466.

Zemsky, Beth. 1998. "Homophobia." In *The Reader's Companion to U.S. Women's History*, edited by Wilma Mankiller, Gwendolyn Mink, Marysa Navarro, Barbara Smith, and Gloria Steinem, 259–260. Boston: Houghton Mifflin.

A Kiss on the Train

Autism, Asexuality and the Conventions of Romantic Comedy

SONYA FREEMAN LOFTIS

> There's no denying that I have feelings for you that can't be
> explained in any other way. I briefly considered that I had
> a brain parasite, but that seems even more far-fetched. The
> only conclusion was love.
> —Sheldon Cooper to Amy Farrah Fowler,
> *The Big Bang Theory*

In recent years, there has been an explosion of films, television shows, and books that suggest a popular interest in the subject of autistic people falling in love. Matt Fuller's award-winning 2015 documentary *Autism in Love* is one example of this trend. Although the documentary follows the lives of autistic people involved in romantic relationships, the film's opening seems to suggest that some audiences may mistakenly view autism as a condition that is somehow antithetical to romance. The film opens with written definitions of its two key terms, "autism" and "love," juxtaposed on the screen. The documentary clearly implies its main question in this opening sequence: if autism impairs one's ability to establish relationships (autism is "characterized by difficulty in ... forming relationships with other people"), then how can autism be reconciled with "love" ("a profoundly tender, passionate affection for another person")? This neurotypical curiosity about autistics in love has also become common in fiction: specifically, autistic characters are increasingly appearing in romantic comedies—the perfect venue in which to exploit social disability for potential laughs. Popular television shows such as *The Big Bang Theory* and best-selling novels such as *The Rosie Project* (2013) feature protagonists with recognizable autistic traits involved in romantic plotlines. These eccentric characters are frequently used for comic effect. In fact, audiences are invited to laugh at aspects of their social disability. The majority of these comedies feature male protagonists who struggle to establish a relationship with female characters. Furthermore, in these works, disability serves to fulfill some of the basic conventions of romantic comedy by having bumbling lovers struggle to express their feelings and to achieve intimacy, leading to comic misunderstandings galore. Although such comedies have been extremely popular, their plots frequently employ and manipulate stereotypes about autism. *The Big Bang Theory*'s Sheldon Cooper has proven to be a controversial figure in the autism community for this very reason. Although Sheldon's character may help to dispel some autism stereotypes, he strongly embodies and perpetuates others. Perhaps most disturbing is the sitcom's treatment of Sheldon's asexuality. Because the cultural imagination of America frequently casts people with autism as asexual, Sheldon is presented as an asexual character. In the course of the sitcom's romantic plotline, Sheldon's implicit autism diagnosis leads to mockery, infantilization, and an eventual "triumph" in which normative heterosexual love conquers all—thus leaving Sheldon's perspective as an autistic and asexual character largely misunderstood and ignored by both the other characters and popular audiences.

Although playing autism for laughs is problematic (and could even be encouraging viewers to bully or discriminate against autistic people), producers and screenwriters have not hesitated to use autism as a comic plot device. Perhaps the most lauded and popular of these representations has been the socially awkward physicist Sheldon Cooper on CBS' *The Big Bang Theory*. In 2014, the romantic comedy that focuses on the misadventures of multiple eccentric couples was "the most watched show on American television" (Locker 2014). Viewers have been asking if Sheldon has autism ever since the show premiered, but the sitcom's creators have been adamant about refusing to label Sheldon as mentally disabled (Sepinwall 2009). The show's creators claim that Sheldon "certainly has traits in common with people with Asperger's" (Sepinwall 2009). However, they claim that "calling it Asperger's creates too much of a burden to get the details right. There's also the danger that the other characters' insults about Sheldon's behavior—in other words, 90 percent of the show's comedy—would seem mean if they were mocking a medical condition as opposed to generic eccentricity. In general, it's more responsibility than … a relatively light comedy can handle" (Sepinwall 2009).

In spite of this blatant denial on the part of the show's creators, Sheldon's autistic traits are so obvious that they present a caricature of common Asperger's stereotypes (Koyanagi 2015). As Sheldon explains himself to his friends and fellow scientists, Howard and Raj, "You may not realize it, but I have difficulty navigating certain aspects of daily life—understanding sarcasm, feigning interest in others, not talking about trains as much as I want to—it's exhausting" (season six, episode eight).

Sheldon is a socially awkward genius with an eidetic memory and an IQ of 187, but he frequently makes socially inappropriate remarks at work. He insists on so strict of a routine that it even includes a bathroom schedule made out for anyone who stays overnight at his apartment. He also engages in stimming (self-stimulating behaviors, such as rocking, pacing, and hand-flapping are common in people on the autism spectrum). In one episode, Howard and Raj discover that Sheldon regularly spends time stimming with a hacky-sac in a basement room at the university. He is also hypersensitive to touch—so much so that his decision to finally give Penny a hug is the climax of one first season episode. In what appears to be a heavy-handed reference to the diagnostic criteria for Asperger's Syndrome presented in the DSM-IV, he even has a special interest in trains. Although special interests in transportation are relatively rare among autistic people, the diagnostic criteria in the DSM-IV listed "trains" as an example of a special interest. Since then, the stereotype of the autistic with a special interest in trains has become widespread. Sheldon also has significant impairments. He needs help from Leonard in many everyday self-care tasks. For example, it is specified in the roommate agreement that Leonard must take Sheldon to the dentist—not just because Sheldon cannot drive, but specifically because Sheldon needs help at the dentist's office. Indeed, it is not perfectly clear whether Sheldon can live independently or not. In fact, when Leonard and Penny get married, they continue to live with Sheldon part-time. Although the show's creators have avoided labeling the character as disabled, Sheldon clearly has many autistic traits. More importantly, these autistic traits are used as a comic device. The audience is expected to have sympathy for poor neurotypical Leonard, compelled by the roommate agreement to shepherd Sheldon at the dentist's office. Both the characters' and the studio audience's responses become models for social responses to disability—and the laugh track punctuates almost everything Sheldon does. As Monika Bednarek (2012) argues, "Insofar as viewers accept such stereotyping unquestionably, they might be said to be co-constructing such stereotypes in a collective process" (225). It is possible that laughing at Sheldon on screen may encourage viewers to laugh at autistic behavior in real life.

Sheldon's implicit autism diagnosis (we know that Sheldon has autism but we do not know that Sheldon has autism) has made this comedic figure very controversial in the autism community. Some autistic people and their families enjoy and applaud the sitcom. For example, the website Interacting with Autism presents Sheldon as an autistic figure who is "a good role model for finding and adapting to living a life on one's own despite his social setbacks" (Jay 2016). The show has even been used as an educational tool for autistic youth. In some social skills classes for teenagers on the spectrum, clips from *The Big Bang Theory* are used to open discussion about social behavior: "The teacher uses clips from the show with Sheldon, stops the clip, and they all discuss what was socially inappropriate and what should have been said or done" (Park 2016). One autistic self-advocate writes that "Sheldon shows that dreams we hope for our own kids like having a job, being in a relationship and living independently can become reality" (Magro 2016). As a professor, Sheldon has achieved the stereotypically ideal job for autistics. I am certainly not downplaying the advantages of a job in which one is paid to talk about one's special interest. Nevertheless, it continues to be a stereotype in the autism community that the goal of *every* autistic child should be to become a professor in his or her area of interest (even though this career path is not achievable for many autistics *nor desired* by all autistics). Shannon Walters (2013) also notes this problem: Sheldon's depiction as a university professor may "risk normalizing cognitive difference because it may imply that there is only one way to be Aspergian" (277). It also strikes me as odd that, when we are setting goals for the fair representation of autistic people in the media, our goals should be so humble that the depiction is acceptable if the person has a job, has a romantic relationship, and moves out of his parents' house. The stereotypes implied, of course, are that autistic adults are expected to be unemployed, socially isolated, and dependent on their parents.

Even still, although *The Big Bang Theory* has received little attention in disability studies, what attention it has received has been largely positive. For example, Margaret Weitekamp (2015) argues that "the Sheldon character is a new take on the stereotype of the narrowly focused, socially inept and physically awkward scientist.... He does have friends. And … the group tolerates his preferences in their collective pursuit of nerdy fun" (82). Shannon Walters (2013) argues that the sitcom "show[s] people with autism … as integral elements to their communities and social circles, resisting the stereotype that people with autism are asocial or isolated" (272). It is true that the fictional figure of Sheldon Cooper defies many stereotypes. However, there are many troubling (and far subtler) autism stereotypes that *The Big Bang Theory* leaves intact: Sheldon is infantilized, depicted as lacking in empathy, and imagined as valuing objects (trains) over people (like his girlfriend Amy). These stereotypes are then repeatedly used as punchlines for the show without questioning the damage that they can do in representing autism at large.

Others in the autism community online find the show's treatment of Sheldon's autistic traits irresponsible. Specifically, some autistic bloggers have objected to the show's refusal to say the word "autism," arguing that the decision to avoid the term may encourage cultural taboos that discourage discourse about mental disability (Anonymous 2015). Mayim Bialik, who plays

Sheldon's girlfriend Amy Farrah Fowler, suggests that the show advances a positive message regarding mental disability because of its lack of diagnostic labeling. "I think what's interesting and kind of sweet and what should not be lost on people is we don't pathologize our characters. We don't talk about medicating them or even really changing them" (Gill 2015). Interestingly, both the show's creators' and Balik's comments focus on the perceived danger of disability labels. The show's creators worry that a diagnostic label would be too heavy for a comedy, while Balik seems to suggest that disability labels and psychiatric medications are inherently negative. The assumption that the depiction of disability must bring weight to a comedy is in itself a troubling disability stereotype (Koyanagi 2015). In a sense, it means that disabled characters are understood as too tragic to appear in comedies, indicating that disability must always be presented as a serious subject (Koyanagi 2015). As autistic self-advocate Jacqueline Koyanagi (2015) wonders, "Why is autism even seen as a grave, weighty issue rather than a normal aspect of life?" Balik's comments make the decision not to use a disability label sound like an act of kindness. It's "kind of sweet" to protect a character from being "pathologi[zed]." Her comment inherently implies that having an autism label is a bad thing. In fact, Balik is suggesting that it would be better to avoid any conversation that acknowledges disability as an identity directly. Her response ignores issues of autism pride and casts having an autism diagnosis as inherently negative. In short, the autism community has rightly questioned the show's refusal to label Sheldon as disabled.

In spite of the creators' comments about mental disability being "too heavy" for comedy, the show does use labels for mental difference. However, instead of using specific terms for mental disability that have been accepted within the disability community, *The Big Bang Theory* falls back on nebulous, ableist, and pejorative terms. The other characters on the show do not describe Sheldon as "autistic" for instance. Instead they use terms such as "crazy," "insane," and "special." In fact, the subject of Sheldon's sanity is a repeating comic refrain in the show:

> HOWARD: Sheldon, don't take this the wrong way, but, you're insane.
> LEONARD: That may well be, but the fact is it wouldn't kill us to meet some new people.
> SHELDON: For the record, it could kill us to meet new people. They could be murderers or the carriers of unusual pathogens. And I'm not insane, my mother had me tested [2.4].

His mother herself confirms this interpretation, "Oh no. He's not crazy. I had him tested. However, I do regret not following up with that specialist in Houston" (3.1). Every time Sheldon insists that he is not "crazy" viewers are reminded that he is through some comedic punchline that follows, such as his mother wondering if she should have followed up with the last test.

The implication seems to put a pejorative burden on those of us who have been "tested" for mental disabilities. The term "special" is another example of a condescending label that many people with disabilities consider offensive, which comes up repeatedly. This is especially the case when Leonard is defending Sheldon to authority figures. In one episode, Sheldon is stumped by a particularly vexing physics problem. As a result, he breaks into a local children's restaurant in the middle of the night in order to use their pit of plastic balls to help him visualize carbon atoms. Of course, the security guard contacts Leonard, who is often called upon to act as Sheldon's "guardian":

> LEONARD: Thanks for not calling the cops.
> SECURITY GUARD: Oh hey—it's no big deal. My sister has a kid who's special.
> LEONARD: Yeah, well, he's extra special.... Hey, Shelly, what you doin'?
> SHELDON: Size ratio was all wrong. Couldn't visualize it. Needed bigger carbon atoms [3.14].

The term "special," like "crazy," is a nebulous way of suggesting that Sheldon has an unnamed mental disability. Leonard and Sheldon's extremely shy friend Raj is also labeled during the course of the sitcom. The character repeatedly self-identifies as having "social anxiety disorder" and "selective mutism" (1.15). In one episode, Raj tries an experimental medication for social anxiety (1.15). In another episode, we find out that Stewart, who owns the local comic book store the characters visit weekly, takes antidepressants (9.13). These characters are clearly labeled, pathologized, and medicated. Avoiding the word "autism" does not stop the show from labeling mental difference.

Unfortunately, many of the ableist jokes in *The Big Bang Theory* imply that Sheldon is less than human. Playing on one of the most popular tropes for depicting autistic characters, Sheldon is frequently compared to a robot:

> HOWARD: Sheldon, if you were a robot and I knew and you didn't, would you want me to tell you?
> SHELDON: That depends. When I learn that I'm a robot will I be able to handle it?
> HOWARD: Maybe. But the history of science fiction is not on your side [1.5].

The implication here is that Sheldon is not human. However, more than that he is also not fully aware of the extent of his difference from the human characters around him. The joke about being a robot in this scene is clearly about Sheldon's implied autism diagnosis. Howard could well be asking, "Sheldon, if you were autistic and I knew and you didn't, would you want me to tell you?" In fact, the robot is frequently used as a figure for autistics because autistic people are often imagined as being less-than-fully-human—largely because of stereotypes that cast autistic people as unemotional and lacking in empathy (Loftis 2015, 17; Murray 2008, 68; Osteen 2008, 11). Imagining autistic people as emotionless machines has serious consequences. A cultural devaluing of autistic humanity and subjectivity may contribute to real world abuse and discrimination—and even to tragedies such as autistic filicide (Loftis 2015, 61).

Later in the show, when Sheldon complains about how over-emotional Leonard is about his failed relationship with their co-worker Leslie Winkle, Raj suggests the best way for an unemotional robot to deal with his overly-emotional human roommate:

> SHELDON: Oh, I've seen that look before. This is just going to be two weeks of tedious Emo songs and calling me down to pet stores to look at cats. I don't know if I can take it.
> RAJ: You could power down [1.5].

Jokes that develop this Sheldon-is-a-robot theme appear in multiple episodes. For example, when Penny is unable to convince Sheldon to purchase a birthday gift for Leonard, Howard intervenes, "Just tell him it's a non-optional social convention" (1.16). After hearing these words, Sheldon immediately acquiesces. Penny is shocked, and asks, "How did you do that?" (1.16). Howard responds as though his autistic friend were a machine: "He came with an operating manual" (1.16). When Sheldon does demonstrate strong emotions, and begins crying, Penny calls his mother for help. She complains that the Sheldon-machine has malfunctioned, "Mrs. Cooper? Hey, it's Penny. I think I broke your son" (4.14). In short, the tired trope of the autistic as machine is alive and well in *The Big Bang Theory*.

The other characters also frequently infantilize Sheldon, joking that his autistic traits and resulting dependency on Leonard make him child-like. Like stereotypes that regard autistic people as inhuman, the all-to-frequent infantilization of autistic adults in media depictions also has real world consequences. My own experiences as an autistic adult have shown me that chance acquaintances are often unwilling to recognize and treat me *as an adult*—condescension and an assumption of incompetence is all too often the norm. Although Leonard may have Sheldon's safety in mind, his attempts to keep track of his eccentric roommate sometimes crosses the line into a condescending violation of Sheldon's privacy:

> LEONARD: I haven't heard from Sheldon in a while, do you think he's okay?... I'm going to see where he is.... I can track his phone.
> PENNY: You do that?
> LEONARD: Not always ... but ever since he wandered off at the swap meet chasing a balloon, I get worried.
> PENNY: He can take care of himself. Look, we went over stranger danger and gave him that whistle [7.24].

Some autistic adults are prone to "wandering behaviors," where they may leave a safe and familiar area and disappear without explanation into a less safe environment. When it happens in real life, it can be terribly dangerous and not at all funny. In fact, autistics are more likely to be the victims of violent crimes and sexual assaults than their neurotypical counterparts (Loftis 2015, 157). However, the desire to protect autistic adults from potential victimization need not include infantalization and condescension. For Penny, Sheldon's wandering behavior offers an opportunity to envision him as a child who needs to learn "stranger danger." For the neurotypical Leonard, taking care of his disabled roommate is an opportunity to earn praise from Penny and to affirm how heroic and "good" he is:

> LEONARD: I don't care. It's dark out, and he's alone. I don't like it. Let's go get him.
> PENNY: It's sweet how you look after him. You're a good guy [7.24].

When the couple find Sheldon at the train station, Leonard entices him to come home with a reward one might offer to a child. He says, "Come home with us and tomorrow I'll take you to Legoland" (7.24). When Sheldon refuses, saying that he is going to travel across the country by himself, both Leonard and Penny are concerned. Some autistic adults struggle with traveling, and Sheldon's desire to travel by himself seems unsafe and unrealistic to Leonard:

> PENNY: Maybe we need to let him go.
> LEONARD: You know he can't take a trip like this by himself.
> PENNY: He's a grown man.
> LEONARD: No, he looks like a grown man. You've seen freaky Friday. Sometimes little kids end up in big person bodies.
> PENNY: Leonard, we can't protect him forever [7.24].

The debate about whether Sheldon can or cannot travel by himself becomes a conversation not about disability but about adulthood. Instead of debating whether an autistic adult with Sheldon's particular impairments can safely travel across the country alone, Leonard and Penny debate Sheldon's status as an adult. In this conversation, disability and dependency are implicitly linked to childhood, to being a "little kid" in a "big person bod[y]."

Another troubling point in the show is the overarching heteronormative romantic plotline into which Sheldon's character is eventually subsumed. Although the other characters in the show seem to recognize Sheldon as asexual (and Sheldon certainly makes his preferences clear), the other characters tend to interpret Sheldon's asexuality as a further sign that he is either inhuman or childlike:

> PENNY: What's Sheldon's deal? Is it girls? Guys? Sock puppets?
> LEONARD: Honestly, we've been operating under the assumption that he has no deal.
> PENNY: Oh, come on. Everybody has a deal.
> HOWARD: Not Sheldon. Over the years, we've formulated many theories about how he might reproduce.... I'm an advocate of mitosis.... I believe one day Sheldon will eat an enormous amount of Thai food and split into two Sheldons.

LEONARD: On the other hand, I think Sheldon might be the larval form of his species and someday he'll spin a cocoon and emerge two months later with moth wings and an exoskeleton [2.6].

Penny is unable to even imagine asexuality as a possibility, while Leonard and Howard use Sheldon's asexuality as fodder for jokes about how he is less than human. Interestingly, Leonard and Howard's jokes ultimately rest on the same premise as Penny's dismissal. The two scientists seem unable to imagine asexuality as a possible orientation. Even in jest, they cannot conceive of a human that is not driven by the desire to procreate. In fact, this is a common misconception about asexuality: "Coming to identify as asexual requires that individuals reject a widely-held cultural ideology of sexuality as biologically based and … draw attention to an oft overlooked social assumption—that all humans possess sexual desire" (Decker 2015). Again and again, being asexual and aromantic is taken as a sign of Sheldon's inhumanity. When Sheldon sees his mother flirting with the chair of the physics department, he is clearly confused by her behavior:

LEONARD: What happened?
SHELDON: I'm not quite sure. It involves a part of the human experience that has always eluded me.
LEONARD: Well, that narrows it down [1.4].

Indeed, Sheldon's disinterest in sexual activity is often presented as a lack of knowledge about sexual activity. For example, before Sheldon consummates his relationship with Amy, Penny feels a need to tell Sheldon about the birds and the bees and to describe "what girls like." Likewise, Sheldon is confused by courtship behavior. He does not understand what is happening when a girl asks him out on a date:

HOWARD: Sheldon, do you have any idea what just happened?
SHELDON: Yes. Apparently, I'm getting a free dinner [2.6].

Ultimately, when the other characters view his asexuality as a sign of his robotic nature and inhumanity, Sheldon is forced to comically defend himself as biologically male. He states, "For the record, I do have genitals. They're functional and aesthetically pleasing" (5.1). Thus, the depiction of asexuality in *The Big Bang Theory* builds on multiple disability stereotypes. First, disability (especially autism) is strongly associated with asexuality (Loftis 2015, 67). Second, asexuality is interpreted by the other characters as a further sign that Sheldon is inhuman (perhaps he is able to reproduce through mitosis) and child-like (not knowledgeable about sex and courtship, rather than simply disinterested in sex and courtship). This series of jokes exploits tropes that advance attitudes that marginalize both asexual and autistic people. Stereotypes that imagine asexual people as immature or child-like are widespread (Decker 2015). As Decker (2015) points out, "Asexuality is not a signal that a person is … stunted emotionally or physically and feeling sexual attraction or inclination is not the line everyone must cross to be treated like an adult." In short, the show proves as unwilling to accept asexuality as a social identity as it is unwilling to accept autism as a social identity.

In Sheldon's relationship with Amy, the series finds opportunities to comically manipulate multiple autism stereotypes. For example, the show sometimes depicts Sheldon as caring more about his special interest in trains than about relationships with other people. Sheldon's special interest is imagined as being in direct competition with his relationship with Amy. In fact, heterosexual romance is symbolically aligned with—and sometimes juxtaposed with—Sheldon's special interest. Oddly, neurotypicals often employ romantic love as a metaphor for explaining the deep interests of autistics (Loftis 2015, 42). Perhaps because having a special interest is a uniquely neurodiverse experience (an experience of strong emotion that neurotypical people usually do not have), it is often explained using metaphors of romance (an experience of strong emotion that neurotypical people often *do* have). Popular conceptions of romantic love may seem to capture the joy and fulfillment that some autistic people experience in their areas of deep interest. In *The Big Bang Theory*, Amy tries to connect with Sheldon on a romantic level by invoking his deep interest in trains.

> AMY: We are going to have Valentine's Day dinner on a fully functioning vintage train … an ALCO FA4 diesel locomotive leading a train of meticulously restored 1915 Pullman first class coaches.
> SHELDON: Wow. I'm feeling the urge to hug you [7.15].

But Sheldon's "urge to hug" does not turn into a hug, and Amy quickly finds that her efforts at achieving a romantic night with Sheldon are in competition with his other "romantic interest"—his autistic special interest, trains.

Indeed, the idea that time invested in autistic deep interests might take away from developing relationships with other people seems to be a common neurotypical misconception. It is almost as if the special interest is imagined as superseding or replacing the need for a human partner. In the show, Sheldon's passion for trains is very much in competition with Amy's desire for a night of heteronormative romance. When Sheldon meets another train aficionado, he changes tables, leaving a disappointed Amy alone with Howard and his girlfriend Bernadette.

> SHELDON: How many trains have you been on?
> ERIC: Tons. A box fell on my head at UPS six years ago. Now I just collect disability and ride trains.
> SHELDON: Wow. Your life is amazing.
> ERIC: Not always. A box fell on my head at UPS six years ago. Now I just collect disability and ride trains [7.15].

Eric's mental disability (traumatic brain injury) is even more obvious to the average viewer than Sheldon's implicit autism. By putting them together on the ALCO FA4, the show's writers effectively make their point to viewers— no one can possibly "love" trains as much as Sheldon does—unless that person has a mental disability. Bernadette makes it obvious that we are to compare Eric and Sheldon as mentally disabled characters when she comments, "Great. Now there's two of them" (7.15). More importantly, Eric can personify Sheldon's special interest as he becomes set up as the social competition for Sheldon's attention while Amy struggles to keep her romantic plans on track.

Symbolically, Amy has to wrest Sheldon away from Eric, away from his deep interest, away from trains—away from his autism. Sheldon cannot have a "romantic" evening (at least, not the kind that Amy will enjoy) with Eric and Amy simultaneously. Amy is disappointed and maybe the implied neurotypical and heteronormative viewer is too:

AMY: We are supposed to be having a romantic weekend.
SHELDON: Oh, really? Because I remember you saying this trip was going to be something we could both enjoy. Did you mean that or were you just trying to trick me?
AMY: I deserve romance [7.15].

Sheldon responds with a diatribe of mockery that ends with a mock kiss—a mock kiss that very quickly turns into a real kiss. Although Sheldon is initially standing far away from Amy and leaning far forward in order to kiss her, he steps closer until he is finally touching her, resting his hands on her hips. Amy certainly seems satisfied because the mock kiss transformed into one that seemed both sexual and romantic:

AMY: That was nice.
SHELDON: Good. Um. The conductor said that if I come back to the engine room, he would show me how to take the train through a crossing.
AMY: Okay, have fun.
SHELDON: Do you want to come with me? [7.15].

Sheldon's invitation to share his interest with Amy is a distinctively (if stereotypically) un-autistic move, intended to suggest a romantic intimacy between the two characters. This implies that Sheldon's earlier conflict of interest is now resolved. Ultimately, even Eric is invited to join the couple in the engine room. The very fact that Amy and Sheldon's long awaited first kiss happens on a train suggests the primacy of *The Big Bang Theory*'s interest in autism stereotypes: the kiss is a symbol of heteronormative romance (Sheldon's relationship with Amy) wrapped in a symbol of autistic "romance" (Sheldon's "love" for trains).

While the sitcom initially presents Sheldon as asexual and aromantic (and the other characters implicitly recognize Sheldon as asexual and aromantic), the plotline of the series eventually shows Sheldon engaged in a sexual and romantic relationship. Although the kiss on the train may suggest (at least symbolically) that autism and romance can co-exist, Sheldon's romantic relationship with Amy gradually changes his character. More specifically, Amy seems to target Sheldon's autistic traits as characteristics that need to be changed. Certainly, the sitcom plays on the idea that romantic love changes people for the better. When Sheldon gets a song stuck in his head, he realizes that it is a song about how Amy has changed him as a person: "I know why the song was in my head. It's about Amy. It's about how she made my life better. Consider the lyrics, 'I was living like half a man. Then I couldn't love but now I can, more soul than I ever had. I love the way you soften my life'" (9.10). It is commonplace for romantic comedies to show how romance can transform one into a better person, completing someone who was "incomplete" when single. Throughout the course of the sitcom, Amy teaches Sheldon (often very explicitly) about social skills and social relationships. The half of Sheldon that is "missing" seems to be the social half. For example, Amy teaches Sheldon about empathy:

> AMY: Everyone tried to take care of you and you were nothing but mean to them … just apologize to them … maybe you could try apologizing because you actually feel bad. It's called empathy. It's something you could work on.
> SHELDON: I have empathy. Watch—Leonard made me soup and I was mean to him. [Sheldon makes an exaggerated sad face.]
> AMY: Great. Now try it as if this isn't your first day as a person.
> SHELDON: Fine. Leonard made me soup and I was mean to him. Hey! I felt a little something…. I was mean to him. He must have felt terrible. Now I feel terrible. Neat! [9.13].

In *The Big Bang Theory*, the "transformative power" of Amy's love apparently targets traits that are stereotypically autistic such as having difficulty with empathy. Can love cure autism? *The Big Bang Theory* seems to think so—falling in love appears to be making Sheldon into a better (read: less autistic) person. This is clearly an example of the disability "cure or kill" trope discussed by Rosemarie Garland-Thomson (2001, 355). Disability is a problem that the narrative must solve. In short, Sheldon cannot continue to exist as an autistic character unless he gradually becomes more neurotypical. Ultimately, Sheldon's place as an asexual and autistic character is subsumed into the larger narrative arc of the sitcom's romantic comedy plotline.

Although Sheldon apparently has no desire to sleep with Amy, he eventually decides to have sex with her. He explicitly tells Penny that he engages in sexual activity "in order to show Amy how much I care about her" (9.11). The image of the two lying in bed together, Amy disheveled and Sheldon composed, clearly hints at Sheldon's continued indifference to sex:

SHELDON: Well, I enjoyed that more than I thought I would.
AMY: Me too!
SHELDON: I look forward to your next birthday when we do it again.
AMY: That works for me [9.11].

While audience members may laugh at the idea of sex that is reserved as a birthday celebration, Sheldon makes it very clear that sex is a sacrifice he makes for Amy's sake. He enjoyed it—but only more than he thought he would. Some asexual people do become sexually involved with their partners as Sheldon does in the course of the show. As Decker notes, some asexual people "want romance. Some don't. Some are willing to have sex. Some aren't. Some are virgins. Some aren't. Some masturbate, or have a libido, or want children. Some don't" (Decker 2015). However, the show is as unwilling to say the word "asexual" as it is to say the word "autism." This refusal causes Sheldon's asexual identity and preferences to be overshadowed by his union with Amy. Sheldon's perspective as an autistic and asexual character is overlooked by the other characters and probably by many viewers of the show. The narrative arc of the romantic comedy continually invites the viewer to focus on Amy's heteronormative, romantic, and neurotypical perspective.

In the end, *The Big Bang Theory* is successful partially because it gets laughs, partially because it offers a twist on the classic romantic comedy motifs, and, perhaps most importantly, because Sheldon is a sympathetic and likable character. As Sheldon puts it, "I'm an odd fellow … and sometimes I say the wrong thing … but I mean well in my heart" (9.13). The bonds he forms with the other characters are both humorous and endearing. As Sheldon explains it (in a funny video recording his life for his future self): "This is Leonard. He's your best friend in the world … sometimes he gets cranky, but you can trust him with your life. And he does more things for you than I can even begin to list" (9.10). The actor who plays Sheldon, Jim Parsons, sees the character as being happy with and accepting of his social and mental differences: "Sheldon, for the most part, as far as we know from what's been written so far, *is* okay with it [being different]. He actually is, in a lot of ways, quite pleased with himself. He enjoys the life he leads, and is very comfortable with himself" (Murray 2009). Although Sheldon may be "quite pleased with himself" as he is, Amy may not be. She requires Sheldon to change and act more neurotypical in order to "move forward" with their relationship. It would seem that the largely neurotypical and heteronormative audience of *The Big Bang Theory* is uncomfortable with Sheldon's "difference." His disability and asexuality, rather than being diverse identities that the show is able to acknowledge and explore, become repressed possibilities that the show can only engage superficially and stereotypically before ultimately erasing them. In the end, Sheldon *has to* consummate a sexual relationship with Amy in order for this comedy to have a happy ending.

REFERENCES

Anonymous. 2015. "Mayim Bialik's Take on Sheldon Cooper and Autism Is Wrong." *Crippled-scholar*, June 17. https://crippledscholar.com/2015/06/17/mayim-bialiks-take-on-sheldon-cooper-and-autism-is-wrong/.

Bednarek, Monika. 2012. "Constructing 'Nerdiness': Characterisation in *The Big Bang Theory*." *Multilingual: Journal of Cross-Cultural and Interlanguage Communication* 31(2–3): 199–229.

Cendrowski, Mark. 2007–2016. *The Big Bang Theory*. Perf. Johnny Galecki and Jim Parsons. Amazon streaming.

Decker, Julie Sondra. 2105. *The Invisible Orientation: An Introduction to Asexuality*. New York: Skyhorse.

Fuller, Matt. 2015. *Autism in Love*. CG Entertainment. Netflix streaming.

Garland-Thomson, Rosemarie. 2001. "Seeing the Disabled: Visual Rhetorics of Disability in Popular Photography." In *The New Disability History*, edited by Paul K. Longmore and Lauri Umansky. New York: New York University Press.

Gill, James. 2015. "Is Sheldon Autistic? *The Big Bang Theory* Actress Mayim Bialik Gives This Brilliant Response." *RadioTimes*, June 15. http://www.radiotimes.com/news/2015-06-15/is-sheldon-autistic-the-big-bang-theory-actress-mayim-bialik-gives-this-brilliant-response.

Jay, Shelbi. 2016. "The Big Bang Theory." *Interacting with Autism*. http://www.interactingwithautism.com/section/understanding/media/representations/details/5.

Koyanagi, Jacqueline. 2015. "Context Matters: On Labels and Responsibility." *Disability in Kid Lit*, April 17. http://disabilityinkidlit.com/2015/04/17/context-matters-on-labels-and-responsibility/.

Locker, Melissa. 2014. "Critics Be Damned—Here's Why *the Big Bang Theory* Is an Unstoppable Force with Fans." *The Guardian*, October 7. https://www.theguardian.com/tv-and-radio/tvandradioblog/2014/oct/07/the-big-bang-theory-critics-fans.

Loftis, Sonya Freeman. 2015. *Imagining Autism: Fiction and Stereotypes on the Spectrum*. Bloomington: Indiana University Press.

Magro, Kerry. 2016. "Why Our Autism Community Loves Sheldon Cooper." *Autism Speaks Blog*, August 13, 2014. https://www.autismspeaks.org/blog/2014/08/13/why-our-autism-community-loves-sheldon-cooper.

Murray, Noel. 2009. "Interview: Jim Parsons." *A.V. Club*, May 9. http://www.avclub.com/article/jim-parsons-27415.

Murray, Stuart. 2008. *Representing Autism: Culture, Narrative, Fascination*. Liverpool: Liverpool University Press.

Osteen, Mark. 2008. *Autism and Representation*. New York: Routledge.

Park, Terri. 2016. Comment on "Why Our Autism Community Loves Sheldon Cooper." *Autism Speaks Blog*, August 13, 2014. https://www.autismspeaks.org/blog/2014/08/13/why-our-autism-community-loves-sheldon-cooper.

Sepinwall, Alan. 2009. "Reader Mail: Does Sheldon from 'Big Bang Theory' Have Asperger's?" *The Star-Ledger*, August 13. http://www.nj.com/entertainment/tv/index.ssf/2009/08/reader_mail_does_sheldon_from.html.

Simsion, Graeme. 2013. *The Rosie Project*. New York: Simon & Schuster.

Walters, Shannon. 2013. "Cool Aspie Humor: Cognitive Difference and Kenneth Burke's Comic Corrective in *The Big Bang Theory* and *Community*." *Journal of Literary and Cultural Disability Studies* 7(3): 271–88.

Weitekamp, Margaret. 2015. "'We're Physicists': Gender, Genre and the Image of Scientists in *The Big Bang Theory*." *Journal of Popular Television* 3(1): 75–92.

"Making Invisible Disability Visible"

Productive Paradoxes of the Seen and Unseen in Recent Social Media Campaigns Produced by Disabled People

SUSAN G. CUMINGS

As countless scholars and critics have shown, traditional "media outlets" (mainstream film, broadcast and print media, as well as their digital name-sakes and descendants), shaped by and infused with ableism, have not contributed very positively or accurately to the representation of disability as a mode of living (see, e.g., Longmore 1985; Gartner and Joe 1987; Keller, Hallahan and McShane 1990; Norden 1994; Nelson 1994; Norden and Cahill 1998; Safran 1998; Mitchell and Snyder 2001; Larson and Haller 2002; Titchkosky 2005; Gill 2006; Haller 2010; Samsel and Peripa 2013; Devotta, Wilton, and Yiannakoulias 2013; Zhang and Haller 2013). In response, many in the disability community increasingly take advantage of new media platforms and technologies to create and share more accurate, multimodal representations, that is, representations combining two or more modes of communication such as text, audio, and visual components. This essay examines three recent examples, focusing specifically on the rhetorical use of photography as a medium and "invisible disability" as a subject, and addressing the apparent paradox in choosing a visual medium to "depict" something that cannot be "seen." Each multimodal example—one uses an independent website cross-promoted through broadcast descendants, another is a sharing platform dedicated to disability and mental health stories, and the last is a mainstream social media application—prompts and is in turn (re)shaped and extended through open participation by online viewers. These examples reflect the participatory cultural system made possible by new media logics, at least when new venues for media are accessible to particular dis/abled users. Taken together, these examples have much to tell us about the importance of persons with disabilities being producers of these representations, and thus they imply, too, the necessity for deliberate, intensive, continuous vigilance in making and keeping such media platforms accessible (Ellcessor 2016), so that not only "able disabled" individuals may participate.

The Productive Paradox

Disability is problematic as an *identity* category because impairments are so varied—I am one handed, or do not hear, or have chronic headaches, or have legs that are paralyzed, for instance. However, the social model of disability helps make clear what people with disabilities have in common: the fight against attitudinal, bureaucratic, material, and ideological barriers rooted not in the body but in the built environment, institutional practices, and the habits of thinking that shape them. The three projects studied in this essay focus on public misperceptions of ambiguous or "invisibly" anomalous bodies. These are bodies said to "look fine" but not experienced that way due to pain, fatigue, and other limitations both physical and the misguided expectations of others concerning what disability "looks like."

Each of these projects depends significantly on the impact of photographs that purport to "make invisible disability visible," and thus relies on a linguistic, philosophical paradox: the use of highly *visual* media (photography, and social media and the Internet in general) to convey something that is supposedly *unseeable*, even for the conventionally sighted. Most obviously, this suggests drawing on the metaphorical (read: social and political) meanings of invisibility: the sense of being unrecognized, ignored and disempowered. Thus, the first case example illustrates participants in the Suffering the Silence campaign who cover their mouths to indicate that they are silenced, while diagnoses as varied as HIV, Lyme, and scoliosis are written on their arms, which makes them "visible." Yet through interplay with the *literal* visuality of these media, disabled activists also reframe understandings of the body as a signifier, of coerced disclosure and shifting boundaries of privacy for people with disabilities (Franits 2016) and the formation of healthy disability identity. Blogger Danielle Myers, in the second case example, uses the autobiographical photo essay genre to offer conventional visual representations of disability—portraits of her pleasant "public" face and struggles in the "privacy" of home—to twist those conventions by emphasizing and manipulating the point of view through juxtaposing varied images of what she looks *like* and what she looks *at*. In doing so, she breaks the "object of pity" convention of disability representation without resorting to its equally problematic mirror-twin, the "supercrip" who "overcomes" and thus "inspires" (Schalk 2016; Silva and Howe 2012). In the third example, Stephen "Ste" Walker posts paired photos on Facebook, one of himself as a sleek, young, and out-on-the-town person, the other of himself exposing the tubes and stoma bag hidden by his trendy clothing. He manifests the exasperation of the non-visibly disabled when encountering puzzlement, suspicion, or open hostility from the uninformed who cannot "see" their experience or their needs. The photos illustrate, too, how persons with disabilities are frequently forced to compromise privacy to satisfy "gatekeepers," whether professionals such as doctors or insurance adjustors who control resources, or self-appointed amateurs who police public space (Pryal 2016).

These case examples all deploy the Internet's visual and multimodal dimensions to promote a redefinition of wholeness. Participants "recapture their bodies and re-mobilize their meanings" (Kuppers 2003, 10). This happens in ways that privilege proximity, integration, and interaction, not judgment, folding the metaphorical sense of visibility (as enfranchisement) in with their literal visibility in (virtual) public space. By positing that any see-able whole must be reunderstood as inevitably holding ability and disability in tension, they displace misleading and potentially disempowering misunderstandings of the relationship between signifier and signified rooted in ableist constructions of the transparency and stability of wellness and illness. Furthermore, #SufferingTheSilence and the #SickButInvisible hashtag born of Walker's rant provide space, structure, and encouragement to unknown others in a (counter)public (Asen 2000; Warner 2002) with whom they claim communal ties, creating virtual communities and organizational coalitions with real benefits. Each campaign succeeds, I argue, because disabled persons act as producers—not just appear as products—of media, controlling their own images, expanding the social imaginary by careful public pedagogy based on disability experience. In doing so, they also encourage the formation of disability identity as a valid social identity not defined by what Garland-Thomson terms "normate" conventions of appearance or behavior (1997).

Nomenclatures: Invisible, Illegible, Hidden, Episodic, Obscure

A key goal of these projects, and this essay, is educating the public about what is often referred to as invisible disability. Terms like "invisible illness" or "invisible disability"—or for invisible substitute variations such as non-visible, hidden, or illegible—are understood as labels applied to bodies that "pass" as normatively abled but are not experienced that way. Using words like invisible or non-visible gives privilege to sight as a means of understanding, and to the onlooker, over the person in question as the arbiter of meaning. Moreover, this labeling allows assumptions of normativity and what McRuer (2002) calls compulsory able-bodiedness to dominate modes of interaction, without challenging the means by which judgment is practiced and acted upon. Shifting terminology from "invisible" to "illegible" does little to change this. Even if it does foreground the agency in the act of interpretation (reading) over visibility as an inherent quality, the structured power relation remains the same. When the subject and object are constructed through language as fixed positions, the "invisibly disabled" are situated as objects of the "nondisabled gaze," without agency or perspectives of their own. This "nondisabled gaze" can be understood as analogous to Mulvey's "male gaze" (1975), a conditioned habit of viewing and interpreting that is shaped by hegemonic subject positions. In such situations, the viewer may themselves not appear to occupy the position technically, but have absorbed the dominant interpretation in order to consequently deploy it. That is, Mulvey argues that many women, shaped by social conventions, view cinema with a "male gaze" without being themselves male. Thus, I point out that viewers, and not only nondisabled ones, may be prone to a gaze structured by hegemonic ableism. While this understanding of a "nondisabled gaze" differs slightly from that of Bill Hughes, it shares the suspicion of a "binary marking out of the world" as a consequence of how disability is dominantly interpreted (1999, 157).

The adjective "hidden" is equally as problematic in that it risks implying that someone is actively doing the hiding, and grants agency to people with disabilities only in a limited sense with the pejorative suggestion that they (we) are acting to deceive. "Episodic" disability, the term used by Lightman et al. (2009), brings temporality and fluctuation into the equation. However, despite its claims to the contrary, it largely resituates that which disables within the body rather than account for the disabling effects of attitudes *toward* that body and systems not designed *for* that body.

Whatever the particular term used for designating them, however, non-visibly dis/abled bodies provoke what Marjorie Garber calls a "category crisis" (1992, 10). This is not because, as Tobin Siebers (2004) observes, "people have sufficient genius to disguise their identity," but rather that there remains an untrained, overprivileged, general population with a "tendency to repress the embodiment of difference" (3). Passing, then, whether deliberate or arrived at through the misrecognition of others, becomes "a site of conflict between those who derive power from defining the boundaries of normalcy and those who lose rights when they are labeled deviant" (Brune and Wilson 2013, 4). The second part of this Catch-22 is that persons with non-visible disabilities must often actively seek a label of "pathology"—a conventional medical diagnosis of some deemed "deficiency"—in order to secure certain rights and benefits. This, as Brune and Wilson dryly observe, "has further complicated these issues of passing" (9).

Lenard Davis suggests that to the general onlooker "the disabled body must always be explained" (1995, xvi), but Andrew Harnish (2016) has observed that supplying a diagnostic label, a common way to seek legibility through a "familiar script," too often *does little to dissipate the obscurity of the lived experience* of one's condition(s). Chelsea Bruner's (2016) lament concerning the misrecognition of her experience with rheumatoid arthritis (RA) brings Harnish's legibility/obscurity distinction into focus. Bruner, a teacher in her 30s, writes that telling others she has RA brings responses along two general lines: (a) RA, that's stiff joints, right? and/or (b) isn't that an old-people thing? Bruner experiences severely debilitating chronic pain and immobility to the point where she misses meals rather than attempt to hold a utensil to feed herself. She is socially isolated and has anxiety and depression not only in dealing with the immediacy of physical pain, but in worrying whether she can continue in the career she loves. Her medications are frequently either unavailable or unaffordable. Bruner experiences every waking hour as a struggle, yet considers *not* telling people she has RA anymore because the familiar script they assume is "stiff joints" (i.e., a nuisance but not that bad) and "old people" (i.e., can't really be her). RA is a "legible" term that actually results in people knowing *less* about her experience and doubting her struggle *more*. Such obscuring of "how people experience, live with, and think about" their impairments (Wendell 2001, 23) illuminates the dire need for multimodal disability pedagogies such as those I will analyze in the remainder of this essay. The case studies I present challenge false binaries of well and ill, able and disabled, and direct their audiences not to seek or settle for seemingly easy labels, but to attend to the complex phenomenology of living with disability.

#SufferingTheSilence

The first case study, Suffering the Silence, a project started by Allie Cashel and Erica Lupinacci, came to my attention when it was covered by U.S. Public Broadcasting (PBS) with the headline "Photos Give Powerful Visibility to Chronic Illness" (Sessa-Hawkins 2015). The visual dimension of the project consists of the 11 original photographs by Amanda Crommet, including one each of Cashel and Lupinacci (Crommet 2015). Crommet's images follow a standard layout. Against a bright blue, textured but undecorated wall, a person is seen from the chest up, looking directly at the camera and covering their mouth with their left hand. On their left forearm, a medicalized diagnostic term is written in block letters with contrasting paint—white paint on darker skin tones, black paint on lighter. Diagnoses include chronic Lyme, lupus, scoliosis, HIV+, hemophilia, endometriosis, ulcerative colitis, asthma, Crohn's, rheumatoid arthritis, fibromyalgia, and scoliosis. The PBS article features six of these photos, depicting four women and two men from a variety of racial/ethnic backgrounds. Accompanying each photo is a statement from the subject about their experience, signed with their first name (Sessa-Hawkins 2015; Crommet 2015). Through the codification of the image production, the sameness (background color, pose, size of the figure in the frame, as well as style and size of lettering) and the difference (race, letter color, age, gender presentation, and condition) are both observable. In accentuating visually both sameness and difference, the images convey both community and coalition.

The project offers a Twitter hashtag that serves as an invitation for others to extend this "community" on social media by posting tagged photos that associate the name of their condition with their public face, and the experience of being silenced or misread. Cashel tells PBS' Margaret Sessa-Hawkins: "A lot of people reached out and have said they've used the portrait to communicate to their loved ones what it's really like to live with this…. And that's what we wanted from the start, we wanted this to be a platform to use to help people communicate their experience" (Sessa-Hawkins 2015). On the project's website, the introduction states: "When someone doesn't look visibly sick, one can often forget what their life is like behind the scenes" (Crommet 2015). "Behind the scenes" suggests there is a different space to which only some have access. It also suggests a certain mechanics behind the performance (though the word choice risks an additional unintended connotation not only of spectacle but of deception). These conditions or impairments "behind the scenes" of these photos, the invisible or illegible, are sparsely represented by the words inscribed onto the bodies in paint to render them "visible" or "legible."

The familiar script of a medicalized diagnostic term does not, however, convey the lived experience, so participant statements address this "obscurity." Common experiences include the need to repeatedly self-disclose, to keep reminding employers or even family members who "know" but find it easy to forget what they've been told in the absence of (to them) observable reminders. Servers, for example, share how they are frequently still expected to carry heavy trays or be perceived as lazy. Others have faced the challenge of being overly pitied, being seen as completely incapable or as having no interests outside their conditions, as if their illness were a totalizing status. One participant, Ty, tells readers, "Just because I have something like this doesn't mean that I still can't go out and sing and do the things that I am meant to do. It doesn't mean that I can't date, that I can't love, it doesn't mean that I can't do any of those things. I'm still a person, I'm still human"

(Crommet 2015). All of the respondents ask not to be judged, dismissed, or forgotten, but to have their concerns remembered and perspectives taken seriously.

Hundreds from across multiple continents joined the #sufferingthesilence hashtag community within months of its inception by submitting their own mouth-covering, diagnosis-revealing photos. While Twitter limits their accompanying statements to 140 characters, some participants like Wendy Gikono (aka @mctdwarrior) link their Twitter posts to their own blogs where they write in greater depth about their experiences. Others have utilized the project's postcard.com link where they can upload a photo and a statement that is turned into both a physical postcard sent to them, and a virtual postcard that is archived as part of an activist "mosaic" on the Suffering the Silence web page. At Cashel's invitation, many more who prefer to participate without photographs have instead posted hundreds of messages of identification and solidarity, with comments like "breaking my silence on #lyme, first time ever," or "I don't have any other way but to struggle out to find place in insanity, pain and world [*sic*]," or "I have Lyme disease and want to encourage Avril and all to #live." The project is achieving its goal of helping people break the individual "silences" and make their non-visible disabilities known. The comment to "Avril," a previous respondent in the feed, also suggests participants are successful in connecting to and encouraging each other in a community of understanding, mutual support, and nascent disability pride of the type called for in Rosemarie Garland-Thomson's recent (2016) *New York Times* piece, "Becoming Disabled." The project's Twitter handle, after all, is @ststogether—"together," no longer alone.

Privacy on Display

The visual rhetoric of my next case study, an August 2015 multimodal essay by blogger Danielle Myers, uses elements such as color saturation and image manipulation to explore imperatives of passing, the supposed divide between public and private, and the complex intersubjectivity of disabled living. Myers also challenges conventions of disability depiction by shifting the point of view, claiming visual agency rather than remaining solely an "object observed."

Myers' work appeared on The Mighty, a web platform proclaiming its dedication to "building a community" among those with impairment, disease, and mental illness, specializing not in the exchange of medical information but in "stories of living." Myers' essay will not be free of "medical moments" (for example, images in treatment rooms) but, true to the stated goals of its publishing platform, its focus is on modes of living that are varied, complex, and interpersonal. The fact that The Mighty has come under scrutiny by a growing number within the disability community for ableism and reproducing tropes of stigma and tragedy since I began working on this essay shows how tenuous it is to build community around disability as a tethering identity, and the necessity for more work to be done (Sutton 2015; Nichols 2015; Griffo 2015; UnBoxed Brain 2016; Hiari 2017). While it is beyond the scope of this essay to weigh in on the specific controversy, it is worth noting that Meyers' work has since been republished by several other outlets (Yahoo Health 2015) and is not specifically the target of such criticism.

Although this notion of building a community among those *living with* certain impairments or conditions may imply an audience of disabled persons, Myers appears to address onlookers who lack personal experience with invisible disability. At the same time, it is common for disability writing on the web to seek to inform the uninformed, knowing that it will also, if done well, elicit an "amen" from those in the audience who share similar experiences. Myers opens with the simple statement "I want to invite you into my life." This life, she goes on to explain, is a family life that includes and is marked by her own rheumatoid arthritis (RA) and fibromyalgia, having four children, and attending to the additional needs of one of her sons, who lives with tuberous sclerosis complex, autism, and epilepsy. Addressing the ways that illness and disability are often not perceived much less understood by onlookers, she gently reminds readers that most will not expect and thus not take into account the complexity of her family's days. Her images also let (sighted) readers "face," visually, what she faces, by including photos taken not *of* her but *from* her literal point of view. The photographs are curated and digitally enhanced to help bring various aspects of her experience to the fore, enriched by her verbal commentary.

Myers' essay is titled "Why I'm Showing These Private Photos of My Life with Chronic Illness." The word *why* immediately acknowledges that she is doing something that must be justified or explained. The rest of the title labels her supposed transgression: "showing" something deemed "private." But why is it deemed private, and by whom? Myers' first photograph presents the sort of public face that passes as nondisabled. A fair-haired young white woman wearing a colorfully-striped t-shirt looks up at a camera from the slightly awkward angle typical of certain selfies, and a caption tells the audience that this is how "you might see me in public on a typical day." The hedging present in the word *might* is initially ascribed not to illness but the ordinary busyness of family life. Mothers of four children, she reminds us in her textual comments, can't always find time to put on makeup or fix their hair. What "private" seems to mean, at a first reading of the essay's next images, is photographic glimpses from inside the home, without the public face and cheerfully colored clothing. We will see her in a nightgown, or with her arms around her husband, next to their bed, neither of them facing the camera, caught, it appears, in a "private moment." Because of the relative cheerfulness of the first colorful image, we might see this private space inside their home as warm and unchallenging. Even the fact that the next photos move from color to muted sepia tones may go initially unnoticed, until Myers' captions address potential misperceptions. Thus, what looks like an embrace, even a dance, for instance, is captioned to disclose: "At the peak of my flare, the morning hours gave me the most pain, and I had difficulty getting out of bed so my husband began to help me" (Myers 2015). Pain must be named in order to invite recognition in another; it cannot be somatically shared (Scarry 1985). The privacy viewers are invited into is at once as "ordinary" as a woman in pajamas, a husband and wife in the bedroom, and is also a privacy of the body's disability, difficulty, and pain that is usually hidden from public view in the privacy of a home she won't leave when she is experiencing a higher intensity of her symptoms.

Myers also approaches what counts as "private" through photographs of swollen and discolored parts of her body—here depicted in color to render them vivid—such as her enlarged hand, or her bare, white legs with a bruised inner thigh. People are expected to cover areas of their bodies their societies deem "private," and in North America, where Myers lives, these typically include the groin area, for women the breasts (an area that before the 1930s U.S. men, too, were expected to cover in public), and in some communities the list is longer. The leg bruise photos, or more specifically, her inclusion of leg bruise photos in a series labeled *private*, conveys expectations not just that one protect one's own modesty, but that one avoid "intruding" on others by allowing what is considered unsightly to be seen in public. Such prohibitions value some bodies (for example, the unbruised or unswollen) above others, and hold people with illness or disability responsible not only for managing their own bodily experiences but the "sensitivities" (ableist expectations) of others, a doubled task.

Myers' disablement is also made more conventionally "visible," that is, legible, through props that mark disability, such as the rolling walker, or "rollator." Her husband helps her reach it, but Myers (2015) continues to press to clarify: "[The rollator] helped with my mobility … [but my] hands hurt so bad that I could hardly grasp the handles." Such verbal contributions address the photographs' limitations, suggesting depiction alone still presents only a partial truth, increased legibility still paired with the lived experience's obscurity. It may be reasonably clear that there is disability requiring an assistive device, but that says nothing of how it *feels*, or the device's limitations in addressing the totality of the lived moment. Myers also coaxes the visual medium to reveal more thanks to the manipulability of digital images with just a simple cell phone and home computer editing capacities. She uses cropping and edge blurring, for example, to make a long, narrow corridor seem all the more so, in an image where she pushes her rollator alone. This enhances the impression of isolation and confinement for the solitary, hunched figure depicted.

The images discussed so far have been of Myers as a figure to be looked at, but to suggest this is true of the whole series is misleading. Right after her initial selfie, she claims ownership of perspective, and begins including photographs not of how she looks but what she sees. Some images focus on trays of needles, for example, and are taken in or contain details suggestive of hospitals or treatment facilities. "Yes, I 'look normal,'" one caption reads, "yet I am very different. Here is life from my perspective." Filters help her emphasize this perspective: a screen shot of the overly wordy diagnosis of her "shredded shoulder," for example, is blurred and distorted, conveying visually how dizzying and difficult it is to decipher.

Some of the most emotional photos Myers shares involve her children. She appears in a few, such as a black and white close-up where she holds her baby daughter. The baby looks toward the camera while sucking a pacifier, nestled into the mother, whose face is turned away from the camera. The lace of Myers' shirt, the escaping tendrils of her tied-back hair, and the patterns of the sofa where the two figures sit form delicate designs in black, white and grays. The invoked artistic aesthetic of black and white photography helps the picture to seem quietly "perfect." Contrast this with another picture, drab but in color: Myers holding her son, a young, dark-haired boy, who clings to her, a large bruise visible on his forehead. "I pray for days when we cuddle just for the sake of cuddling," the caption reads, "[and not] because a seizure has prevented him from moving his own body." Myers expresses determination to find strength, even on days her symptoms are worse, to comfort her children when they need it. Most affecting perhaps, then, is a photo not of Myers but of what she sees, this time a photo of her same son, who lies on the floor alone because she was unable to reach him before he fell during a seizure. This photo is in black and white, but lacks the soft grays and artful patterns of the daughter photo. It is too bright, seems overexposed, conveying a stark scene devoid of comfort or beauty. Together, these images suggest how varied Myers' daily experiences of family life are.

Myers' photo essay ends back in the "public realm" outside the home with two shots that return to cheerful bright colors. Of course, though they remind us of those conventional public-private divisions, in and outside the home, *every* image included in this publically available multimodal Internet essay is now public. One of the concluding pictures is a sunny family holiday snap with a river and city skyline in the background, and the other is a shot of Myers' husband and daughter watching a pink ball roll down a bowling lane. Any visual semblance of a "return to normalcy" (read: "overcoming" of disability) is diverted by the captions that continue to emphasize what's "really" going on, or to put it better, what *else* is *also* going on. The joys are real, they are simply never uncomplicated. The bowling alley photo is taken by, and does not feature Myers, because while she was able to accompany her family, her hands hurt too much to bear the weight of a bowling ball. As a viewer, I watch with her, able like her to witness her husband and daughter's enjoyment, but also like her only as a bystander. It reminds us that for those with chronic illnesses, the story is always bigger than the picture, and whether symptoms are "visible" or not, distance is always felt, even in the presence of a loving family. Myers' disability pedagogy calls for attention not just to what's in the images but what isn't, thus working to reduce experiential obscurity, and in turn to mitigate somewhat that sense of isolation.

Going on a *"Rant"*

Unlike Myers' project, published through a web platform aimed at an interested audience, or Suffering the Silence, that deliberately initiates an online movement, my third case study arose simply as a frustrated rant to nobody in particular. Thanks to the near infinite "spreadability" of social media, it took on a life of its own, and in turn changed the direction of the ranter's life. Ste Walker, a 20-year-old white British man with Crohn's disease, became exasperated after his umpteenth encounter with variations on the phrase "You don't look sick," and took to his personal Facebook page to fume about it. Walker's (2015) post laments the imposed convention that vulnerability must carry specific visible markers of posture, coloring, age, and speed of movement. This imperative, because it is experienced by persons with disabilities and crime victims alike (Danica 1988, 1995), as well as highlights our cultural habit of thinking that those with illness or impairments are "victims." (Had Danielle Myers shown only her bruises or the hunched figure with the walker, without images of cuddles and holidays as well, she would have stayed within this convention.) The demand for pitiable self-presentation produces, in certain situations, what I (2016, 123) have called "the coerced lie" or what Bill Shannon (2011; 2012) calls the "blowfish" strategy. This is an exaggeration of symptoms, whether postural (such as limping more) or verbal ("the pain is *unbearable*!!!") that offers a public simulation of the "worst day," irrespective of the person's actual current state or the fluctuations of symptoms, in order to fit whatever ill-fitting but authorized script will result in their receiving needed support. The history of "poster children" and telethons, as Paul Longmore (2013) has chronicled, is rife with such objectifying and totalizing images of exaggerated weakness and stasis. Deployed in fundraising, they maintain an ontological line of distinction between pitying viewers and the objects of their pity, counting on the sense of moral redemption "we" (nondisabled donors or onlookers) get from helping "them" (the disabled persons coded as tragic, who in this type of image have little or no agency of their own). Those who do not appear vulnerable enough, or in the "right ways," are then deemed the *un*deserving. They risk the disbelief and sometimes hostility of others, inviting "denial" and "mockery" or accusations of "fraud" or "malingering" (Samuels 2003, 242, 247), exactly as Ste Walker experienced.

"People are too quick to judge these days," Walker (2015) opens; "just because I look normal and speak normal, that doesn't mean I don't have a major disability … to look at me I look like any normal guy my age, but that's because I want you to view me like that." Walker immediately lays claim to his agency in controlling how he is seen. The accompanying pair of photographs pushes us to think, too, as did Myers' images, about what we consider private. The photo on the left is a typical selfie: a young, white man holds a mobile phone, taking the photo in a mirror. His stance is casual, his chin is carefully stubbled, he wears a close-fitting, fashionable t-shirt, and his short hair is slicked back. In the photo on the right, the same man is shirtless, with a variety of medical paraphernalia prominently in view, including a line into his chest, a tube into his nose, and an ostomy bag with a clear window showing a stoma, a red opening in the abdomen wall from which bodily waste can emerge to be collected in the bag. Another bag containing yellow fluid bears the printed words "universal" and "bile bag."

The visual lesson, here, if we are to talk of a disability pedagogy embedded in this project, is not simply the exposure of the technologies that go into allowing Walker to get out about the town, nor is it as simple as a disclosure of illness. Although there is a growing genre of "visual autopathography" (Tembeck 2016), from #hospitalglam to the #getyourbellyout "stoma selfies" begun by Bethany Townsend in 2014, the juxtaposing of these two photographs accomplishes a number of things visually that posting them separately would not. Privacy, for one, is more directly addressed and recast. For example, the contrast of wearing clothes and not serves as a reminder that it is not just the walls of the dwelling that are the boundaries of privacy. Similarly to Myers' bruised legs, clothing covers aspects of the body that are customarily expected to be hidden in public, especially when there is waste evacuation involved. Moreover, tubes entering/exiting Walker's body in multiple places also remind the viewer that the body itself is not a private space because the boundaries of a body with disabilities are often of necessity more permeable, with borders transgressed in service of providing support and, rarely, relief. Showing a bag full of extracted bodily fluid and a stoma exiting the abdomen wall also brings the inside out in a very literal way. Here some of the processes and products customarily invisible inside the human body are made visible in the photo, and made public through a web distribution unrestricted by any "privacy settings."

The juxtaposition of the two photos makes the point, again, as Myers' images do, that no one photo, *or visual impression gleaned in a personal encounter*, can convey the entire reality of any person. A viewer seeing only the t-shirted, slicked back selfie would too likely fail to imagine the medicalization this body endures, as Walker laments. On the other side, if there were only the shirtless photo with medical tools so prominently in view, viewers could fall easily into a solely medicalized reading of Walker as a "case" and would be tempted to interpret the figure as passive, stripped of identity, "purely ill," and "globally incapacitated" (Wendell 2001, 17). The juxtaposition underscores the false binarity that opposes wellness and illness, disability and able-bodiedness, and limits our capacity to interpret either image when presented alone.

Alongside the photographs is a lengthy description of the psychological and social toll of Walker's diagnoses, symptoms, medical managements, and the judgments of others. He describes pain, incapacitation, and a "mental battle raging inside me all the time," given that he has "not been able to eat a meal in 2 years, or only been at home for 4 weeks in the last 18 months, been away from my family and friends, seeing what my illness does to them" (2015). While he makes clear having his illness is difficult, painful, and exhausting, he also stresses that it is not only this but *others' presumption in misreading him and mistreating him based on those projections* that have pushed Walker over the edge, so to speak, and into this post. The arrogance and hostility of others are what he can no longer tolerate and wishes to address. He concludes his long post—its lax spelling and grammar continued evidence that he does not have any particular public audience in mind—by reemphasizing this point, saying:

> So the next time someone says to me "well you look perfectly fine, why are you using that disabled toilet, or parking in that disabled spot, your [*sic*] conning the system, your [*sic*] not disabled, you don't need that walking stick" just stop and think maybe I just want TO BE FINE or to feel normal, you don't know [*sic*] what I go threw [*sic*] on a daily basis and you have no right to judge me just on your perception of me that you can see because you don't no [*sic*] what goes on inside … so stop and think before you speak, think about the struggle I've gone threw [*sic*] just to get out of bed and get dressed and tried [*sic*] to look "normal" …
>   Sorry for the super long post but I needed to rant :)
>   #SickButInvisible
>   #CrohnsDisease [2015].

As he ends, Walker uses the invented hashtag #SickButInvisible as the encapsulation of a message: that he is sick but not recognized and therefore is disempowered (capturing the literal and metaphorical senses of invisibility).

To this he adds a second hashtag providing the name of his illness, Crohn's disease, seeking to invoke a recognizable script. The lesson he wants to share is both about his body and about the modes of experience ignored by those who presume to judge. The two photographs represent the same person, during the same period of time, who has experienced these events, and who, by implication, continues to have further experiences that neither photo captures. The variability of dis/abled experience breaks through, particularly when accompanied by the "rant" text. Walker's invitation to "look abit [*sic*] closer, tho [*sic*], or ask me questions," makes use of both literal visuality (look at these two photos of one body) and of "looking closely" as metaphor (seek to learn more than you currently know), while issuing a call to ask questions and forge relationships.

Clearly, this post purporting to address Walker's judges found an unanticipated but real audience ready to offer "Amens," given the speed with which it went viral. Comments, 12,000 in the first two months, came mainly from Facebook users with invisible disabilities or illnesses themselves, with typical messages amounting to "Me too" and "I hate when that happens" and "People are stupid" and "Hang in there." Walker was clearly unprepared for the volume of response, and initially answered every comment personally, thanking each writer—and these were mainly strangers—for their interest and support. Three months after his initial post, however, he reposted his "too quick to judge" photos and text more deliberately and purposefully. This repost, framed by the same dual selfies, was to "refresh people's minds" and "for people who haven't seen it yet," but was also a harbinger of a new project inspired by responses to the initial rant. Walker (2016a) writes: "we want ALL OF YOU to be involved." Reiterating that his interest is in image, looks, and illness, he states: "the stigma associated with invisible illnesses and the misconception about what disability looks like really needs to change, and with all your help, we may make a slight difference so please give this a share, and be on the look out for my little project that will be uploaded later" (2016a). His follow-up, in late January, then encourages others to post their own photos, and to use his hashtag as a deliberate linking mechanism: "all you have to do is upload a photo of yourself with #SickButInvisible hashtag, we all upload selfies constantly so let's just add my hashtag to them PLEASE, PLEASE GET INVOLVED, SHARE THIS POST, UPLOAD YOUR PICTURES WITH THE HASHTAG, LETS [*sic*] TRY AND MAKE A DIFFERENCE…. Not all disabilities are visual, so please, help me try and change that" (2016b).

Walker's initial 2015 post spoke to those who confronted and doubted him as "you," relying on what Litt and Hargittai call a "phantasmal tie," that is, addressing particular entities or individuals "even at times when [the writer knew] it was unlikely or in some cases impossible for such entities to see or respond to the post" (2016, 6). That is, Walker does not have an actual tie that would direct the message to the individuals whose crass behavior inspired it, and therefore does not expect to reach the actual people who had mistreated him. Unlike Myers or Suffering the Silence, Walker is not, in his initial rant, engaging in deliberate activism or reaching out to established communities through dedicated platforms. He's just tired and angry, and turns to his personal social media account for an outlet. After his initial post, however, the subsequent revival post seems to address a different audience. His "you" now relies on what Litt and Hargittai (2016) call "communal ties" (6) with a much expanded, responsive community of *new* followers who have chosen to *establish* connection with him because of their common experience. His call-out is no longer a vaguely-aimed admonition, but has become an invitation to a specific, growing community to fight stigma and educate others together. Its hashtag, once simply a linguistic distillation, has become a "linked conversation anchor" (Jackson and Banaszczyk 2016, 395). It acts as a rallying point across multiple social media platforms for a campaign fighting "stigma against ALL invisible illnesses and disabilities" (2016c). Walker and his friend Lauryn Morgan soon after set up a dedicated #SickButInvisible Facebook page, Twitter, and Instagram accounts separate from their personal ones, and have made a strong effort to form supportive and activist coalitions with diverse organizations addressing Crohn's and colitis, depression, severe anxiety and other mental health concerns, autism, discrimination against the deaf, and so on. They encourage consumer pressure, organizing campaigns of complaint against a fast food chain where a chronically ill man was refused use of the accessible restroom (Gladwell 2016), and of public praise to a UK supermarket chain for new "not all disabilities are visible" signs on their accessible restrooms (Mulroy 2016). This is social media turned citizen media, to use Ellis and Goggin's (2015) term, with people with disabilities (and their allies) acting as citizens who "make" and "shape" media to encourage other democratic practices of mutual social responsibility (79). The hashtag has since received attention from mainstream news outlets like the *Cork* [Ireland] *Independent* ("It's Okay Not to Be Okay") and the new organization also provides direct encouragement through "You Are Visible" goodie boxes sent once a month to a person with an invisible illness/disability nominated by community members. Out of one off-the-cuff, but creatively constructed social media post, Ste Walker has found a full-time vocation, and many are benefitting from the activism he and Morgan facilitate and the community they are building.

Conclusion: Agency Over Obscurity

Attending to media images produced by persons with disabilities expands understandings both of modes of disability living and of the potential of the media themselves. In *Status Update,* Alice Marwick (2013) declares that the democratizing possibilities lauded in the early days of social media have devolved into exclusion, elitism, and a preoccupation with status and attention; social media, she proclaims, is "intrinsically focused on individuals" and "neoliberal subjectivity" (7). Intrinsically? Surely not. The media projects described in this essay present each self as complex and of worth without needing to be classified in neoliberal terms. They stress solidarity, community building, and the value of interdependence over individuality or earning potential. Over and against the mainstream edited and polished self(ie) they stress that there are many interrelated yet highly diverse images that only *together* can begin to represent a person. They emphasize that modes of experience vary, and deliberately reveal complex selves through word and image, including making the supposedly private or discomforting public, in contrast to the types of perfectly constructed image-people and imitation celebrities from whose media use Marwick is drawing her conclusions. These disability activists, harnessing the paradox of "making the invisible visible," shake up habits of perception and judgment and encourage others, through online forums and hashtag activism, to join in this crowdsourced disability pedagogy and activism. Walker, Myers, and *Suffering the Silence* actualize the potential for Internet sharing sites with interactive functions to be for the disability community simultaneously a means of educating others, of making connections, and an "outlet for creative expression" (Bromley 2008, 1). This is not Marwick's brand of self-obsessed, neoliberal individuality, and reminds us that attending to disability perspectives both reveals aspects of disability living and corrects misleading generalizations about broad phenomena such as social media.

To build on the models studied here, though, accessibility remains key. Virtual social spaces, including those pre-dating the internet, showed early promise for persons with disabilities by offering ways to circumvent some of the many barriers that made physical social spaces inaccessible, such as narrow entrances, stairs, loud noise, and low or flashing lights (Shakespeare et al. 1996, 188). Asynchronous contact also meant potential adaptability to "crip time," a widely used colloquial phrase in the disability community that Alison Kafer (2013) sums up as involving "an awareness that disabled people might need more time to accomplish something or arrive somewhere" (26). When websites and applications don't comply with technical and access standards, they present new forms of barriers to fully independent interaction (Hollier 2017; Hollier 2012; Boudreau 2012). Control functions and navigation tools that interface easily with screen readers, alternative text for images, and captions for video, for example, can be built in, but many platforms need remediation or intervention. Third-party adaptive applications and alternative portals are often designed by disabled users themselves, a testament to such users' wish not for disability-specific social media sites but for access to "the same popular social media tools used by the broader online community" (Hollier 2017). "The mere act of participating," observes Verlanger (2008), "becomes a political act." The users I study in this essay do not discuss the accessibility of the internet or the sites or applications they use, which suggests that they enjoy a degree of "able-disabled" privilege, finding no notable technical or economic barriers to their own participation. This should not lessen the need to attend to these issues. It should be noted, for example, that while images in Myers' article are all tagged with alternative text, the images on the Suffering the Silence website are not. This reminds us that even advocacy that purports to be coalitional and social justice-oriented can reproduce habitual inequalities.

The meaning of our bodies is "produced in continuous, lifelong negotiations between how we see ourselves and how our culture sees us" (Holmes 2001, 27), and there is often "violence" (Siebers 2006, 174) in the (mis)interpretation of dis/abled bodies (Jones 1997; Lolo 2017). All three case studies in this essay (*Suffering the Silence*, Myers, and Walker) question definitions of public and private, and break "object of pity" visual conventions without erasing struggle, challenging audiences to take responsibility for a collective cultural failure to recognize the complexities of disability living (Montgomery 2001). Through strategic uses of the visuality of the internet and the availability (to them) of digital photographic and editing technologies, they disrupt economies of passing and expose compulsory ablebodiedness through the simultaneous visual depiction of passing and disclosing. One might construct equations for the images in each example, with the variables spelled out. In Suffering the Silence (2015), stylized composition and framing present the formula as "diverse passing bodies + arm label + symbolic silencing by covering the mouth, emphasizing both variety and shared experience." Myers' (2015) formula reads: "passing body + assistive technologies + visual distortions + a gaze turned outward to expose the customary voyeurism to which persons with impairments are subjected."

Walker's (2015) rant and its image juxtaposition offers "passing body + non-passing/medicalized body as coterminous, not mutually exclusive."

Together, these projects address the objectification of disability and the disabling effects of objectification. They expose the false binary of well and ill. They address the difficulties of living with conditions considered by the mainstream as illegible and explore how obscurity persists, and in some cases may deepen, even when one presents a supposedly "legible script" such as a diagnostic term or visible medical or assistive device. Above all, each asks that we understand how little information a single view affords, and how disability as a mode of living is complex, variable, and subjective, as are all modes of living. Each of these projects claims the authority of people with disabilities to tell their own stories through the use of photography and various mediatized public platforms, to express their truths, and to form and celebrate supportive community. One might say: This is voice. This is visibility. Better, though, to avoid metaphors that still rely on the body, and on ableist paradigms of seeing and hearing (cf. Marshall 2014). This is *political and social empowerment*. This is *community-building* and *public pedagogy*. This is *autotheory* (Young 1997). This is *activism*. The case studies presented in this essay demonstrate how, as long as economic and technical accessibility are pursued and assured, media tools at the disposal of disabled persons in charge of their own representation facilitate creative multimodal storytelling that challenges all of us to be better receivers, interpreters, and carriers of each other's stories, stories that are at once multiple and singular, fragmentary and whole.

REFERENCES

Asen, Robert. 2000. "Seeking the Counter in Counterpublics." *Communication Theory* 10(4): 424–446. doi: 10.1111/j.1468–2885.2000.tb00201.x.

Bromley, Barbara E. 2008. "Broadcasting Disability: An Exploration of the Educational Potential of a Video Sharing Web Site." *Journal of Special Education Technology* 23(4): 1–13.

Brune, Jeffrey A., and Daniel J. Wilson. 2013. "Introduction." *Disability and Passing: Blurring the Lines of Identity.* Philadelphia: Temple University Press.

Bruner, Chelsea. 2016. "Untitled [if this thing taking away my health]." Facebook post, 5 September (also earlier posts, passim).

Crommet, Amanda. 2015. "Suffering the Silence: Portraits of Chronic Illness." *Suffering the Silence*, September 9.

Cumings, Susan G. 2016. "In/Visible Disability, Stare Theory, and Video's Ecologies of Seeing/Seeing Whole: Bill Shannon in Perspective(s)." In *Seeing Whole: Towards an Ethics and Ecology of Sight*, edited by Mark Ledbetter and Asbjørn Grønstad, 119–172. Newcastle upon Tyne: Cambridge Scholars.

Danica, Elly. 1988. *Don't: A Woman's Word.* Charlottetown, PEI: gynergy books.

_____. 1995. *Beyond Don't: Dreaming Past the Dark.* Charlottetown, PEI: gynergy books.

Davis, Lennard. 1995. *Enforcing Normalcy: Disability, Deafness, and the Body.* New York: Verso.

Devotta, Kimberly, Robert Wilton, and Niko Yiannakoulias. 2013. "Representations of Disability in the Canadian News Media: A Decade of Change?" *Disability & Rehabilitation* 35(2): 1859–1868. 10.3109/09638288.2012.760658.

Ellcessor, Elizabeth. 2016. *Restricted Access: Media, Disability, and the Politics of Participation.* New York: New York University Press.

Ellis, Katie, and Gerald Goggin. 2015. "Disability Media Participation: Opportunities, Obstacles and Politics." *Media International Australia* 154 (February): 78–88. http://dx.doi.org/10.1177%2F1329878X1515400111.

Franits, Linnea. 2016. "Privacy Settings: Disability Breaks the Rules." Southern Humanities Council Conference, Louisville, KY, January 29. Presentation.

Garber, Marjorie. 1992. *Vested Interests: Cross-Dressing and Cultural Anxiety.* New York: Routledge.

Garland-Thomson, Rosemarie. 1997. *Extraordinary Bodies: Figuring Physical Disability in American Culture and Literature.* New York: Columbia University Press.

_____. 2003. "Towards a Poetics of the Disabled Body." In *The Meaning of Difference: American Constructions of Race, Sex and Gender, Social Class and Sexual Orientation*, Third Edition, edited by Karen E Rosenblum and Toni-Michelle C. Travis. Boston: McGraw-Hill.

_____. 2016. "Becoming Disabled." *New York Times*, August 21.

Gartner, Alan, and Tom Joe. 1987. *Images of the Disabled, Disabling Images.* New York: Praeger.

Gill, Michael. 2006. "The Disabled Male Gaze: Expressions of Desire and Emotion in Rory O'Shea Was Here." *Disability Studies Quarterly* 26(4): n.p. http://dsq-sds.org/article/view/806/981.

Gladwell, Hattie. 2016. "Man with Crohn's Disease Denied Use of McDonald's Toilets Despite Showing 'Can't Wait' Card." *Metro* [UK], August 17. http://metro.co.uk/2016/08/17/man-with-crohns-disease-denied-use-of-mcdonalds-toilets-despite-showing-cant-wait-card-6070957/

Griffo, Megan. 2015. "Editor's Note: Why We Removed a Story." TheMighty.com, December 21. http://archive.is/NksxV#selection-1583.11–1583.69.

Haller, Beth. 2010. *Representing Disability in an Ableist World: Essays on Mass Media.* Louisville, KY: The Avocado Press.

Harnish, Andrew. 2016. "'A Part of Me Died Suddenly': 'Minimally Invasive' Surgery, Illegible Disability, and Technocultural Confusion." Disability, Arts and Health Conference, Nordic Network for Gender, Body, Health, University of Bergen, Norway, September 2. Conference Presentation.

Hiari, Twilah. 2017. "Why I Resigned from *The Mighty.*" *Mad in America: Science, Medicine and Social Justice,* February 16.

Hollier, Scott. 2012. "Sociability: Social Media for People with a Disability." Word Document accessible from mediaaccess.org.au.

_____. 2017. "The Growing Importance of Accessible Social Media." *In Disability and Social Media: Global Perspectives,* edited by Katie Ellis and Mike Kent, 77–88. New York: Routledge. Proquest Ebrary ebook, Ch. 6, n.p.

Holmes, Martha Stoddard. "Working (with) the Rhetoric of Affliction: Autobiographical Narratives of Victorians with Physical Disabilities." In *Embodied Rhetorics: Disability in Language and Culture,* edited by James Wilson and Cynthia Lewiecki-Wilson, 27–44. Carbondale: Southern Illinois University Press.

Hughes, Bill. 1999. "The Constitution of Impairment: Modernity and the Aesthetic of Oppression." *Disability and Society* 14(2): 155–172. http://dx.doi.org/10.1080/09687599926244.

"It's Okay Not to Be Okay." 2016. *Cork Independent* [Ireland]. March 17.

Jackson, Sarah J., and Sonia Banaszczyk. 2016. "Digital Standpoints: Debating Gendered Violence and Racial Exclusions in the Feminist Counterpublic." *Journal of Communication Inquiry* 40(4): 391–407. doi: 10.1177/0196859916667731

Jones, Megan. 1997. "'Gee, You Don't *Look* Handicapped…': Why I Use a White Cane to Tell People That I'm Deaf." *Ragged Edge/Electric Edge,* July-August.

Kafer, Alison. 2013. *Feminist, Queer, Crip.* Bloomington: Indiana University Press.

Keller, Clayton E., Daniel Hallahan, and Edward A. McShane. 1990. "The Coverage of Persons with Disabilities in American Newspapers." *Journal of Special Education* 24: 271–282. doi:10.1177/002246699002400302.

Kuppers, Petra. 2003. *Disability and Contemporary Performance: Bodies on the Edge.* New York: Routledge.

Lightman, Ernie, Andrea Vick, Dean Herd, and Andrew Mitchell. 2009. "'Not Disabled Enough': Episodic Disabilities and the Ontario Disability Support Program." *Disability Studies Quarterly* 29(3): n.p. http://dsq-sds.org/article/view/932

Litt, Eden, and Eszther Hargittai. 2016. "The Imagined Audience on Social Network Sites." *Social Media + Society* 2(1): 1–12. doi: 10.1177/2056305116633482.

Lolo. 2017. "Things Not to Say to Someone in a Wheelchair—Top 3." YouTube video, 9:47. Posted by SittingPrettyLolo, January 15.

Longmore, Paul. K. 1985. "Screening Stereotypes: Images of Disabled People." *Social Policy* 16: 31–37.

_____. 2013. "Heaven's Special Child: The Making of Poster Children." In *The Disability Studies Reader,* 4th edition, edited by Lenard J. Davis, 34–41. New York: Routledge.

Marshall, Caitlin. 2014. "Crippled Speech." *Postmodern Culture* 24(3): n.p. Project Muse via ProQuest Premium. doi:10.1353/pmc.2014.0020

Marwick, Alice. 2013. *Status Update: Celebrity, Publicity, and Branding in the Social Media Age.* New Haven: Yale University Press.

McRuer, Robert. 2002. "Compulsory Able-Bodiedness and Queer/Disabled Existence." In *Disability Studies: Enabling the Humanities*, edited by Rosemarie Garland-Thomson, Brenda Jo Brueggemann, and Sharon L. Snyder, 88–99. New York: MLA Publications.

"The Mighty: Apologize for The Harm You Do to the Disability Community!" n.d. [2015]. Online Petition. Change.org.

Mitchell, David, and Snyder Sharon. (2001). *Narrative Prosthesis: Disability and the Dependencies of Discourse*. Ann Arbor: University of Michigan Press.

Montgomery, Cal. 2001. "A Hard Look at Invisible Disability." *Ragged Edge* 2.

Mulroy, Zahra. 2016. "ASDA Are Being Praised for New Toilet Sign Showing 'Not All Disabilities Are Visible.'" *The Daily Mirror* [UK], August 5. http://www.mirror.co.uk/news/uk-news/asda-being-praised-new-toilet-8568413.

Mulvey, Laura. 1975. "Visual Pleasure and Narrative Cinema." *Screen* 16(3): 6–18.

Myers, Danielle. 2015. "Why I'm Showing These Private Photos of My Life with Chronic Illnesses." *The Mighty*, August 18. https://themighty.com/2015/08/intimate-photos-of-life-with-fibromyalgia/

Nelson Jack A. 1994. "Broken Images: Portrayals of Those with Disabilities in American Media." In *The Disabled, the Media, and the Information Age*, edited by Jack A. Nelson, 1–24. Westport, CT: Greenwood Press.

Nichols, Meriah. 2015. "Why I've Had It with *The Mighty*." Blog post. *The 365 Days with Disability Project*. MeriahNichols.com, November 16.

Norden, Martin. 1994. *The Cinema of Isolation: A History of Physical Disability in the Movies*. New Brunswick: Rutgers University Press.

Norden, Martin, and Madeleine Cahill. 1998. "Voice, Women, and Disability in Tod Browning's Freaks and Devil Doll." *Journal of Popular Film and Television* 26(2): 86–100. Accessed September 12, 2014. http://dx.doi.org/10.1080/01956059809602778.

Pryal, Katie Rose Guest. 2016. "This is What Accessibility Looks Like (Part 2)." KatieRose GuestPryal.com, April 5.

Safran, Stephen P. 1998. "The First Century of Disability Portrayal in Film." *The Journal of Special Education* 31(4): 467–479. 10.1177/002246699803100404.

Samsel, Maria, and Prithvi Perepa. 2013. "The Impact of Media Representation of Disabilities on Teachers' Perceptions." *Support for Learning* 28(4): 138–145. doi:10.1111/1467-9604.12036.

Samuels, Ellen. 2003. "My Body, My Closet: Invisible Disability and the Limits of Coming-Out Discourse." *GLQ: A Journal of Lesbian and Gay Studies* 9(1–2): 233–255. muse.jhu.edu/article/40803.

Scarry, Elaine. 1985. *The Body in Pain: The Making and Unmaking of the World*. Oxford: Oxford University Press.

Schalk, Sami. 2016. "Reevaluating the Supercrip." *Journal of Literary and Cultural Disability Studies* 10(1): 71–86. muse.jhu.edu/article/611313

Sessa-Hawkins, Margaret. 2015. "Photos Give Powerful Visibility to Chronic Illness." *Art Beat: PBS Newshour*, September 2.

Shakespeare, Tom, Kath Gillespie-Sells, and Dominic Davies. 1996. *Sexual Politics of Disability: Untold Desires*. London: Cassel.

Shannon, Bill. 2011. "Unique Security Requirements." *Bill Shannon: What Is What*, November 4. WhatIsWhat.com.

_____. 2012. "Skateboard Graphic Strategy to Validate Medical Usage." *Bill Shannon: What Is What*, July 2. WhatIsWhat.com.

Siebers, Tobin. 2004. "Disability as Masquerade." *Literature and Medicine* 23(1): 1–22. *Project MUSE*. doi:10.1353/lm.2004.0010.

_____. 2006. "Disability in Theory: From Social Constructionism to the New Realism of the Body." In *The Disability Studies Reader*, edited by Lennard J. Davis, 173–183. New York: Routledge.

Silva, Carla Filomena, and P. David Howe. 2012. "The (In)validity of *Supercrip* Representation of Paralympian Athletes." *Journal of Sport and Social Issues* 36(2): 174–194. http://dx.doi.org/10.1177%2F0193723511433865.

"Still Waiting for *The Mighty* to Do Better." 2016. Petition update, 3 January. Change.org.

Sutton, Michelle. 2015. "Neurodiversity vs. *The Mighty.*" MichelleSuttonWrites.com, December 21.

Tembeck, Tamar. 2016. "Selfies of Ill Health: Online Autopathographic Photography and the Dramaturgy of the Everyday." *Social Media + Society* 2(1): 1–11. http://dx.doi.org/10.1177%2F2056305116641343.

Titchkosky, Tanya. 2005. "Disability in the News: A Reconsideration of Reading" *Disability and Society* 20(6): 655–668. http://dx.doi.org/10.1080/09687590500249082.

Un-Boxed Brain. "Open Letter to *The Mighty.*" Un-BOxedBrain.com. Blog post. n.d.

Verlanger, Kestrell. 2008. "Disability and Participatory Culture." *Beyond Broadcast: Mapping Public Media,* February 9, 2008. Conference presentation. beyondbroadcast.net/blog/?p=124.

Walker, Ste. 2015. "Untitled [People are too quick to judge these days]." Facebook post, October 25.

_____. 2016a. "Untitled [I'm giving this another share]." Facebook post, January 27.

_____. 2016b. "Untitled [Right guys and girls]." Facebook post, January 29.

_____. 2016c. "Untitled [Life's been a bit crazy since the viral post I did last year]." Facebook post via Crohns & Colitis UK, April 29.

Warner, Michael. 2002. "Publics and Counterpublics." *Public Culture* 14(1): 49–90. *Project MUSE*, muse.jhu.edu/article/26277.

Wendell, Susan. 2001. "Unhealthy Disabled: Treating Chronic Illnesses as Disabilities." *Hypatia* 16(4): 17–33. http://www.jstor.org/stable/3810781.

Young, Stacey. 1997. *Changing the Wor(l)d: Discourse, Politics and the Feminist Movement.* New York: Routledge.

Zhang, Lingling, and Beth Haller. 2013. "Consuming Image: How Mass Media Impact the Identity of People with Disabilities." *Communication Quarterly* 61(3): 319–334. http://dx.doi.org/10.1080/01463373.2013.776988.

Between Representation and Reality

The Sighted and Sightless
in Blind Massage

Jason Ho Ka Hang

Disability studies has gained attention and prominence in academia in the last decade or so, but not much has been written about people with disabilities in the Asian context. This is alarming, particularly in China, since the context—culture, demographics, population density, sociopolitical atmosphere—is totally different from the West. Western media representations do not necessarily demonize people with disabilities explicitly. Rather they have different tendencies to sympathize as a way of further marginalizing disability and disabled people. Paul Longmore (2003), for that matter, points out that "disability is a punishment for evil; disabled people are embittered by their 'fate'; disabled people resent the nondisabled and would, if they could, destroy them" (134). Most if not all of the films that depict various disabled populations are made by the able-bodied, resulting in one-dimensional and often biased portrayals of disability. As Martin Norden (1994) rightly suggests, "moviemakers photograph and edit their works to reflect an able-bodied point of view" (2), with one-sided representations of disabilities and marginalities not uncommon in contemporary films and media. What Longmore (2003) and Norden (1994) observe can be vividly traced in Western disability cinema since the millennium. This is the case in films such as Jessie Nelson's *I Am Sam* (2001), Julian Schnabel's *The Diving Bell and the Butterfly* (2007), Olivier Nakache and Eric Toledanolike's *The Intouchables* (2011), Jacques Audiard's *Rust and Bone* (2012), Ben Lewin's *The Sessions* (2012), and of course James Marsh's *The Theory of Everything* (2014) that is based on the real-life

142

story of Stephen Hawking. The scenario of Asian/Chinese disability cinema, however, is quite different from its Western counterpart. One very typical example would be Lee Chang-dong's *Oasis* (2002), a Korean melodrama featuring a surreal love story between a female protagonist with cerebral palsy and a sociopath. Unlike the above Western disability films which tend to be realist and directly confront the pain and suffering of people with disabilities, this Korean piece contains a lot of dreamy and surrealistic moments that offer audiences an alternative space to imagine and contemplate the situation of having a disability in a Korean/Asian context. Not a lot of analysis, however, has been done in the context of China.

This essay precisely seeks to fill the gap between Western and Asian disability studies by examining Lou Le's *Blind Massage* (2014), a Mainland Chinese film that sways between textual representation and reality to critically evaluate the distance between mediated disabilities and what disabled people encounter as performed by disabled actors. *Blind Massage* features a group of blind masseurs who express their love, lust, and desire within the parlor in which they work. Serving able-bodied people while striving hard to lead a sightless life, these masseurs face pressure and hardship from both themselves and the sighted. The double marginalization they embody while trying to build a connection between the two worlds is suggestive of how conservative Mainland Chinese society perceives disability in an able-bodied and able-minded world. While not necessarily a tear-jerker, the film aptly positions sightlessness on a fair and objective plane for audiences to respectfully contemplate the situationality of people with disabilities. This film is analyzed because it offers viewers more than the typical one-dimensional representation about people who have blindness or other disabilities.

Ultimately, as Thomas Hoeksema and Christopher Smit (2001) argue, "what a film says is not as important as what a film makes the viewer think about" (39). The thin line between representations/fictionality and reality/authenticity provides a vast space for viewers and critics alike to explore experiences of visually impaired people in the Asian context. By evaluating blindness in this film, therefore, I will uncover differing manifestations of disability in media through various genres in cinema. Media and filmic representations matter a lot to the perception of disability, because cinema—mainstream and artistic alike—plays an important role in shaping, constructing, and distorting audiences' outlook and attitude towards disabled people. Different forms of media inform how viewers perceive disability, which brings about the intricate interrelationship between media studies and disability studies. I will also outline the critical connection between Western and Asian disability studies, and recognize the opportunities for doing disability studies—which has been, more or less, a Western construct—in a Chinese context.

Blindness and Massage in Mainland China

Blind Massage is not the first film in which director Lou Ye tackles sensitive issues and marginalized characters. As compared to other Mainland Chinese filmmakers of the Sixth Generation after Zhang Yimou—one of the most recognized Fifth Generation Mainland Chinese filmmakers by Western critics and audiences, Lou is "more rebellious and edgy" (Cheung 2010, 14). Cheung is, of course, referring to *Summer Palace* (2007) and *Spring Fever* (2009), which are radically different from another Sixth Generation filmmaker Jia Zhangke, whom she is more interested in her analysis. *Summer Palace* (2007) is a direct portrayal of youths growing up during the period when the Tiananmen massacre took place in Beijing in 1989, which was expectedly banned in China but was well-circulated in international film festival circuits. Lou Ye naturally caught global attention after that and his subsequent film, *Spring Fever* (2009), was financed by French investors. It is a story about homosexuality which is, once again, a taboo in the mainland, but his tendency to intermingle the personal with the political can be traced to these two films. Thus, these films successfully brand Lou Ye as a filmmaker who belongs to the art-house circuit but make him a banned director in China at the same time: he cannot produce films in the mainland and his films cannot be shown in China either.

If second-wave feminists argue that the personal is the political, the same applies to other forms of gender expressions, alternative sexualities, and marginalities, which explains why Lou Ye is equally interested in other groups of people at the margins, such as those with blindness in *Blind Massage*. Having been detached from his home country for almost a decade, Lou Ye returns to China and makes this very locally-specific film that deals with a timely and unique issue in the mainland. In terms of critical reception, the film captured the Best Film Award at Taiwan's Golden Horse Awards and Hong Kong's Asian Film Awards. Despite the lukewarm box office reception to the film in the mainland, one cannot deny that *Blind Massage* is easy to relate to for Chinese audiences, owing to the very fact that it is precisely about massage, an activity and pastime that many Chinese people engage in and can identify. For example, *China Labour Bulletin* (2005) reports that "there are about 30,000 to 40,000 massage workers working in some 3,000 massage parlors in Shenzhen alone," and these numbers show how much Mainland Chinese people are enthusiastically involved in massaging.

Within the context of Asia, alongside Thailand, China is another country where many massage parlors can be found, serving both locals and visitors. A few things that distinguish these Mainland Chinese parlors from, for instance, those in Bangkok would be that many of these Chinese parlors hire, or are even owned, by blind people—people who rely on labor work even more so than the able-bodied population. For example, one popular parlor in Shenzhen's Luohu Commercial City where a lot of Hong-Kongers and Westerners frequent is precisely called "Blind Bing," operated by a blind person named Bing. While Thai massage emphasizes massaging the body and the feet, Chinese massage—or *tui na*, the Chinese film title of *Blind Massage*—very often involves acupuncture and cupping therapy, where acupoints, accuracy, and preciseness are crucial. This explains how and why a lot of blind people in the mainland choose this career and sometimes gain enormous success in this particular business. Another characteristic of masseurs in China, be they blind or not, is that most if not all of them are drifters. After the open-door policy, many Mainland Chinese people move from rural areas or villages to first-tier cities like Shanghai and Shenzhen or second-tier ones like Chongqing and Nanjing to earn a living. Very often, these labors, with no skills and barely any education, have to obtain physical jobs like waiters, constructor workers, and of course masseurs as well as sex workers. Willa Dong and Yu Cheng (2017), for instance, note that "Shenzhen is a particularly important example for other metropolises in China as the first city to adopt market-based economic reforms that are being implemented throughout the country" (186) in their analysis of migration and sex work in Shenzhen. Li Xueying (2013) also reports that her therapist "had come to the southern boomtown city to make his fortune" when she visited a Shenzhen massage parlor. Since the 1990s, China has stepped away from traditional socialism and entered a new mode of capitalism. It is a form of capitalism with Chinese characteristics, or what Zhang Xudong (2008) calls post-socialism, "a system more open to the construction of a social world which transcends the dogmas of capitalism or socialism to get in touch with the productive forces of a world of life with all its social and cultural specificities and complexities" (16). These labor forces, including but not limited to those who are sightless, seize the opportunity to earn fast money and lead a stable life by moving to bigger, developed cities. However, for some individuals who are blind, they may face even more frustration and insecurity. In any case, *Blind Massage* captures this sentiment by narrating the drama involved with such a massage parlor in Nanjing. Ma Yingli, the scriptwriter of the film, adapts Bi Feiyu's (2008) novel *Massage* which beautifully conveys that blind people—as in other forms of marginalities and disabilities—eat, love, make fun, have joy, make love, have dignity, and make sacrifices—just like any other people. This is also what disability studies scholars have long been fostering: the normalization and neutralization of disability. For instance, Tobin Siebers (2012), among others, boldly puts forward the following:

> If sex is walking together on a beach, if it is running across a field of flowers to meet an embrace, what is the nature of sex apart from the ability to walk or to run? If a

person's wheel chair gets stuck in the sand or if low vision makes it unfathomable to dash across a field, does it mean that this person will have little chance of having sex? Clearly people who do not do these things or go to these places manage to have sex, but that is not exactly the point. The point is to ask how the ideology of ability determines how we think about sex [44–45].

Whether it is fair, or in what capacity to represent people with disabilities is one thing, and whether casting sighted actors and actresses to reenact blind people's lives is appropriate is another. This essay seeks to interrogate these issues as well as the possibilities of disability empowerment when sightlessness is depicted on screen, and the readerly model of interpretation helps to center the empowerment of people with disability so that their voices, very often ignored, neglected, or distorted by mainstream media, can be fairly heard.

Partly since it is adapted from a piece of literature, *Blind Massage* remains rather poetic throughout the entire narrative and is indebted to is original fiction. It is also full of clichés: both literary and stereotypical ones regarding sightlessness, but that does not diminish the value of the film in terms of portraying blind life in Mainland China. The film's aesthetic and realist dimensions both account for its acclamation. The adapted screenplay is acknowledged and recognized by Taiwan's Golden Horse Awards, though one may find some lines too poetic and romanticized for a film that deals mostly with blindness—a disability after all. Disability studies critics are often concerned with the over-sentimentalization of disability experiences, be it suffering or life as a whole. Rosmarie Garland-Thomson (2009), for instance, contends that the "sentimental produces the sympathetic victim or helpless sufferer needing protection or succor and invoking pity, inspiration, and frequent contributions" (63). In contrast to the Western context, the script of *Blind Massage* as a Chinese piece uses neither apathy nor sympathy to scrutinize visual impairment, but rather poeticizes and even aestheticizes blindness. This is rather unique in a film portraying disability issues. I argue, nevertheless, that Lou Ye manages to strike a balance between romanticizing and actually narrating the lives of those who are sightless.

Through the use of a wide range of filmic techniques such as the shaky handheld camera, overexposure, blank/black screen, distorted close-ups, and subjective, yet blurry, and out-focused point of view, a rather realist approach is adopted. Similar to his Sixth Generation contemporaries like Jia Zhangke, Lou adopts an observational and documentary-like approach to depict and explore sightlessness. There is always a dilemma by saying that media representations, and films are becoming something non-commercial, alternative, or even artsy when people with disabilities are shown on screen, as they are involved in the marginality discourse. On the one hand, viewers may worry about exploitation, as portraying people with disabilities inevitably involves appropriation. On the other hand, representing people with visual conditions on screen also means that they have a presence in the mainstream media, despite the stereotypes and stigmatizations that often accompany marginalized groups when showcased in the media. Lou Ye, as someone who strays between the mainstream/commercial and the art-house/alternative, successfully narrates *Blind Massage* as a story about blind people without further mythicizing blindness. He artfully allows both those with visual conditions and those without to identify with bits and pieces of the narrative. Within the first five to ten minutes, he demonstrates the ways in which *Blind Massage* blends fictionality and authenticity to formulate a picture that aptly represents the experience of disability by this group of masseurs.

The film opens with something rather banal: a brief explanation of how and why one of the main protagonists, Xiao Ma, loses his eyesight in a traffic accident when he was young. After the accident, as a result of struggling to fit in and get along with his peers, he tries to commit suicide. Throughout the rest of the film, the camera randomly pans to the scar on his neck as a constant reminder of his painful past. This serves as a strong contrast to the end of the film because Ma is the only character who ends up living a fulfilling life by marrying an able-bodied woman and opening his own massage parlor. As a film that portrays disability, it suitably gives presence to the experiences of people with disabilities by continually switching between a first and third person point of view to tell the stories of the characters. While there is an omniscient voice narrating the entire story, her voice does not dominate the narrative and she is only heard from time to time throughout the film. The blind characters themselves also have their own stories to tell, and do so directly. For instance, after narrating Ma's childhood, the viewer is introduced to another male protagonist, Fu Ming, who introduces himself to the audience. When he tells others who he is, he says, "Fu Ming," "Fu" as in resume, and "Ming" as in brightness, which indicates his name is definitely not random. In other words, his name can be literally translated as resuming brightness, which is of course an utmost irony for a blind man. This opening scene is interesting and significant in the sense that it separates the sightless from the sighted. Ma is sent to a special school for the blind and Fu Ming is refused as a potential suitor in a "blind" date scenario by an able-bodied girl's parents for being sightless. Fu Ming even says that where there are eyes, there is the mainstream, and that the blind precisely does not belong to this mainstream society. Thus, the two are cast as unbelonging in mainstream society, a theme that resonates throughout the entire film.

This foretelling is even followed by a special way of filmmaking that is unique. Unlike a "normal" film where opening credits usually scroll in writing on the screen, for this film, the narrator actually speaks the words out aloud. For instance, the word "director" and the name of the director himself are said aloud along with the entire cast and titles of the film. This suggests that the filmmaker seeks to provide accommodations so that everyone may "watch" the film, ironically a film about blindness. And in a macro sense, this bridges the gap between ability and disability via something unusual and out of the norm, like narrating the credits aloud. This outset of the film prepares audiences to be immersed into an alternative world and subtly suggests that for one, the barrier between the blind and the seeing is and will always be there, but for two, while they live and lead their own lives, it is still possible that the two groups can coexist. The coexistence in question may inscribe something hierarchal, like what Longmore (2003) observes: "Typically, disabled characters lack insight about themselves and other people, and require emotional education, usually by a nondisabled character. In the end, nondisabled persons supply the solution: they compel the disabled individuals to confront themselves" (137–138). The hierarchy might be solid, but massage, as I would argue, is being used as a metaphor to soothe things and relieve the pressure in question.

Beyond Blindness: Love and Desire

> "To be obsessed with a concept. The concept of love. The scent of love is the scent of danger. You see it all when you are blind."
>
> —Lou Ye, *Blind Massage*

As the plot unfolds, the audience is left to question whether the able/disabled dichotomy is necessarily significant when Lou Ye asks if there are values, such as beauty, that go beyond eyesight. For instance, possessing proper eyesight does not essentially mean having the ability to envision, and sometimes it is those with visual disabilities rather than the sighted who maintain and acquire vision. This also hints at the rather poetic, literary, if not romanticized and aestheticized side of the film: sentimentalism may be subject to criticism, yet it is also an effective tool to dissect the issues surrounding disability, suffering, and loss brought about by being disabled that some Western disability films tend to highlight. When it comes to sight and seeing, beauty always comes to the forefront. The notion of beauty has been interrogated by feminist and queer critics alike. Some understand beauty as a site of systemic oppression and thus critique it as an extension of the patriarchal order, while others criticize standardized modes of beauty as heteronormative regimes. As Ann Pointon and Chris Davies (1997) remind us, "It is also too simplistic to talk about 'negative' compared with 'positive' images because although disabled people are in general fairly clear about what might constitute the former, the identification of 'positive' is fraught with difficulty" (1). In the realm of disability studies, it is often asked whether more diverse and inclusive forms of recognition are available to tackle the intricate relationship between beauty and disability, especially in different forms of cultural productions like theater, dance, music, and poetry. For example, Sally Chivers and Nicole Martotić (2010) "do not intend an emphasis on physical disability per se but an emphasis on the transformation of physical difference into cultural patterns of spectacle, patterns that replicate a range of pathologizing practices that oppress people" (8–9). A case in point would be the text *Beauty Is a Verb: The New Poetry of Disability* (2011) edited by Jennifer Bartlett, Sheila Black, and Michael Northen, which is precisely an attempt to explore these issues. While clichés and stereotypes suggest blind people do not and need not care about outer beauty and thus appreciate inner beauty more, *Blind Massage* has a slightly different take. This is obvious when the female lead, Du Hong, is introduced because she is beautiful to those who can see, but to her, beauty does not matter. Her customers are amazed by how beautiful she is, and go so far as to say her beauty makes her "just like normal." The claim is alarming because it suggests that beauty only belongs to the those who can see. This statement takes us back to a fundamental issue within disability studies that keeps asking and urging for the answer: what defines ab/normality and normalcy? Within queer studies, Michael Warner (1999) argues that queers ought to stay abnormal, because resuming "normal" would mean going back to if not succumbing the heterosexual system. One must question: what would be the case if people with disabilities did the same? He asserts, "Variations from the norm, in other words, are not necessarily signs of pathology. They can become norms…. The question of what is right or healthy is something that cannot be answered simply by natural laws of the biological organism" (Warner 1999, 58). If that's the case, it can be equally argued that the blind can embrace their sightlessness which enables them to perceive the world in a radically different perspective. The notion of beauty as being understood as a norm and normal is thus suggestive.

Later on in the film, Du Hong herself also mourns that beauty is meaningless for a blind girl like her; it is a disaster. In other words, since she is blind she cannot love like the ways able-bodied people do. As shown in the film, precisely because they are not seeing, they are able to "see" more, echoing the general belief that people with disabilities like the deaf and the blind are extra if not hypersensitive regarding their senses and the sensual. Without light, they touch and caress more intensely. They rely on smell and scents, just like Xiao Ma uses her sexual fantasy's underpants to masturbate. Apparently boundless, they can be even more anxious. This swinging between feeling free and constrained is channeled throughout the entire narrative, and the urge to depict the sightless as normal is constantly contested by the ways they are seen and maltreated by the sighted. These, of course, include the discriminatory remarks they receive as well as different forms of humiliation they have to face on a daily basis. I thus argue that the massage parlor serves as a platform for love and desire to blossom. Disabled people do not only have the same right to love and be loved, but they can also enjoy sex even within the more conservative Chinese context. While admitting and acknowledging their sexual libido and deprivation, Lou Ye is trying to see love beyond vision and any boundaries regardless of their eyesight.

From the Chinese legend *The Butterfly Lovers* to Chen Kaige's *Farewell My Concubine* (1993), from established and prominent Fifth Generation Mainland Chinese filmmakers like Zhang Yimou to the Sixth Generation like Jia Zhangke, Mainland Chinese love stories always feature tragic, dramatic, and sometimes over-exaggerated moments that at times are breathtaking yet sentimentalized. In *Blind Massage*, love, lust, and desire among the blind are not only dramatized but philosophized. As mentioned above, one of the reasons would be that the literary component remains as an adapted screenplay. This, nonetheless, also brings about a rather philosophical dimension of blind love that distinguishes this film from its western counterparts situated within world cinema. The prime example in the film, undoubtedly, would be Xiao Ma and his prostitute girlfriend. This unlikely couple starts off as sex trading, but they eventually become bonded emotionally regardless of one having a disability and one without. What's more, it is precisely because of their shared marginality—one's disability and the other's work as a prostitute—that further tightens their bond. First as friends, they tell each other stories, which for Xiao Ma does not matter as to whether these stories are fake or not. In fact, throughout the entire film, "blindness" is at least taken on two levels: it represents those who are literally blind, and those who may be sighted but fail to see reality.

For instance, when Ma's girlfriend is teased for dating someone who cannot see, she defends her relationship by yelling that it is the sighted who are ultimately blind. This scene echoes the tone of the whole film that when able-bodied and people with disabilities connect, the results could be disastrous, but also fruitful. David Mitchell and Sharon Snyder (2015) state that the "strategy of intimacy and prolonged exposure to disabled bodies, communication modes, perceptual capacities, and appearances reduce feelings of estrangement from disabled people's differences" (123). While differences are understandably very difficult to eradicate, *Blind Massage* manages to record the tension and tug-of-war between the sighted and the sightless. While Ma eventually marries his girlfriend and opens a parlor of his own, other parts of the plot highlight the seemingly impossible reconciliation between the two different worlds. At one point, the barrier between the two worlds is narrated as being like light and darkness. People with sight are omniscient with their eyes, and the sightless to them are almost like another species: respected, but to be maintained at a distance. Conflicts inevitably exist, and there is hardly any harmonious, perfect reconciliation. That explains in one way or another how and why the film ends rather poetically: the narrator murmurs that the sighted and the sightless are both superstitious. In other words, they believe in destiny. They, however, cannot clearly see fate, and they are thus similarly blind in that regard. Again, this refers to some banal clichés that the blind eventually see it all, but their sightlessness offers them an alternative horizon to come to terms with hardships and perceive the world differently. Lou Ye himself also believes this stance as revealed in interviews, claiming that "the world of the sightless is broader and greater" (Zhou Xin 2014).

Lou Ye pertinently captures this essence of blindness by employing both professional actors and sight-impaired amateurs to partake in this film, forming a kaleidoscope of the love and lust in a blind massage parlor. The film thus remains a fair, objective, and ethical depiction of blind lives, be it within or outside the narrative. For instance, Lou Ye mentions that the set had to be meticulously prepared so that the blind amateurs would find it easier to adapt to the filming environment. He describes, "No grip track nor lighting cable was allowed to run across the set to avoid possible stumbles. Once a prop was in place, it could not be moved or else the blind actors and actress wouldn't be able to reach it working from their memory" (Zhou Xin 2014). In any case, if massage is taken as a metaphor to emphasize the significance of human, sensual touch for blind people, then the desire to be seen and recognized from the disabled population is complicated by the fact that *Blind Massage* is, after all, a filmic mediation. While some may question or even challenge whether it is legitimate and ethical to reenact blind people as such, I would argue that when it comes to mediating disability, there could not be a stainless, legitimate representation that is perfect. All media representations are political in the sense that power and power struggles are involved, and at the end of the day, it is hard to conclude whether we are empowering or disempowering people who are sightless. Disability empowerment is ultimately crucial, and I believe that the sighted can play an equally important role in giving space and voice to the sightless in mediating blindness on screen and in various media platforms. As Hoeksema and Smit (2001) remind us, "Without a multifaceted interpretation, disability films will eventually be seen simply as political commentary, never receiving their proper critique" (41).

To that end, this essay has attempted to provide a comprehensive analysis and critique of Lou Ye's *Blind Massage*—among other Asian disability films—to offer an alternative perspective to interrogate and go beyond the dichotomy of the sighted and sightless. Hopefully, this will let readers have a sense of how a Mainland Chinese film deals with disability, and take a glimpse at the reality of blind people in the Asian context. Additionally, this analysis has also proven the inseparable relationship between disability and cinema, and disability studies and media studies in a macro sense. Understandably, people with disabilities and disability scholars have different concerns and agendas. These include basic rights, laws, policymaking, social welfare system, and mental health care, among others. From a cultural, and especially film studies point of view, however, how and why various disability communities are represented in various media forms is equally important if not more significant than the well-being of people with disabilities. It is because media representations play an extremely influential role in affecting the ways in which the general public looks at and recognizes disability experiences. As mentioned above, we are not seeking something perfect and flawless. Perfect people have no stories to tell, and it is precisely the flaws and imperfections of people with disabilities that entail their countless, heartfelt narratives mediated on the cinematic screen. This awareness—the ability and power that the media has and will always have—is something that media studies scholars ought to bear in mind when they explore disability.

REFERENCES

Bartlett, Jennifer, Sheila Black, and Michael Northen. 2011. *Beauty Is a Verb: The New Poetry of Disability*. El Paso: Cinco Puntos Press.
Cheung, Esther M. K. 2010/1. "Realisms within Conundrum." *China Perspectives*.
China Labour Bulletin. 2005. "Masseuses in China: Long Working Hours and Low Awareness of Occupational Health Risks." March 11. http://www.clb.org.hk/content/masseuses-china-long-working-hours-and-low-awareness-occupational-health-risks.
Chivers, Sally, and Nicole Markotić. 2010. *The Problem Body: Projecting Disability on Film*. Columbus: Ohio State University Press.
Dong, Willa, and Yu Cheng. 2017. "Sex Work, Migration, and Mental Health in Shenzhen." In *Learning from Shenzhen: China's Post-Mao Experiment from Special Zone to Model City*, edited by Mary Ann O'Donnell, Winnie Wong, and Jonathan Bach. Chicago: University of Chicago Press.
Garland-Thomson, Rosmarie. 2009. *Staring: How We Look*. Oxford: Oxford University Press.
Hoeksema, Thomas B., and Christopher R. Smit. 2001. "The Fusion of Film Studies and Disability Studies." In *Screening Disability: Essays on Cinema and Disability*, edited by Anthony Enns and Christopher R. Smit. Lanham, MD: University Press of America.
Li, Xueying. 2013. "Tales from a Shenzhen Massage Parlour." July 30. http://www.straitstimes.com/asia/tales-from-a-shenzhen-massage-parlour
Longmore, Paul. 2003. *Why I Burned My Book and Other Essays on Disability*. Philadelphia: Temple University Press.
Mitchell, David T., and Sharon L. Snyder. 2015. *The Biopolitics of Disability: Neoliberalism, Ablenationalism, and Peripheral Embodiment*. Ann Arbor: University of Michigan Press.
Norden, Martin. 1994. *The Cinema of Isolation: A History of Physical Disability in the Movies*. New Brunswick: Rutgers University Press.
Pointon, Ann, and Chris Davies. 1997. *Framed: Interrogating Disability in the Media*. London: British Film Institute.
Siebers, Tobin. 2012. "A Sexual Culture for Disabled People." In *Sex and Disability*, edited by Robert McRuer and Anna Mollow. Durham: Duke University Press.

Warner, Michael. 1999. *The Trouble with Normal: Sex, Politics, and the Ethics of Queer Life.* New York: Free Press.

Zhang, Xudong. 2008. *Postsocialism and Cultural Politics: China in the Last Decade of the Twentieth Century.* Durham: Duke University Press.

Zhou, Xin. 2014. "Interview: Lou Ye." June 30. http://www.filmcomment.com/blog/interview-lou-ye/.

What's Disability Got to Do with It?

Media Accounts of Oscar Pistorius Before and After the Death of Reeva Steenkamp

Clare Harvey

Oscar Pistorius is the South African world renowned double-amputee Paralympian. As a baby he had Polio, and both of his legs were amputated at the knees when he was 11 months old. Pistorius fatally shot his girlfriend, Reeva Steenkamp, on Valentine's Day 2013. He claimed not guilty for murder maintaining that he mistook Reeva Steenkamp for a house intruder. Initially, he was convicted of culpable homicide (manslaughter) in 2014 and served one year in prison. An appeals court then overturned this decision. In 2016 he was sentenced to a six-year jail sentence for the murder of Reeva Steenkamp (Press Association 2016). Perhaps inevitably, the media's portrayal and societal view of Pistorius changed after the death of Reeva Steenkamp and within the subsequent court cases. He went from being deemed as a hero who had "overcome" his physical limitations (Davis 2014a) to a vulnerable disabled individual. Further, various media formats, including social media platforms and the print media, began to place greater, and negative, emphasis on Pistorius' disability. The essay will highlight how the media portrays individuals with disabilities, referencing examples from the media coverage of the legal case of Pistorius. Typically disabled people are represented as weak and atypical in the media, which perpetuates ableism in the public arena. Those in the media must be cognizant of the importance of holistic reporting taking into account both disability theory at large, and representations of disability, rather than focusing on literal legal issues, as was the case in the media rendering of Pistorius. It will be argued that the psychosocial reasons for the shift in media perceptions and portrayal of Pistorius reproduce ableist assumptions and representations. These ableist depictions were, of course, present, albeit in a different form, before the death of Reeva Steenkamp and the trials.

The term *media* is used in this essay to refer to South African and International news agencies. It refers to newspaper print media, as well as news and sports television channels. This term also refers to social media posts including those on Twitter and Facebook, of which there were countless daily posts during both of the Pistorius trials. These posts are made by members of society (who are also often employed by media agencies).

The analysis will begin by defining the term *disability* and understanding how disability is designated as a label. The original model of understanding disability is a medical one (Ryan 2005). Proponents of this model believe disability is solely located within the person's physical body. The medical model is known as the deficit model because it focuses on the biological and often pathological aspects of disability within the person (Watermeyer 2012). In contrast to the medical model of disability, the social model suggests disability is external to the individual. One experiences oneself as disabled due to constraining institutional and societal structures (Barns and Mercer 2005). Thus "disability" is experienced outside of the body due to social conditions. The social model importantly differentiates disability and impairment (Shakespeare 2006). Disability is a result of social exclusion; whereas impairment is a physical limitation. Hence, according to this model, disability is a form of social oppression as a result of one's impairment(s) (Prilleltensky 2004). However, the two labels, disability and impairment, are often used interchangeably because in many cases impairment gives way to societally-constructed disabilities, as evident in the existence of centralized stairs instead of ramps in most buildings, amongst other examples.

More recently there has been a growing call for disability to be conceptualized through a psychological, specifically psychoanalytic, lens (Marks 1999; Watermeyer 2012). Traditionally, psychoanalytic understandings of disability have been greatly criticized. When psychoanalysis was originally applied to disability experiences it supported the deficit or medical model since many of the psychoanalytic theories served to pathologize and institutionalize people with disabilities (Goodley 2011). However, various theorists contend that psychoanalytic theory is a most relevant method for understanding the internal emotional experiences and psychic processes of disabled people (Marks 1999; Watermeyer 2006; Harvey 2015). Furthermore, a psychoanalytic model of disability can be utilized to understand how able-bodied/minded people perceive and experience disability. Thus, the essay focuses on exploring the reactions that both able-bodied and people with disabilities have toward people with disabilities. Such responses most often incorporate the psychological defense mechanism of splitting (Klein 1946; Hinshelwood 1998). The discussion will provide insight into how disability produces anxiety often causing the person to engage with disability negatively. Thus, the argument will demonstrate the need to attend to the psychological, and specifically psychoanalytic, experiences of disability, and the subsequent portrayal of disabled people so that ableism is not perpetuated. The discussion will specifically refer to the case of Pistorius to highlight such reactions and tendencies.

The Two Faces of Disability

Disability is often approached by society and the media in an ambivalent manner because people often engage in what psychologists call the defense mechanism of splitting (Klein 1946). When feelings of anxiety are experienced in relation to another, the person often unconsciously splits the subject into a binary to manage the overwhelming feelings. The binary is a purely good/bad perception, or an only positive/negative awareness (Klein 1946). Defending against anxiety by splitting results in an unintegrated psychical function since the individual does not recognize the other as a complete person. This is because it is too anxiety provoking to be aware of perceived weakness and badness in another. Splitting in adults is an unhealthy defense mechanism because its use suggests a person is experiencing great difficulty in holding psychical organization together as a whole (Klein 1946). Engaging in splitting suggests the person cannot tolerate mixed feelings such as love and hate, pleasure as well as angst within the self, and within others. People resort to splitting to manage their overwhelming emotions. The converse is a non-split and integrated psychological self that functions in a state of healthy ambivalence in which both difficult and positive feelings can be consciously felt for the self and others. Those who have disabilities can also split in relation to other people with disabilities. Disabled people can engage in pitying others with disabilities, particularly those whose disability is perceived as "worse" than their own.

Accordingly, one construction of disability, by the media and society, is as something that elicits shame for the person living with the disability. Feelings of self-pity are split off and projected onto the disabled individual. The defensive maneuver of projection and splitting (Klein 1946; Hinshelwood 1998), results in able-bodied people no longer feeling uncomfortably sorry for their own vulnerable, fallible aspects because these intolerable character-istics are felt to reside in the disabled other. Subsequently acts of kindness and assistance by non-disabled people are elicited in an attempt to make themselves feel better about their own "fortunate" unimpaired state. Thus they do not have to think about, and feel, the accompanying feelings related to their own sense of weakness and bodily mortality—aspects everybody has.

The other viewpoint of disability is as something that a person "overcomes" and thus disability no longer exists in ways that negatively impacts on the person's life. Consequently, a disabled person is given heroic status, a role Pistorius was granted before the death of Reeva Steenkamp. Some even viewed him as "superabled" (Booher 2011) which is a form of splitting, and thus psychologically unhealthy. This suggests that people do not engage with Pistorius as a whole person and subsequently he is never portrayed fully, with strengths as well as flaws. The media, including newspaper headlines, has often referred to Pistorius as the "Blade Runner." Indeed this is the title of his autobiography (Pistorius 2009). The "fastest man on no legs" (Sokolove 2012) is another media phrase used to refer to him. These terms effectively accentuate Pistorius' otherness, and people are drawn to the fact that he has successfully "beaten" his physical impairments. In this discourse, disability is the focus and is viewed positively. Consequently, able-bodied people feel reassured that should they acquire a disability, it would only be a hindrance if they were unable to work hard to overcome it. Thus, their anxiety, and other challenging feelings, is subdued. Further, those living with a disability feel less anxious since they too may believe that disability does not have to be a limitation.

Indeed, Pistorius was awarded the Helen Rollason award at the BBC Sports Personality of the Year in 2007, which is awarded to athletes for "outstanding achievement in the face of adversity" (Lindsay 2013). Consequently, he has had many followers who enthuse about his triumph over hardship. After Pistorius' ambition was achieved in the 2012 Olympic Games by competing against able-bodied individuals, he became a superstar and was granted role-model status as having "'overcome" his impairments. This performance "seemed the ultimate indication that the athlete had, indeed, triumphed over his disability. It was easy to believe his claim not to see himself as disabled" (Davis 2014a). Garland-Thomson (2013) believed this achievement illustrated how disability may benefit the individual, rather than hinder, which is a popular viewpoint taken by the media. Shortly after this, *Time Magazine* named Pistorius one of the hundred most influential people in the world (Gregory 2012).

Within media discourse, Pistorius became like the general able-bodied population. He was "not" disabled. His disability was not perceived as something negative and hence he did not need to be pitied. Since Pistorius overcame his odds, the rest of society could rest assured that their potential fallibility and bodily vulnerability could also be transcended, if need be. Up until the death of Reeva Steenkamp, and the consequent legal trials, Pistorius was portrayed optimistically by the media, as a phenomenal individual who had "overcome" his disability. However, as with anything that is constructed as binary, the other aspects that make up Pistorius were "forgotten" and buried in his, and the public's, psyche. This erasure comes at great cost to an individual's psychical organization and functioning since the accompanying difficult feelings of these hidden aspects remain in the background and can cause psychological distress.

The media was not the only entity that portrayed Pistorius' disability as a binary. Pistorius himself, in various formats, continuously minimized his disability. *The New York Times* quoted him as saying, "I don't see myself as disabled. There's nothing I can't do that able-bodied athletes can do" (Longman 2007). He has also said that he does not feel a particular exhilarating sensation in beating non-disabled athletes as this would imply he was dwelling on his disability. "You have to move past it," he said. "Everyone has setbacks. I'm no different. I happen to have no legs. That's pretty much the fact" (Sokolove 2012). Hence, Pistorius controls his anxiety by focusing on ableist perspectives and disavowing his disability. This serves to entrench an ableist mind-set in a very public figure who has a disability. Such an ableist perspective has influenced how the public perceives disability, or in some cases, pushes disability entirely into the periphery of people's minds.

Pistorius' mother appears to have had a strong influence in his tendency to split his identity and downplay his impairments. This propensity to not acknowledge his disability may have contributed to him wanting to achieve. However, he is also left not being perceived as a whole, psychologically integrated individual. From a very young age, his disability and accompanying potential vulnerabilities were not acknowledged within his family. Pistorius' mother wrote a letter to him at the time of his amputation: "The real loser is never the person who crosses the finishing line last. The real loser is the person who sits on the side. The person who does not even try to compete" (Pistorius 2009, vii). According to the psychologist's report from his legal trial, "the word disabled was never mentioned" during his childhood (Davis 2014a). In Pistorius' interview with *The Telegraph* in 2005, he is quoted as saying, "I could not have wished for better parents because they brought me up exactly the same way as my elder brother … and younger sister." This is reminiscent of Pistorius' tendency to go to great lengths to be perceived as "normal," not disabled. Society tends to portray disabled individuals as abnormal. He goes on to say, "Anyway, what is disabled? Some people view themselves as disabled because they have one or two disabilities. But what about the millions and millions of abilities they have?" This suggests Pistorius' inclination to "ignore" and downplay his disability; rather than consider it as one of the many different aspects of himself. He is relying on the psychological defense mechanism of splitting, as well as denial (Freud 1964; Bowins 2004). Individuals block and reject from consciousness those aspects that cause them to feel anxious and ashamed. Further, Pistorius tends to engage in passing, a phenomenon whereby individuals attempt to minimize or hide their disability so that they are perceived as able-bodied (Goffman 1968; Bogart 2014). Passing has the potential of causing serious harm to one's sense of self and self-esteem.

The Telegraph 2005 article ends with the words "Pistorius is not a disabled gold medallist and world record holder, merely a gold medallist and world record holder with no legs." This is an indication that the author too, like so many, has conformed to the common social narrative of describing Pistorius as having "overcome" his disability, thus exceptionalizing him in relation to others who have not "transcended" their disabilities. Indeed, for Swartz (2013), "Pistorius has become such a mainstream icon that his impairments seem irrelevant" (1159). The media and societal tendency to view disabled people in such a binary fashion, and specifically a celebrity role model in such a divided way, is harmful for all people with disabilities. It is potentially problematic for those who are faced with their more difficult feelings surrounding their disability and who are not managing to incorporate their strengths into their overall functioning. These people may feel pressure to conform to Pistorius' way of managing his disability by downplaying it and even discounting its presence.

A different narrative has emerged since the fatal incident involving Reeva Steenkamp, Pistorius' deceased girlfriend. According to Davis (2014), the "image of Pistorius as having transcended disability has been largely shattered by his murder trial." Pistorius' disability was linked with negativity and difficult emotions during his two trials and the accompanying accounts by the media. One of the main arguments made by his legal team was the sense of vulnerability Pistorius experiences in relation to his disability. The defense's witness, Wayne Derman, the chief medical officer for the 2012 South African Paralympic team, testified that "Pistorius justifiably feared more for his safety than an able-bodied person, because disabled people are more likely to be the victims of attacks" (Davis 2014a). The lead defense counsel, Barry Roux, took this argument further when he compared Pistorius' fear of being a target because of his disability as akin to a woman fearing domestic abuse from a violent husband. This woman develops "an exaggerated response to danger" and a low frustration tolerance, and could potentially kill her husband as a result (Phipps 2014). Barry Roux stated that Pistorius feels insecure and vulnerable, especially without his prostheses, and that this "fear is consistent with the responses of a disabled man with a 'slow burn' of insecurities" (Phipps 2014). Accordingly, disability is negatively equated with vulnerability and burdensome, which is the deficit viewpoint of the medical model of disability.

During Pistorius' 2014 trial sentencing, ableist issues of pity and vulner-ability related to disability were focused upon at length. Pistorius' defense team utilized his disability as a reason for him to receive a lighter sentence, arguing that he is "afflicted by too severe a disability to serve a jail sentence" (Duggan 2014). They raised concerns that prisons could not adequately cater for his disability. However, the CEO of the QuadPara Association of South Africa (QASA) Ari Seirlis (2014), angrily retaliated, saying that allowing Pis-torius to be a "law unto himself ... could be devastating to others with dis-abilities." Ari Seirlis (2014) requested that Judge Masipa not accept that Pistorius' disability makes him too vulnerable to be punished because of the potential negative ramifications for people with disabilities. Hence, he stated, people with disabilities "will be cursed if we are perceived as vulnerable and unpredictable." Further, State Chief Prosecutor Gerrie Nel accused Pistorius of using his disability when it suits him (City Press 2014). Thus, disability was continued to be cast in a negative light.

Mental health professionals also narrated Pistorius' life with a disability during the trial. These narratives were closely aligned with the pre-existing and powerful medical model of disability. Dr. Merryl Vorster, a forensic psy-chiatrist, testified that his upbringing and early amputation made Pistorius feel threatened. She diagnosed Pistorius with a generalized anxiety disorder (Riccobono 2014). Jonathan Scholtz, the lead clinical psychologist in Pistorius' forensic psychological assessment, described Pistorius' attitude to his dis-ability, "it's interesting that his biggest dream was to race against able-bodied athletes, perhaps an attempt to give psychological credence to his mother's position that he was not disabled" (Smith 2014). Jonathan Scholtz further found that when Pistorius felt physically threatened "a fear response follows that might seem extraordinary when viewed from the perspective of a normal-bodied person, but normal in the context of a disabled person with his history" (Smith 2014). Yet again, this testimony aligns disability with weakness, whereby its pathology is reminiscent of the medical models under-standing of disability. Jonathan Scholtz explained that Pistorius suffered "extreme self-consciousness and anxiety about being ridiculed or embar-rassed" (Davis 2014b). Indeed, in Pistorius' testimony during the trial, he admitted to feeling "shy" and "embarrassed" when people see his prostheses (Davis 2014b). Pistorius' own discomfort aligns with how others felt when forced to witness his disability. For example, some social media commentators admitted feeling unnerved when they saw Pistorius' legs without his artificial prostheses in court (Davis 2014b). This reinforces the earlier point in this essay, that non-disabled people often feel apprehension to disability. Pistorius' reaction to being seen without his prostheses suggests he is an insecure, fear-ful, and psychologically wounded individual because of his disability. This is a very different Pistorius to the one known before the death of Reeva

Steenkamp, who was a strong and powerful sporting hero who had "transcended" his disability (Bansel and Davies 2014). Thus, since disability is popularly linked with negativity and weakness, those seeking to save Pistorius from prison argued his disability alone gave him reason enough to pull the trigger. This narrative, of course, is at odds with the super-achiever and fearless athlete portrayed before Reeva Steenkamp's death.

However, many media commentators and scholars in disability studies have expressed concern that the "use of disability in his defense may have elements of expedience" (Davis 2014a and b). Some within the disability community argue that the Pistorius trial perpetuated the negative assumptions and prejudices surrounding disability. For instance, Carol Glazer, the president of the National Organization on Disability in the United States, suggested that coupling Pistorius' reactions to having a physical disability with mental illness equate to "exploitation" (Lupkin 2014). During the trial, it was argued that Pistorius has an anxiety disorder, stemming from his perceived helplessness, that triggered his fight or flight responses the night he murdered his girlfriend. On Valentine's Day 2013, when Pistorius heard a noise in his bathroom, he could not flee because he was not wearing his prosthesis. Consequently, his defense team and the media suggested his anxiety and fear left him with no better option than to shoot. However, various disability groups disagreed that Pistorius' disability could be to blame for the shooting of Reeva Steenkamp. Carol Glazer went on to say that there tends to be a "'knee-jerk' reaction to assume that becoming disabled is 'the most traumatic experience on earth,' but it's not true because people adapt" (Lupkin 2014). Furthermore, to suggest that someone with a disability automatically feels helpless or in the weaker position, and therefore, any action taken in such a position, such as murder, should be excused as a mistake is a problematic assumption. The narrow perspective that disability is essentially a traumatic, weak experience corresponds with the traditional, deficit medical model of disability, and continues an ableist tradition.

Additionally, Garland-Thomson (2013) was concerned about the potential inferences that may be made between disability and a character flaw due to the shooting and trials. In the case of Pistorius, this character flaw includes his feelings of anxiety and rage. Since the shooting of Reeva Steenkamp, Pistorius' history of anger and aggression towards women was highlighted by the media. Garland-Thomson (2013) further worried that Pistorius' actions would be understood by larger society as arising from feelings of resentment which people are assumed to develop because of their disability. Consequently, disability may be related to a character flaw because disability is easily associated with a disadvantage in a person. This is most certainly not the case since it suggests disabled people are "abnormal" and need to be "fixed." Taken further, while the Pistorius of the pre–Reeva Steenkamp shooting was seen as the exceptional person who had "transcended" his disability to the extent that he was no longer conscious of it, the Pistorius on trial was seen as psychologically wounded because of his disability.

A second court case was held in 2016 when South Africa's Supreme Court of Appeal upgraded Pistorius' conviction from culpable homicide to murder. During this second trial, Pistorius' physical disability was highlighted more than it was during the initial court case. Since Pistorius was not wearing his prosthetic legs when he shot Reeva Steenkamp, he stated that it left him vulnerable and needing to defend himself. During the sentencing hearing, defense lawyer Barry Roux asked Pistorius to remove his prostheses to demonstrate his "physical vulnerability" (AFP 2016). The courtroom saw him walk unsteadily on his amputated stumps while crying. This was an apparent attempt at gaining able-bodied people's pity for the accused. The dramatic scene served dual purposes; the first was to illustrate that Pistorius was vulnerable to an intruder, and second, to prove he was ill-suited for jail because of his vulnerability. The scene created much pity for the accused. Chainey (2016) argued that pity has been unhelpful to disabled people because it objectifies the person "as less than fully human." Of course, people with disabilities are fully people, who possess both weaknesses and strengths. However, as Young (2013) wrote, Pistorius' dual portrayal, both pre- and post-trials, suggests that as a role model, those who achieve great things are *only* great. This is an impossible ideal to live up to. It is challenging for the general population to view role models as complex and flawed, even more so when these role models have disabilities. However, role models are imperfect and contain weaknesses as well as strengths, as all individuals do. Young (2013) continued, "in a world that barely accepts the idea of a disabled man who would protest a victory on the track [when Pistorius lost the 200m at the Paralympics in 2012 he lodged a protest against the winning athlete], we are ill-prepared to cope with the idea of a disabled man charged with murder." Consequently, this binary outlook maintains inequality, and disabled people are perceived as incompetent and hopeless.

Before Pistorius' lawyer, Barry Roux, asked him to walk without his prostheses Roux stated to the court, "I don't want to overplay disability ... but the time has come that we must just look [at Pistorius] with different eyes" (Press Association 2016). Barry Roux continued to highlight the effects of Pistorius' disability: "It is three o'clock in the morning, it is dark, he is on his stumps ... his balance is seriously compromised and ... he would not be able to defend himself. He was anxious, he was frightened" (AFP 2016). This is a very partial view of Pistorius, and of disability, as someone/something vulnerable and bad. Further, the perception that disability is not integrated as one part of Pistorius' personhood is prevalent.

Following this demonstration, Judge Masipa agreed that Pistorius should not be judged as the individual who "won gold medals" but rather like the "vulnerable" man without prostheses that he was (Press Association 2016). The tendency to split representations of disability is obvious. "The life of the accused will never be the same.... He is a fallen hero who has lost his career and been ruined financially. He cannot be at peace," continued Judge Masipa (Munusamy 2016). Hence, Pistorius is portrayed as a broken man, who is less than. Judge Masipa persisted, Pistorius the Paralympian and Pistorius without his legs are "two different persons" and "ignoring this fact would lead to an injustice" (Press Association 2016). The binary view of Pistorius (and consequently of disability) is blatant which has implications for disabled people who attempt to integrate their disability as one aspect of their multifaceted identities. Further, this view entrenches an ableist outlook in society, continuing the perception that disabled people are weak and need to be pitied.

Gerrie Nel, State Chief Prosecutor, insisted during the hearing that "pity will play no part in this sentence" (Chainey 2016). However, the suggested minimum jail sentence for murder in South Africa is fifteen years, and Pistorius received a lenient sentence of six years. Thus, it is difficult to believe that pitying disabled people did not play a major role in this legal case, as well as in the media coverage thereof. Further, Chainey (2016) argued that the "fear of disability is so deeply embedded in our cultural psyche that it could not have been far from the judge's mind." Hence, able-bodied people continue to fear their own vulnerability; and disabled people are viewed in a binary mode, as not fully psychically integrated and completely human.

Conclusion

With the shooting and consequent death of his girlfriend Reeva Steenkamp, Pistorius' disability, as well as disability in general, is viewed by society and the media more negatively. Specifically, disability is seen as a weakness and thus the disabled person needs to be pitied. The resulting portrayal is that because of his disability Pistorius is vulnerable and thus needed to shoot. It is difficult and demanding for disabled and non-disabled people to engage with this viewpoint. It has been argued in the essay that able-bodied people struggle to engage with notions of disability since it reminds them of their own sense of mortality and bodily vulnerability, and the resulting shameful, discomforting feelings that are evoked (Marks 1999). These intolerable thoughts and accompanying emotions are often psychologically defended against because they are too anxiety provoking to think about. People do not want to be reminded of what could have been, or what could still happen to them, that they may become dependent on others and thus perceived as a burden. According to Watermeyer and Swartz (2008), notions surrounding disability evoke haunting and anxiety-provoking experiences for non-disabled individuals. If Pistorius' disability was portrayed by the media as more of an integrated aspect of who he is, his followers would have to admit that he too is at times vulnerable and flawed. Consequently, this would speak to non-disabled people's sense of weakness and potential for bodily flaws. Instead, people revert to the psychological defense mechanism of splitting.

Disability needs to be represented in a more appropriate and psychologically diverse manner, as an integrated aspect of a person's identity. People with disabilities need to be recognized as fully human rather than as particularities with possibly different moral and psychological principles. Accordingly, Pistorius' disability should be portrayed in the media as shaping aspects of his more positive characteristics and strengths, *as well as* his weaknesses and more negative characteristics. This is a more appropriate way to regard the presence of disability in a person's life, rather than the traditional societal and media response as being something to pity or to overcome, as epitomized in the Pistorius example. Everyone's story needs to be understood as everyone has elements of dependence and vulnerability.

References

AFP. 2016. "Oscar Pistorius Walks Without Prosthetics in Court to Highlight Disability Ahead of Sentencing." *First Post*, June 15. http://www.firstpost.com/sports/oscar-pistorius-walks-without-prosthetics-in-court-to-highlight-disability-ahead-of-sentencing-2836958.html.

Bansel, Pete, and Bronwyn Davies. 2014. "Assembling Oscar, Assembling South Africa, Assembling Affects." *Emotion, Space and Society*. http://dx.doi.org/10.1016/j.emospa.2014.04.002.

Barns, Colin, and Geof Mercer. 2005. *The Social Model of Disability: Europe and the Majority World*. Leeds: Disability Press.

Bogart, Kathleen R. 2014. "The Role of Disability Self-Concept in Adaptation to Congenital or Acquired Disability." *Rehabilitation Psychology* 59(1): 107–115.

Booher, Amanda. 2011. "Defining Pistorius." *Disability Studies Quarterly* 31(3). http://dsq-sds.org/article/view/1673/1598.

Bowins, Brad. 2004. "Psychological Defense Mechanisms: A New Perspective." *The American Journal of Psychoanalysis* 64(1): 1–26.

Chainey, Naomi. 2016. "The Light Sentencing of Oscar Pistorius Is an Insult to People with Disabilities." *Daily Life*, July 11. http://www.dailylife.com.au/news-and-views/dl-opinion/the-light-sentencing-of-oscar-pistorius-is-an-insult-to-people-with-disabilities-2016 0710-gq2ekp.html.

Davis, Rebecca. 2014a. "Oscar Pistorius Murder Trial: What's Disability Got to Do with It?" *The Guardian*, July 8. https://www.theguardian.com/world/2014/jul/08/oscar-pistorius-murder-trial-disability

_____. 2014b. "Oscar Pistorius and the Paradox of the Disabled Super-Athlete." *Daily Maverick*, July 11. http://www.dailymaverick.co.za/article/2014-07-07-oscar-pistorius-and-the-paradox-of-the-disabled-super-athlete/#.VBGMRsKSySq.

Duggan, Oliver. 2014. "How Gerrie Nel and Barry Roux Argued the Sentencing of Oscar Pistorius." *The Telegraph*, October 21. http://www.telegraph.co.uk/news/worldnews/oscar-pistorius/11174966/How-Gerrie-Nel-and-Barry-Roux-argued-the-sentencing-of-Oscar-Pistorius.html.

Freud, Sigmund. 1964. "The Neuro-Psychosis of Defense." In *The Standard Edition of the*

Complete Psychological Works of Sigmund Freud, Volume 3, edited by James Strachey, 45–61. London: Hogarth Press.

Garland-Thomson, Rosemarie. 2013. "Elegy for Oscar Pistorius." *Aljazeera*, March 14. http://www.aljazeera.com/indepth/opinion/2013/03/20133148645751304.html.

Goffman, Erving. 1963. *Stigma: Notes on the Management of Spoiled Identity*. Harmondsworth: Penguin.

Goodley, Dan. 2011. "Social Psychoanalytic Disability Studies." *Disability & Society* 26(6): 715–728.

Gregory, Sean. 2012. "Oscar Pistorius." *Time*, April 18. http://content.time.com/time/specials/packages/article/0,28804,2111975_2111976_2112134,00.html.

Harvey, Clare. 2015. "Maternal Subjectivity in Mothering a Child with a Disability: A Psychoanalytical Perspective." *Agenda* 29(2): 89–100.

Hinshelwood, Robert. 1998. *A Dictionary of Kleinian Thought*. London: Free Association Books.

Klein, Melanie. 1946. "Notes on Some Schizoid Mechanisms." *International Journal of Psychoanalysis* 27: 99–110.

Lindsay, Jamie. 2013. "Oscar Pistorius: Timeline." *The Telegraph*, February 18. http://www.telegraph.co.uk/news/worldnews/africaandindianocean/southafrica/9879016/Oscar-Pistorius-timeline.html.

Longman, Jere. 2007. "An Amputee Sprinter: Is He Disabled or Too-Abled?" *The New York Times*, May 15. http://www.nytimes.com/2007/05/15/sports/othersports/15runner.html?pagewanted=all&_r=0.

Lupkin, Sydney. 2014. "Disability Does Not Justify Pistorius Shooting, Groups Say." *ABC News*, July 22. http://abcnews.go.com/Health/disability-justify-pistorius-shooting-groups/story?id=24401355

MacDougall, Kathleen. 2006. "'Ag Shame' and Superheroes: Stereotype and the Signification of Disability." In *Disability and Social Change: A South African Agenda*, edited by Brian Watermeyer. Cape Town: Oxford University Press.

Marks, Deborah. 1999. *Disability: Controversial Debates and Psychosocial Perspectives*. London: Routledge.

Munusamy, Ranjeni. 2016. "Oscar Pistorius Sentence: An Homage to Celebrity and White Privilege." *The Guardian*, July 7. https://www.theguardian.com/world/2016/jul/07/oscar-pistorius-sentence-an-homage-to-celebrity-and-white-privilege.

Phipps, Claire. 2014. "Oscar Pistorius 'At Risk of Suicide' Without Further Mental Health Care—Live Trial Coverage." *The Guardian*, July 2. http://www.theguardian.com/world/2014/jul/02/oscar-pistorius-live-trial-coverage-wednesday-2-july#block-53b3becde4b0c1f211705bd2.

Pistorius, Oscar. 2009. *Blade Runner*. London: Virgin Books.

Press Association. 2016. "Oscar Pistorius Jailed for Six Years for Reeva Steenkamp Murder." *The Telegraph*, July 6. https://www.eveningtelegraph.co.uk/fp/oscar-pistorius-jailed-six-years-reeva-steenkamp-murder/.

Prilleltensky, Ora. 2004. *Motherhood and Disability: Children and Choices*. New York: Palgrave Macmillan.

Riccobono, Anthony. 2014. "Oscar Pistorius Case Summary: Key Evidence as Closing Arguments Loom in Murder Trial." *International Business Times*, July 30. http://www.ibtimes.com/oscar-pistorius-case-summary-key-evidence-closing-arguments-loom-murder-trial-1643460.

Ryan, Sara. 2005. "'People Don't Do Odd, Do They?' Mothers Making Sense of the Reactions of Others Towards Their Learning Disabled Children In Public Places." *Children's Geographies* 3(3): 291–305.

SAPA. 2014. "Oscar Pistorius Shamelessly Using Handicap On Call—Gerrie Nel." *City Press*. http://www.citypress.co.za/news/oscar-pistorius-shamelessly-using-handicap-call-gerrie-nel/.

Seirlis, Ari. 2014. "With Disability Comes Vulnerability—or Is Vulnerability a New Disability?" *Daily Maverick,* July 8. http://www.dailymaverick.co.za/opinionista/2014-07-08-with-disability-comes-vulnerability-or-is-or-vulnerability-a-new-disability/.

Shakespeare, Tom. 2006. "The Social Model of Disability." In *The Disability Studies Reader*, edited by Lennard Davis. New York: Taylor and Francis.

Smith, David. 2014. "Oscar Pistorius Traumatised and May Be Suicide Risk, Psychologist Finds." *The Guardian*, July 2. http://www.theguardian.com/world/2014/jul/02/oscar-pistorius-suicide-risk-psychologist.

Sokolove, Michael. 2012. "The Fast Life of Oscar Pistorius." *The New York Times*, January 18. http://www.nytimes.com/2012/01/22/magazine/oscar-pistorius.html?pagewanted=all&_r=0.

Swartz, Leslie. 2013. "Oscar Pistorius and the Melancholy of Intersectionality." *Disability & Society* 28 (8): 1157–1161.

Watermeyer, Brian. 2006. "Disability and Psychoanalysis." In *Disability and Social Change. A South African Agenda*, edited by Brian Watermeyer. Cape Town: HSRC.

_____. 2012. "Is It Possible to Create a Politically Engaged, Contextual Psychology of Disability?" *Disability & Society* 27(2): 161–174.

Watermeyer, Brian, and Leslie Swartz. 2008. "Conceptualising the Psycho-Emotional Aspects of Disability and Impairment: The Distortion of Personal and Psychic Boundaries." *Disability & Society* 23(6): 599–610.

Young, Stella. 2013. "Oscar Pistorius and an Unfathomable Crime." *The Drum*, February 18. http://www.abc.net.au/news/2013–02–19/young-oscar-pistorius-and-an-unfathomable-crime/4527424.

Disability and Cyber-Victimization

ZHRAA A. ALHABOBY, HALA EVANS,
JAMES BARNES *and* EMMA SHORT

People living with disabilities face harassment, discrimination and violence in real life contexts that often results in "traditional" or "offline" victimization. Traditional victimization implies a repeated negative behavior or attention over a period of time, carried by an individual or a group towards the "victim" in a physical context (Kouwenberg, Rieffe, Theunissen, and de Rooij 2012). The introduction of the Internet as a new medium of communication has reshaped these experiences by adding the risk of cyber-victimization. In this essay, we discuss the experiences of cyber-victimization, such as cyberstalking, cyberharassment, and cyberbullying of people with different types of disabilities. We also address the impact upon victims and the potential underlying risk factors specific to online media use. We argue that online content has escalated the risk of cyber-victimization for people with disabilities due to the existing vulnerability and discrimination in the offline context.

There are two ways one might intervene to prevent further impact on vulnerable populations. Firstly, to counteract this form of victimization, it is necessary for supporters to acknowledge the biomedical consequences of socio-cultural practices that lead to cyber-victimization. Secondly, people with disabilities have been using promising approaches to counteract cyber abuse, which could decrease this phenomenon in the longer term. These approaches include empowering each other through their online disability identity, influencing public opinion using online media and promoting a social model through relevant support groups. Through various academic articles, media sources, and interviews with victims, the aforementioned argument will be expanded upon to show the importance of online media's influence on people with disabilities.

The Existing Context: Vulnerability and Discrimination

Discrimination against people with disabilities goes back to ancient history when disabled people were used as "scapegoats" through cultural justifications (Quarmby 2011). Over the years, the construction of disability has been influenced by changes in cultures, communities, and communication. The involvement of the Internet as a new means of communication has created a new context that further reshaped this vulnerability (Wells and Mitchell 2014). It is estimated that 62.5 percent of adults with disabilities in the United States have high-speed Internet access (File and Ryan 2014). Further, one in every five people living with long-term conditions participate in online health discussions (Fox and Purcell 2010). In the UK, 75 percent of people with disabilities have online access, 97.3 percent of adults aged 16 to 24 years with disabilities were recent Internet users in 2016 (ONS 2016). Internet use by people with a physical disability was not significantly different from people without disabilities, but the difference was significant in the case of intellectual disabilities (Wells and Mitchell 2014). These figures might not be fully accurate considering the differences between specific types of disabilities, but they do reflect the instrumental role the Internet plays in everyday life. Hence, recognizing its potential and risks is required.

The quest for disability rights has undergone numerous improvements in recent years. The public has raised their consciousness regarding terminology use for example. People are encouraged to utilize inclusive language instead of passive or stereotypical terminology such as "crippled," "handicapped" or "mentally retarded" (ODI 2014). Despite improvements in recognizing disability rights, people with disabilities still endure discrimination from online disablists who use offensive language (Pring 2016). To understand how the Internet is used to perpetuate this prejudice, it is necessary to understand the context under which the models of disability discourse operate.

The way in which disability is conceptualized by individuals and organizations impacts people's understanding and subsequently influences their language, expectations, and interactions in society (Haegele and Hodge 2016). The medical and social models of disability are the two prominent models that frame disability. From the medical perspective, disability is seen as a "deficit," an impairment in body functions as a result of disease or injury that requires normalization through diagnosis and treatment (Humpage 2007; Forhan 2009). Hence, in this model, disability is perceived as a negative individual trait that overlooks the value and needs of people with disabilities (Haegele and Hodge 2016). The social model views disability as a construct that is imposed on the impairment. Thus, disability in of itself is neither a positive nor a negative attribute. Rather, it is the society's responsibility to be more inclusive towards people with disabilities (Anastasiou and Kauffman 2013). Nevertheless, by shifting responsibility for change toward society, the social model might lead one to overlook an individual's impairment as a part of their lived experience (Haegele and Hodge 2016). Anastasiou and Kauffman (2013) argue that disability is different from other human diversity components, such as ethnicity, due to the underlying biomedical element. The impairment forms part of everyday life that influences people's choices. Thus, people with disabilities will benefit from addressing both the biomedical and social dimensions. This mixture in adopting the medical and the social model has influenced the definition of vulnerability, which is the underlying concept in many victimization cases.

Vulnerability is a term used to describe an individual or a group of people who require protection (Levine et al. 2004). The discourse related to people with disabilities and vulnerability status is multifaceted. One aspect of this complicated discourse is how disability is stereotypically linked with illness. For instance, in the UK, disability is constructed as a long-term physical or mental impairment in the Equality Act (EA 2010), and hence the legal definition is similar to the medical perspective. Another facet is what happens when one acquires a disability status. Once the sick role is legitimized medically, disability is then perceived as a title associated with reward. A good example of this is when one fulfills the legal definition of disability and hence acquires disability benefits in the UK. These individuals are then perceived as consumers and subsequently face offensive language by taxpayers such as being called "scroungers," "workshy" or "cheats" (Briant, Watson, and Philo 2013). Emerson and Roulstone (2014) argue that this approach in identifying disabilities and the subsequent compensations has led to a systematic error in institutions by consistently attaching negative value judgments to disability, which facilitate further stereotyping by the public in linking disability with either severe illness or fraud. These two aspects, linking disability with visible illness and referring to disability as beneficiary status, have contributed to discrimination against disabled people. For instance, the public may assume that only people with visible physical disabilities who use wheelchairs can use accessible parking areas. Should anyone else utilize these spaces, they are then liable of committing fraud by the public. In turn, some disabled people were frequently reported to the police when using accessible parking areas and were called "scroungers" and "bogus claimants" (Quarmby 2015). Taking the UK as an example, due to cost and tax issues, the typical newspaper story about disability is increasingly focused on fraud cases to get disability benefits

(Briant, Watson, and Philo 2013). These assumptions have reinforced the public's willingness to stereotype, and influenced the experiences of discrimination of disabled people in their communities.

A recent UK survey explored the perceived motivation of offenders in disability hate crimes. It found that 89 percent of respondents identified themselves as disabled, and 87.2 percent experienced a minimum of one harassment offense (Quarmby 2015). The motivation of offenders ranged between hate, jealousy, and accusations of fraud because of the relative invisibility of some disabilities. Hence, one of the major aspects surrounding disability discrimination is the immediate socio-cultural context and perceived level of disability. Moreover, being different from the majority of the population, physically (Horowitz et al. 2004), intellectually (Kowalski and Fedina 2011), or in terms of lifestyle (Sentenac, Arnaud, et al. 2011) has consistently contributed to victimizing disabled people. Therefore, vulnerability in this sense is a complex situation enabled by the socio-cultural context, maximizing differences and labeling, all of which ultimately lead to victimization over the years.

Victimization is described as any unwanted attention or negative behavior over time, produced by an individual or a group, against the victim or victims (Kouwenberg et al. 2012). Victimization of disabled people is widely documented as an international issue that is not linked to a specific condition. The research done in victimization constructs the issue in medical terms. For example, in Canada, individuals having epilepsy were victimized in schools. Children aged eight to 16 years with epilepsy were more frequently targets of bullying with a prevalence of 42 percent, compared to 21 percent in "healthy" controls and 18 percent among children with chronic kidney disease (Hamiwka et al. 2009). In Ireland and France, young individuals with chronic conditions such as diabetes, arthritis and cerebral palsy were frequently targeted by their peers with a prevalence of 20.6 percent in Ireland and 16.6 percent in France (Sentenac, Gavin, et al. 2011). Individuals with intellectual disabilities such as Attention Deficit Hyperactivity Disorder (ADHD) and autism were victimized in the United States (Taylor et al. 2010, Chen and Schwartz 2012). Meanwhile, young people with hearing impairments were discriminated against in Netherlands (Kouwenberg et al. 2012). Despite the geographical variations and figures, the impact of victimization is consistent.

The documented impact of victimization includes short and long term consequences such as psychological complications including low self-esteem, anxiety and depression, social isolation, unemployment, and suicide (Hugh-Jones and Smith 1999, Sheridan and Grant 2007). In addition, victimization can lead to health complications including physical health complaints (Sentenac et al. 2013), exacerbation of illness (Zinner et al. 2012), and disruption of health management (Sentenac, Arnaud, et al. 2011). Even though negative stereotypes often stem from adopting the medical perspective, which frames most of the consequences in psychological and wellbeing terms, the supportive channels view victimization as a social problem that denies victims from getting appropriate support. Hence, the effects of victimization on disabled people are devastating, and the introduction of the Internet in everyday communication has added to the complexity.

Online Context and Cyber-Victimization

With the dramatic increase of Internet use, e-mail, text messages, blogs, and social networking websites/apps (including Facebook, Twitter, Instagram, YouTube, and others) are part of everyday life. For example, more than 80 percent of the population in the UK has Internet access, including in the least socio-economically deprived areas (ONS 2015). Internet use presents numerous benefits for facilitating social networking, disseminating health information, and peer support. Subsequently, this virtual context became available for both people with disabilities and ableist offenders. Despite the benefits, the Internet has brought along the risk of online discrimination, or what we could call "cyber-victimization."

"Cyber-victimization" of disabled people is being increasingly reported worldwide (Fridh et al. 2015). It is an umbrella term covering a range of cyber-offenses such as cyber-harassment, cyberbullying, cyberstalking, cyber-disability hate crimes or cyber-sexual exploitation. Each of these terms has a definition that could vary between disciplines. However, they share the criteria of being an antisocial behavior by the "offender" towards the "victim" via electronic communication causing fear and distress (Alhaboby et al. 2016). This is achieved through sending harassing content, insults, creating false profiles, spreading lies, or contacting the social network of the victim. Examples of cyber-victimization in victims' own words include "I caught him posting threatening comments under a false name on the guest book of my website, shortly before he had told me that there was someone out to get me" (Alhaboby et al. 2016, 1140). Another example is a media article addressing how Twitter responds passively to discrimination against people with disabilities. One of the people interviewed was a disabled activist who faced numerous harassing messages on Twitter such as "You're just a disabled bitch that should be put down. Nothing but a lazy workshy, scrounger" (Pring 2016).

Another type of cyber-victimization, "cyberharassment," is recognized as negative attitudes or intimidating behaviors towards the victim involving the use of the Internet and/or cell phone. One study took a cross-sectional segment of the population in Sweden to explore the cyber-victimization of disabled people and used the term cyberharassment (Fridh, Lindström, and Rosvall 2015). In a sample of over 8,000 participants, 762 individuals with disabilities were included. Participants were individuals 12, 15, and 17 years old with self-reported impaired hearing, impaired vision, reading/writing disorders, dyslexia, and attention deficit hyperactivity disorder (ADHD). Cyberharassment in this study was defined as a violation or harassment over the past 12 months, involving electronic communication. Male participants reported a frequency of cyberharassment of 32.1 percent (one incident) to 41.5 percent (several incidents). While female participants reported 28 percent and 35 percent frequencies, respectively (Fridh, Lindström, and Rosvall 2015). The impact upon victims was mainly subjective health complaints.

When the intimidation in harassment is associated with power imbalances, this perceived unequal power relation between the victim and the offender is described as "cyberbullying." Such experiences are common in schools and workplaces due to the nature of relations between parties. Another public health study conducted in Sweden used 413 participants 13 to 15 years old, drawn from a sample of 5,248 participants to explore cyberbullying (Annerbäck, Sahlqvist, and Wingren 2014). The types of conditions included were impaired hearing or vision, limited motor function, dyslexia, Attention Deficit Hyperactivity Disorder (ADHD), asthma, diabetes, epilepsy, and intestinal diseases. "Cyberbullying" was defined as an indirect form of bullying that involves harassment via the Internet or mobile phones in the past two months. It involves using power to control others or cause distress. The impact reported was poor health, mental health consequences and self-harm.

Another cyber-offense is "cyberstalking," which involves repeated unwanted contact triggering fear and distress, with the added characterization of fixation. Hence, scholars identify cyberstalking cases by the repetition of ten harassment incidents over a period of four weeks (Sheridan and Grant 2007). Cyberstalking is either a singular event or part of an evolution that gives offenders new methods to target the victim (Bocij and McFarlane 2003). In Sheridan and Grant's (2007) study, the original aim of the research was to investigate the effects of cyberstalking on its victims in general. However, 11.9 percent of cyberstalking cases were against disabled people. Regardless of the presence of disability, the impact of cyberstalking was comparable to stalking in terms of causing anxiety, fear, depression, self-harm, and paranoia.

The definitions above are not consistent in the literature and vary between disciplines and individual studies. However, there tends to be some overlap. For example, online harassment or cyberharassment may also be referred to as trolling and is also related to cyberstalking. Both cyberstalking and cyberharassment include receiving offending comments, spreading lies, insults or threats online, and frequently cause a significant negative impact on "victims" (Short et al. 2014).

In UK legislation, the Crown Prosecution Service identifies cyberstalking as a type of harassment taking place online that is covered under the legislation, depending on the details related to each specific case (CPS 2016). Some issues surround these definitions. Firstly, when looking at online experiences, it is difficult to identify a threshold for the number of incidents. For instance, whether each e-mail or Facebook comment is an incident, or whether each platform, e.g., Facebook or Twitter is an incident. Secondly, the duration to identify a victimization experience also varies, with some researchers using a lifetime approach (Mueller-Johnson, Eisner, and Obsuth 2014). Other researchers look at weekly, monthly, or yearly experiences (Didden et al. 2009). Thirdly, when cyber-victimization is perceived to be a result of hostility or prejudice, any of these offenses could also be labeled as cyber-disability hate crime that has only recently recognized (Alhaboby et al. 2016). Fourthly, people who went through cyber-victimization do not necessarily identify themselves as victims. Based on issues related to defining the offense, duration, and a number of incidents, the prevalence of cyber-victimization against disabled people cannot be clearly determined. It could range between 2 percent (Didden et al. 2009) to 41.5 percent (Fridh, Lindström, and Rosvall 2015). Despite variations, it could be assumed that these cyber-victimization experiences are potentially more devastating than traditional ones. Online experiences are worse because of the anonymity of offenders, the availability of a broad range of means to employ, the fact that most online comments are permanent, and that the effect does not go away by avoiding physical presence in a specific context (Anderson, Bresnahan, and Musatics 2014). Hence, victims still face an impact that is not acknowledged by others, as one of the victims interviewed stated, "I do not think many people realize how bad harassment can affect you psychologically, especially if it has been going on for some time" (Alhaboby et al. 2016, 1140). In fact, cyber-victimization is further complicated by international offenses whereby offenders are overseas, and the police face difficulties investigating such cases (Sheridan and Grant 2007). Accordingly, cyber-victimization represents a phenomenon building on the existing context of vulnerability and discrimination that adds new dangers that are specific to the online context.

Underlying Factors

In addition to the ongoing vulnerability issues discussed earlier, several factors could increase the vulnerability of people with disabilities in online media. One of these factors is the underestimation of the seriousness of communications taking place online. There is a relatively common assumption that the Internet is "not real" and any unwanted communication could be fixed by shutting down electronic devices or not going online (Short et al. 2014). Such assumptions are not only shared by the public, but also by some of the personnel working at supportive channels such as the police, service providers, and healthcare practitioners (al-Khateeb et al. 2017). Hence, the disavowal of these service providers could influence the quality of support a victim may receive, including health support. Due to training and underestimation issues, some victims ended up changing their mobile phone numbers, jobs, homes, and even country (al-Khateeb et al. 2017). Accordingly, disability in most cases is perceived as a medical issue by supportive channels, but the resultant victimization is seen as a social issue that leaves victims struggling for support (Alhaboby et al. 2016). Moreover, when people underestimate the impact of online communication, harassing others becomes easier. People who might not commit harassment offenses offline could be turned into online offenders (Sheridan and Grant 2007).

The second factor that increases one's level of victimization is related to Internet access and utilization by disabled people. There are anticipated differences in Internet use between people with and without disabilities. One of the differences relates to the general use of the Internet, comparing the frequency and purposes of web surfing (Lathouwers, de Moor, and Didden 2009). For example, it was presumed that people with disabilities spend longer time online due to mobility needs and utilizing online shopping services (Sheridan and Grant 2007). However, despite these assumptions, recent studies did not find significant time differences in Internet use by disabled people (Shpigelman and Gill 2014). Other researchers found no differences in online behavior between people with and without disabilities except in forming close online relationships (Wells and Mitchell 2014). Thus, using the Internet as a means for socialization is another potential underlying factor for victimization.

Forming social relations online was further addressed specifically with individuals having intellectual disabilities because trying to socialize online put them at higher risk of victimization (Sofronoff, Dark, and Stone 2011). The Theory of Mind was used to explain this issue by looking mainly at two constructs, first gullibility which is vulnerability to be tricked, and second credulity as the tendency to believe something (Sofronoff, Dark, and Stone 2011). Researchers in this case attempted to explain victimization experiences by a deficit in communication skills. This resulted in framing the issue socially and, in some cases, misunderstandings in communication while building online relationships resulted in being labeled as bullies and victims at the same time (Yen et al. 2014).

The third factor is the stereotyping that happens by collectively using the term "disability" when referring to a heterogeneous group of conditions. Researchers in various disciplines such as psychology, criminology, and public health have undermined disability in cyber-victimization studies by constructing it as a generic term without further analysis. In some instances, "disability" was used to cover all students from schools with special needs (Didden et al. 2009). Thus, reporting commonly included victims with a "physical disability," "intellectual disability," or special need. Few studies looked specifically at ADHD, Asperger's syndrome, or autism (Yen et al. 2014). Accordingly, research of cyber abuse cases involving people with disabilities tends to overlook a wide range of conditions that exist under the disability umbrella, such as people with invisible disabilities like chronic fatigue syndrome. This contributes to how these individuals are falsely perceived by the general public, resulting in a vicious cycle of stereotyping through research, government statistics, and media representation.

Support to Victims

Response and support available to victims of cyber-offenses can be divided into informal support and instrumental support. Informal support includes approaching friends and family, while instrumental help is the formal support through channels available to victims to help in coping with cyber-victimization (Galeazzi et al. 2009, Reyns and Englebrecht 2014). An example of informal support was shared by a victim of cyberharassment: "The harassment became apparent to my friends and family when I fell ill and they became my carers. They took action to stop it by contacting my harasser directly" (Alhaboby et al. 2016, 1140).

Instrumental support includes accessing health and psychological services such as mental health support, and problem-solving strategies such as employing lawyers and actions by the police. Within the UK there are some legislative acts to respond to cyberharassment such as the Protection from Harassment Act 1997, the Malicious Communications 1988, the Communications Act 2003, the Crime and Disorder Act 1998, and the Equality Act 2010 (CPS 2016). When the victim is labeled disabled, the harassment could also be addressed under the Disability Discrimination Act 1995, the Equality Act 2010, or the Communications Act 2003 section 127 for disability hate crime (CPS 2016). Despite the availability of a number of legal remedies, victims with disabilities still seem to struggle to get support (Alhaboby et al. 2016). This could be either due to the relative ambiguity of cyber offenses accompanied by the unclear thresholds in legal acts, where people working in instrumental support channels lack sufficient training as discussed earlier. The following blurbs explain examples of support received from the police and

Twitter, respectively: "Police were ill informed and actually saw it as a diversity issue about disability. I had to fight them to act under the protection from harassment act 1997—and in interviewing others affected, there was gross disability discrimination" (Alhaboby et al. 2016, 1140) and "They don't care about disabled people being told to die, that we should be beaten. They don't care about people organizing hate mobs to try to ruin disabled people's lives" (Pring 2016).

Another issue relates to how cases of cyberstalking are addressed by authority and supportive figures. In the UK, 50 percent of stalking victims complained that family and friends did not take them seriously, 50 percent were told they were going mad, only 42 percent reported it to police, and 61 percent thought the stalkers were just being helpful (Sheridan 2005). This might not be very different from professionals' responses. The majority of cyberstalking victims had little support, and this was accompanied by blaming the victim, especially by the police (Short et al. 2014). The lack of support given to cyberstalking victims, combined with the vulnerability of people with disabilities to cyberstalking, cause victims to be significantly disempowered (Sheridan and Grant 2007). Hence, supportive measures to ensure people with disabilities are receiving adequate support should include public awareness, among other changes in policies.

The Way Forward: Using Media to Counteract Cyber-Victimization

The Internet, as a medium of communication, presents risks to people with disabilities but also has the potential of generating rewards. Online communities provide potentially huge benefits to people with disabilities. One such benefit is that online communication offers victims of discrimination the opportunity to confront their abusers or raise awareness of such offenses. Thus, viewing the Internet as a means of empowering those who have been traditionally disempowered makes it possible to fight cyber-victimization in the long term. Not only does this allow the victim to confront the victimizer but also generates virtual communities of people who band together to share their experiences and expand their empowerment through group membership. The Internet has provided people living with relatively overlooked disabilities such as myalgic encephalomyelitis (ME) with opportunities to express themselves and support each other. The perspectives of these individuals are being recognized through online campaigns. They are generating awareness and social change regarding the impact of ME as an invisible disability for instance. They are also advocating for the re-categorization of myalgic encephalomyelitis as a neurological condition instead of the psychological one it is currently classified as. The recognition of these efforts can contribute to reshaping how the public perceive disability beyond physical impairments, which could potentially minimize harassing this group for "not looking ill." Hence, it could be assumed that the online social identity developed by people with disabilities and subsequent in-group empowerment is a powerful way to counteract cyber-victimization. This could be explained by Social Identity Theory, which involves a process of categorization, resulting into considering the self as part of an in-group "us" that is different from the out-group "them," with a tendency of bias towards the in-group (Tajfel 2010, Turner, Brown, and Tajfel 1979). Therefore, online disability identity can be based on disabled people experiences rather than medical or research terms when people with disabilities are empowered to construct them for themselves.

One such constructed disability identity is known as the "spoonie" identity, and is commonly adopted by disabled people and shared in online narratives. It is built on the Spoon Theory, which was based on a real experience shared by an online blogger (Miserandino 2003). The blogger uses spoons to illustrate how she manages her daily life with Lupus. This theory was soon adopted by thousands of people with various types of disabilities and chronic conditions who started calling themselves spoonies: "I have used the spoon theory to explain my life to many people. In fact, my family and friends refer to spoons all the time. It has been a code word for what I can and cannot do. Once people understand the spoon theory they seem to understand me better, but I also think they live their life a little differently too. I think it isn't just good for understanding Lupus, but anyone dealing with any disability or illness. Hopefully, they don't take so much for granted or their life in general" (Miserandino 2003). The Spoon Theory acknowledges the impact that chronic illness can impose on the daily lives of people. Hence, it does not dismiss the medical aspect. Using the word spoonie to communicate the online identity demonstrates how the Internet can be a medium where people with disabilities can find and support each other against "outsiders." Unfortunately, outside the boundaries of using the term spoonie by people with disabilities, the use of the word is very limited in research and it mostly appears through narratives of participants as a way to express themselves (Biro 2012, Jackson 2013, Miller 2015).

People with disabilities have also found creative ways to use the Internet to communicate the hardships they have endured through interacting with the public offline. The media has covered a few stories of disabled people being harassed because they are physically different, or due to being labeled "disabled" but not using a wheelchair. For instance, one story relays the experience of a 27 year old Ph.D. researcher in the UK who has had Ehlers-Danlos Syndrome since birth (Cockroft 2016). The condition is a connective tissue disorder that affects her "routine" activities in which her joints could dislocate up to 40 times per day while combing hair, coughing, or walking. She uses crutches and a wheelchair, but upon going out she receives harassing comments from strangers and claims that she is using the crutches to avoid work. Thus, to avoid ostracization and harassment, she often skips using the walking aids. Once while out in public, she used her disability badge to park in an accessible spot reserved for people with disabilities. Upon returning to her vehicle, she was harassed for "not looking disabled" with a note that read "Rot in hell" and "You should be disgusted in yourself. One day I hope you know what it is like to be disabled, then you will know." She responded to the incident by posting a picture of the note online and asking people not judge others by appearance. She wrote, "Trying so hard to not appear disabled due to hurtful comments and try to live a normal life is hard, I was really hurt by it" (Cockroft 2016). Despite the impact, this experience had on her, the courage in sharing it on the Internet helped to spread its impact and increases awareness on her rare condition to decrease stereotyping.

When experiences of ableism are shared through a personalized narrative, such as in the previous example, promising improvements in generating social justice, awareness, and community building can be anticipated. Another example of such social change comes from a video posted on YouTube of a teen with Asperger's syndrome. The video went viral and was covered by a number of media articles (Stout 2015). The 14-year-old boy from Hertfordshire used a selfie stick to attach his mother's video camera and record videos that explain, in his own words, how cyberbullying messages impact him. The selfie stick usually comes with an extendible handle and fits smartphones or cameras to capture a photo or a picture of oneself. It is for anyone's use but could have special importance when used by people with disabilities because it accommodates limited mobility (Berry 2016). Additionally, the creative use of a selfie stick to self-record and share the impact of cyberbullying via the Internet helped in touching the lived-experience of usually isolated victims. The boy's short video was a poignant illustration for how individuals with disabilities suffer from cyber-victimization. As a result, it was shared by thousands of people who felt moral indignation about the incidents. Such initiatives indicate the potential of using the Internet to communicate suffering, fight cyber-victimization, and influence public opinion. However, it should be noted that using the Internet media itself to counteract cyber-victimization has its own risks. For instance, the comments and responses by others could also generate further negative comments and harassment. Despite this potential, the longer term benefits of having an open dialogue about these issues could be a key factor to improve public awareness and prevent future cyber-victimization.

Conclusion

Unfortunately, while ableism existed before the Internet, it has taken further steps with electronic communications that were impossible a few decades ago. The advent of the Internet ushered in a new kind of victimization that takes the forms of cyberharassment, cyberstalking, cyberbullying, and cyber-disability hate incidents. All of these offenses share common criteria and devastating impact upon victims, paralleled by insufficient support. Victimization is often aggravated by the underestimation of what happens online and made worse by disability stereotypes and Internet use. Disability cyber-victimization are characterized using descriptors from both the medical and social models, where the medical perspective perpetuates harmful disability stereotyping and discrimination among the public, yet the consequences are framed as social thereby leading to improper support. Despite these obstacles, people with disabilities have managed to use online communities to empower each other, fight for disability-related causes, and find creative ways to influence public opinion. If we are to continue to counteract cyber-victimization, we must acknowledge the psychological and mental consequences of incidents in the short term while working to improve inclusivity, educate supportive channels and the public about cyber-victimization in the longer term.

REFERENCES

Alhaboby, Zhraa A., Haider M. al-Khateeb, James Barnes, and Emma Short. 2016. "'The Language Is Disgusting and They Refer to My Disability': The Cyberharassment of Disabled People." *Disability & Society* 31(8): 1138–1143. doi: 10.1080/09687599.2016.1235313.
al-Khateeb, Haider M, Gregory Epiphaniou, Zhraa A. Alhaboby, James Barnes, and Emma Short. 2017. "Cyberstalking: Investigating Formal Intervention and the Role of Corporate Social Responsibility." *Telematics and Informatics* 34(4): 339–349. doi: http://dx.doi.org/10.1016/j.tele.2016.08.006.
Anastasiou, Dimitris, and James M. Kauffman. 2013. "The Social Model of Disability: Dichotomy between Impairment and Disability." *Journal of Medicine and Philosophy* 38(4): 441–459.
Anderson, Jenn, Mary Bresnahan, and Catherine Musatics. 2014. "Combating Weight-Based Cyberbullying on Facebook with the Dissenter Effect." *Cyberpsychology, Behavior and Social Networking* 17(5): 281–286. doi: 10.1089/cyber.2013.0370.
Annerbäck, Eva-Maria, Lotta Sahlqvist, and Gun Wingren. 2014. "A Cross-Sectional Study of Victimisation of Bullying among Schoolchildren in Sweden: Background Factors and Self-Reported Health Complaints." *Scandinavian Journal of Public Health* 42(3): 270–277. doi: 10.1177/1403494813514142.
Berry, Kelly. 2016. "Selfie Sticks: Transforming the Selfie." University of London.
Biro, David. 2012. "An Anatomy of Illness." *Journal of Medical Humanities* 33(1): 41–54.
Bocij, Paul, and Leroy McFarlane. 2003. "Cyberstalking: The Technology of Hate." *The Police Journal* 76(3): 204–221.
Briant, Emma, Nick Watson, and Gregory Philo. 2013. "Reporting Disability in the Age of Austerity: The Changing Face of Media Representation of Disability and Disabled People in the United Kingdom and the Creation of New 'Folk Devils.'" *Disability & Society* 28(6): 874–889.
Chen, Pei-Yu, and Ilene S. Schwartz. 2012. "Bullying and Victimization Experiences of Students

with Autism Spectrum Disorders in Elementary Schools." *Focus on Autism and Other Developmental Disabilities* 27(4): 200–212. Doi: 10.1177/1088357612459556.

Cockroft, Steph. 2016. "'Rot in Hell' Note Left to Disabled Driver." MailOnline.

CPS. *Impact and Dynamics of Stalking and Harassment* 2016 [cited 2-2-2016]. http://www. cps.gov.uk/legal/s_to_u/stalking_and_harassment/#a05a.

Didden, R., R.H.J. Scholte, H. Korzilius, J.M. de Moor, A. Vermeulen, M. O'Reilly, R. Lang, and G.E. Lancioni. 2009. "Cyberbullying Among Students with Intellectual and Developmental Disability in Special Education Settings." *Developmental Neurorehabilitation* 12(3): 146–151 6p. doi: 10.1080/17518420902971356.

EA. 2010. "Guidance on Matters to Be Taken into Account in Determining Questions Relating to the Definition of Disability." In *Equality Act 2010.*

Emerson, Eric, and Alan Roulstone. 2014. "Developing an Evidence Base for Violent and Disablist Hate Crime in Britain: Findings from the Life Opportunities Survey." *Journal of Interpersonal Violence.* doi: 10.1177/0886260514534524.

File, Thom, and Camille Ryan. 2014. "Computer and Internet Use in the United States: 2013." *American Community Survey Reports.*

Forhan, Mary. 2009. "An Analysis of Disability Models and the Application of the ICF to Obesity." *Disability and Rehabilitation* 31(16): 1382–1388.

Fox, Susannah, and Kristen Purcell. 2010. "Chronic Disease and the Internet." Pew Internet & American Life Project.

Fridh, Maria, Martin Lindström, and Maria Rosvall. 2015. "Subjective Health Complaints in Adolescent Victims of Cyber Harassment: Moderation through Support from Parents/ Friends—A Swedish Population-Based Study." *BMC Public Health* 15(1): 949–949. doi: 10.1186/s12889-015-2239-7.

Galeazzi, Gian M, Aleš Bučar-Ručman, Laura DeFazio, and Anne Groenen. 2009. "Experiences of Stalking Victims and Requests for Help in Three European Countries. A Survey." *European Journal on Criminal Policy and Research* 15(3): 243–260.

Haegele, Justin Anthony, and Samuel Hodge. 2016. "Disability Discourse: Overview and Critiques of the Medical and Social Models." *Quest* 68(2): 193–206.

Hamiwka, Lorie D., G. Yu Cara, Lorraine A. Hamiwka, Elisabeth M.S. Sherman, Blaire Anderson, and Elaine Wirrell. 2009. "Are Children with Epilepsy at Greater Risk for Bullying Than Their Peers?" *Epilepsy & Behavior* 15(4): 500–505.

Horowitz, June Andrews, Judith A. Vessey, Karen L. Carlson, Joan F. Bradley, Carolyn Montoya, Bill McCullough, and Joyce David. 2004. "Teasing and Bullying Experiences of Middle School Students." *Journal of the American Psychiatric Nurses Association* 10(4): 165–172. doi: 10.1177/1078390304267862.

Hugh-Jones, Siobhan, and Peter K. Smith. 1999. "Self-Reports of Short- and Long-Term Effects of Bullying on Children Who Stammer." *British Journal of Educational Psychology* 69(2): 141–158. doi: 10.1348/000709999157626.

Humpage, Louise. 2007. "Models of Disability, Work and Welfare in Australia." *Social Policy & Administration* 41(3): 215–231.

Jackson, Megan. 2013. "The Special Educational Needs of Adolescents Living with Chronic Illness: A Literature Review." *International Journal of Inclusive Education* 17(6): 543–554.

Kouwenberg, Maartje, Carolien Rieffe, Stephanie C.P.M. Theunissen, and Mark de Rooij. 2012. "Peer Victimization Experienced by Children and Adolescents Who Are Deaf or Hard of Hearing." *Plos One* 7(12): e52174-e52174. doi: 10.1371/journal.pone.0052174.

Kowalski, Robin M., and Cristin Fedina. 2011. "Cyber Bullying in ADHD and Asperger Syndrome Populations." *Research in Autism Spectrum Disorders* 5(3): 1201–1208. doi: 10.1016/j.rasd.2011.01.007.

Lathouwers, Karen, Jan de Moor, and Robert Didden. 2009. "Access to and Use of Internet by Adolescents Who Have A Physical Disability: A Comparative Study." *Research in Developmental Disabilities* 30: 702–711. doi: 10.1016/j.ridd.2008.09.003.

Levine, Carol, Ruth Faden, Christine Grady, Dale Hammerschmidt, Lisa Eckenwiler, and Jeremy Sugarman. 2004. "The Limitations of "Vulnerability" as a Protection for Human Research Participants." *The American Journal of Bioethics* 4(3): 44–49.

Miller, Ryan Andrew. 2015. Intersections of Disability, Gender, and Sexuality in Higher Education: Exploring Students' Social Identities and Campus Experiences. Dissertation. University of Texas at Austin.

Miserandino, Christine. 2003. "The Spoon Theory." http://www.butyoudontlooksick.com/articles/written-by-christine/the-spoon-theory/.

Mueller-Johnson, Katrin, Manuel P. Eisner, and Ingrid Obsuth. 2014. "Sexual Victimization of Youth with a Physical Disability: An Examination of Prevalence Rates, and Risk and Protective Factors." *Journal of Interpersonal Violence* 29(17): 3180–3206. doi: 10.1177/088 6260514534529.

ODI. 2014. "Inclusive Language: Words to Use and Avoid When Writing About Disability." In *Office for Disability Issues: Department for Works and Pensions.*

ONS. 2015. "Internet Access—Households and Individuals." Office for National Statistics [cited 11–2–2016]. Available from http://www.ons.gov.uk/ons/rel/rdit2/internet-access--households-and-individuals/2015/index.html.

_____. 2016. "Internet Users in the UK." https://www.ons.gov.uk/businessindustryandtrade/itandinternetindustry/bulletins/internetusers/2016#25-of-disabled-adults-had-never-used-the-internet.

Pring, John. 2016. "Anger Over Twitter's 'Can't Be Bothered' Attitude to Disablist Abuse." *Disability News Service*, February 25.

Quarmby, Katharine. 2011. *Scapegoat: How We Are Failing Disabled People.* London: Portobello.

_____. 2015. Disability Hate Crime Motivation Survey—Results 2015 [cited 28-9-2015]. https://katharinequarmby.wordpress.com/.

Reyns, Bradford W., and Christine M Englebrecht. 2014. "Informal and Formal Help-Seeking Decisions of Stalking Victims in the United States." *Criminal Justice and Behavior* 41(10): 1178–1194.

Sentenac, Mariane, Catherine Arnaud, Aoife Gavin, Michal Molcho, Saoirse Nic Gabhainn, and Emmanuelle Godeau. 2011. "Peer Victimization Among School-Aged Children with Chronic Conditions." *Epidemiologic reviews*: mxr024.

Sentenac, Mariane, Aoife Gavin, Catherine Arnaud, Michal Molcho, Emmanuelle Godeau, and Saoirse Nic Gabhainn. 2011. "Victims of Bullying Among Students with a Disability or Chronic Illness and Their Peers: A Cross-National Study Between Ireland and France." *Journal of Adolescent Health* 48(5): 461–466.

Sentenac, Mariane, Aoife Gavin, Saoirse Nic Gabhainn, Michal Molcho, Pernille Due, Ulrike Ravens-Sieberer, Margarida Gaspar de Matos, Agnieszka Malkowska-Szkutnik, Inese Gobina, Wilma Vollebergh, Catherine Arnaud, and Emmanuelle Godeau. 2013. "Peer Victimization and Subjective Health Among Students Reporting Disability or Chronic Illness in 11 Western Countries." *European Journal of Public Health* 23(3): 421–426.

Sheridan, Lorraine. 2005. University of Leicester Supported by Network for Surviving Stalking: Stalking Survey. [cited 13-5-2015]. http://www.le.ac.uk/press/stalkingsurvey.htm.

Sheridan, Lorraine P., and Tim Grant. 2007. "Is Cyberstalking Different?" *Psychology, Crime & Law* 13 (6): 627–640.

Short, E., S. Linford, J.M. Wheatcroft, and C. Maple. 2014. "The Impact of Cyberstalking: The Lived Experience—A Thematic Analysis." *Stud Health Technol Inform* 199: 133–7.

Shpigelman, Carmit-Noa, and Carol J. Gill. 2014. "How Do Adults with Intellectual Disabilities Use Facebook?" *Disability & Society* 29(10): 1601–1616.

Sofronoff, Kate, Elizabeth Dark, and Valerie Stone. 2011. "Social Vulnerability and Bullying in Children with Asperger Syndrome." *Autism* 15(3): 355–372. doi: 10.1177/1362361310365070.

Stout, Liz. 2015. "Autistic Teen Told Kill Bullies Uses Selfie Stick Film Video Daily Torment." *Dailymail*, November 24.

Tajfel, Henri. 2010. *Social Identity and Intergroup Relations.* Cambridge: Cambridge University Press.

Taylor, Lloyd A., Conway Saylor, Kimberly Twyman, and Michelle Macias. 2010. "Adding Insult to Injury: Bullying Experiences of Youth with Attention Deficit Hyperactivity Disorder." *Children's Health Care* 39(1): 59–72. doi: 10.1080/02739610903455152.

Turner, John C., Rupert J. Brown, and Henri Tajfel. 1979. "Social Comparison and Group Interest in Ingroup Favouritism." *European Journal of Social Psychology* 9(2): 187–204.

Wells, Melissa, and Kimberly J. Mitchell. 2014. "Patterns of Internet Use and Risk of Online Victimization for Youth with and without Disabilities." *The Journal of Special Education* 48(3): 204–213. doi: 10.1177/0022466913479141.

Yen, Cheng-Fang, Wen-Jiun Chou, Tai-Ling Liu, Chih-Hung Ko, Pinchen Yang, and Huei-Fan Hu. 2014. "Cyberbullying Among Male Adolescents with Attention-Deficit/ Hyperactivity Disorder: Prevalence, Correlates, and Association with Poor Mental Health Status." *Research in Developmental Disabilities* 35: 3543–3553. doi: 10.1016/j.ridd. 2014.08.035.

Zinner, Samuel H., Christine A. Conelea, Gwen M. Glew, Douglas W. Woods, and Cathy L. Budman. 2012. "Peer Victimization in Youth with Tourette Syndrome and Other Chronic Tic Disorders." *Child Psychiatry and Human Development* 43(1): 124–136. doi: 10.1007/s10578-011-0249-y.

About the Contributors

Zhraa A. **Alhaboby** is a qualified medical doctor (MBBS) and holds an MSc in international primary healthcare from Barts and the London School of Medicine and Dentistry. She teaches undergraduate and postgraduate modules in the Faculty of Health and Social Sciences at the University of Bedfordshire (UK).

James **Barnes** is a chartered psychologist and an associate fellow of the British Psychological Society. He has been involved in a variety of projects working with individuals with Parkinson's disease, dyslexia, PTSD, and has been a member of the National Centre of Cyberstalking Research.

Bill **Beechler**, Jr., is a board certified developmental-behavioral pediatrician working in the Riley Child Development Center in Indianapolis. As an assistant professor of pediatrics with the Indiana University School of Medicine, he trains pediatrics, internal medicine, and psychiatry residents as they rotate through the RCDC.

Sara Beth **Brooks** holds a bachelor's degree in communication studies and a minor in history. She has presented at the Creating Change Conference on LGBT Equality and the White House 2015 Briefing on Bisexuality. She was named one of 2013's Top Ten LGBT Student Leaders in the United States by Campus Pride.

Susan G. **Cumings** is a full-time lecturer in writing and critical inquiry at the University at Albany, State University of New York. She holds a Ph.D. from Emory University, and prior to joining SUNY, she was the coordinator of women's studies and an associate professor of English at Georgia College and State University.

Hala **Evans** is a senior lecturer in public health at the University of Bedfordshire (UK). She teaches modules for postgraduate students in health studies. Her research interests are focused on inequality in health, violence/aggression in schools, communicable diseases and non-communicable diseases, and health and lifestyle.

Amber E. **George** teaches online philosophy courses at Misericordia University and Southern New Hampshire University. She has coedited two books: *Screening the Non/Human*, with JL Schatz, and *The Intersectionality of Critical Animal, Disability, and Environmental Studies*, with Anthony J. Nocella II. She is the editor of the *Journal for Critical Animal Studies*.

Mia **Harrison** is a Ph.D. candidate in gender and cultural studies at the University of Sydney. She has worked with Apple on events related to accessibility and education and has written training material on the use of Apple's assistive technologies, as well as on behavior and etiquette for working with people with disabilities.

Clare **Harvey** is a clinical psychologist, lecturer and researcher in the psychology department at the University of the Witwatersrand, Johannesburg. She has worked in government and private clinical settings, including a stint as head of the psychology department at Rahima Moosa Mother and Child Hospital.

Jason Ho **Ka Hang** is an assistant professor in the Department of Comparative Literature at the University of Hong Kong. He has contributed articles to the edited volumes *LGBT Transnational Identity in Media* (2012), *In Critical Proximity* (2007), as well as the inaugural issue of *Trespassing Journal* (2012).

Sonya Freeman **Loftis** is an associate professor at Morehouse College and specializes in Shakespeare and disability studies. She is the author of *Shakespeare's Surrogates* and *Imagining Autism*. Her essays on drama and disability have appeared in many journals, and she serves on the editorial board for *Disability Studies Quarterly*.

Meghann E. **O'Leary** is a doctoral candidate in disability studies at the University of Illinois at Chicago. She has an essay, "Homage to Spencer: The Politics of 'Freedom' and 'Choice' in Neoliberal Times," in the forthcoming anthology *Madness, Violence and Power*, edited by Andrea Daley, Lucy Costa and Peter Beresford.

JL **Schatz** is the director of debate at Binghamton University, where he is a lecturer and teaches courses on media and politics out of the English department. He has published on representations of apocalypse, environment and disability, and subjectivity in relation to teaching pedagogy in debate. He has also coedited a special issue for the *Journal of Critical Animal Studies* and organized several conferences.

Emma **Short** is a chartered psychologist and associate fellow of the British Psychological Society. She is director of the National Centre for Cyberstalking Research, principal investigator for the Electronic Communication Harassment Observation (ECHO) project, and leader of a Home Office–funded project on cyber harassment.

Tyler **Snelling** is in the communication studies MA program at the University of Nevada at Las Vegas. He reviewed submissions for the Disability Issues Caucus and the Political Communication Division at the National Communication Association's 2016 convention.

Fiona **Whittington-Walsh** is the chair of the sociology department at Kwantlen Polytechnic University, British Columbia. She is also the vice president of Inclusion BC, a provincial non-profit organization that strives for the full inclusion of people with developmental disabilities in all aspects of life.

Hailee M. **Yoshizaki-Gibbons** is a doctoral candidate in disability studies and a University Fellow at the University of Illinois at Chicago. Her work has been published in *Review of Disability Studies* and *Intellectual and Developmental Disabilities*.

Index